Oh Canada!

Oh Quebec!

Oh Canada!
Oh Quebec!

REQUIEM FOR A DIVIDED COUNTRY

MORDECAI RICHLER

 ALFRED A. KNOPF *New York* *1992*

THIS IS A BORZOI BOOK
PUBLISHED BY ALFRED A. KNOPF, INC.

Copyright ©1992 by Mordecai Richler Productions Inc.

A portion of this work was originally published in *The New Yorker*.

Owing to limitations of space, all acknowledgments of permission to reprint previously published material will be found following the Selected Bibliography.

Library of Congress Cataloging-in-Publication Data
Richler, Mordecai,
    Oh Canada! Oh Quebec! / by Mordecai Richler.—1st ed.
      p. cm.
    Includes bibliographical references and index.
    ISBN 0-679-41246-8 (hardcover)
    1. Quebec (Province)—History—Autonomy and independence movements—Humor. 2. Nationalism—Quebec (Province)—Humor.
I. Title.
F1053.2.R53 1992
971.4'04—dc20

For Daniel and Jill, Noah, Emma, Marfa, and Jacob

Oh Canada!

Oh Quebec!

One

NINETEEN NINETY. On a perfect summer day in Montreal, local raspberries in season, two tickets to that night's ball game riding in my breast pocket, I went to meet some friends at a downtown bar I favored at the time: Woody's Pub, on Bishop Street. As I arrived, a solemn middle-aged man was taking photographs of the blackboard mounted on the outside steps. He was intent on a notice scrawled in chalk on the board:

TODAY'S SPECIAL
Ploughman's Lunch

The notice happened to be a blatant violation of Quebec's Bill 178, which prohibits exterior signs in any language but French, and the photographer was one of a number of self-appointed vigilantes who, on lazy summer days off from work, do not head for the countryside to cool off in the woods or to fish; instead, they dutifully search the downtown streets for English-language or bilingual commercial signs that are an affront to Montreal's *visage linguistique*—HIYA! VERMONT BASEBALL FANS WELCOME HERE, say, or HAPPY HOUR 5 TO 7. They photograph the evidence and then lodge an official complaint with the Commission de protection de la langue française. Woody was lucky. A chalkboard sign can be erased. However, had he chosen to promote his lunches with an outside neon sign in English only, or even a bilingual one, that would have been something else again. A first offense would get him off with no worse than a warning from one of the commission's inspectors. All the same, a dossier would be opened on him. There would be another visit to his bar and, if he persisted in his obloquy, a letter from a bailiff with a thirty-day warning, and then a period of grace of up to nine months before he might be scheduled to appear in court, where he could be fined a maximum of $570. Woody could easily spin out the process for a couple of years, maybe longer, behave himself for a month, post another English-only or bilingual sign, and start the ball rolling again. The truth is, we have always done things differently in Quebec, our laws seldom being quite what they appear to be. During the forties, for example, gambling casinos and bordellos were both illegal, but in fact Montreal was a wide-open city. Our cops, a considerate bunch in those days, would unfailingly phone the proprietor before making a raid to settle on an appropriate number of sinners to be booked, and, on leaving, would solemnly padlock a toilet rather than the front door, minimizing inconvenience to the clientele once play resumed. Honoring this tradition, the sign law, ostensibly uncompromising, in practice does not so much prohibit exterior commercial signs in languages other than French as slap a surcharge on them.

In 1990, four provincial agencies, with a total annual budget of $24 million, were in place to deal with our linguistic conundrums: the Commission de toponymie, whose function is to rename towns, rivers, and mountains that have English place-names; the Office de la langue française; the Conseil de la langue française; and the already mentioned Commission de Protection, whose inspectors have been dubbed "the tongue-troopers" by ungrateful English-speaking Montrealers.

According to the 1986 census, Montreal has a population of 2,921,357, which breaks down as follows: 1,974,115 whose mother tongue is French, 433,095 whose mother tongue is English, and 514,147 whose mother tongue is Italian, Greek, Portuguese, or other. In the new nationalist nomenclature the population is also classified as Francophone (a.k.a. the collectivity), Anglophone, or, if their mother tongue is neither French nor English, Allophone.

At Woody's Pub, where a number of us used to gather late in the afternoon to review the day's idiocies, the banter slipping from English to French and back again, we did not suffer from a lack of sustenance in the spring or summer of 1990. The snows had hardly melted when the zealots who run Montreal's French Catholic school board shocked even the separatist Parti québécois with a demand that immigrant students who were caught shooting the breeze in English in the schoolyards should be severely punished. Then aging nutters out in smalltown Ontario trampled on a Quebec flag, wiping their shoes on the fleur-de-lis for the benefit of TV cameras. Next to be heard from was the Alliance for the Preservation of English in Canada (APEC), an organization whose president, Ron Leach, a seventy-year-old retired lawyer, claimed 36,000 members.[1] Leach, in an appearance before a parliamentary committee on the Official Languages Act, objected to this 1969 legislation, which had been introduced by Pierre Elliott Trudeau's government. It stated: "The English and French languages are the Official Languages of Canada for all purposes of the parliament and the government of Canada, and enjoy equality of status and equal rights and privileges as to their use in all the institutions of the parliament and government of Canada."[2] The act, he protested, was an intrusive piece of social engineering that discriminated against long-serving Anglophone civil servants, denying them promotion if they were unilingual. APEC, he had claimed in an earlier appearance before another parliamentary committee, "is not now, nor has it ever in the past, been opposed to bilingualism. Nor have we been opposed to the teaching of the French language as a subject in our schools." But if official bilingualism, imposed by Ottawa, is allowed to continue, he argued, Canada as a nation would be destroyed.[3] Furthermore, there was no point in English-speaking Canada becoming officially bilingual when Quebec had clearly rejected the policy. "In the early to mid-seventies," he said, "by a series of legislative enactments, culminating in Bill 101, the Province of Quebec became unilingually French."

Denounced for his "paranoid and bigoted views"[4] by a member of the parliamentary committee, Leach insisted he was not prejudiced. He couldn't deny, however, that he had been inspired to found his organization, in 1977, by his reading of *Bilingual Today, French Tomorrow* by J. V. Andrew. Andrew had once told an APEC meeting that English Canada needed the French language as much as anyone needed the AIDS virus and he anticipated a French takeover of Canada, propelled by a Quebec that has become "an impregnable bastion, breeding pen and marshalling yard for the colonization of the rest of Canada."[5]

Andrew, who served in the Royal Canadian Navy for almost thirty years, retired with the rank of lieutenant commander in 1974. He claims that since *Bilingual Today, French Tomorrow* was first published in 1977—its subtitle *Trudeau's Master Plan for an All-French Canada*—it has gone into ten printings, selling 110,000 copies; this, he says, in spite of timorous book chains refusing to handle it and Trudeau sending out the order to "Government-funded Francophone Associations throughout Canada to buy up the book and destroy it."[6] Certainly the retired sailor is not one to pull his punches. On the very first page, he writes:

A political conspiracy has been taking place in Canada which, if it continues, will shortly lead to a Canadian civil war. This war will almost certainly involve the United States. Other countries, Russia and China included, will take whatever advantages they can from it. Many lives will be lost, and much of eastern Canada will be laid to waste. When it is finally over, nothing will have been resolved thât could not be resolved today, with no loss of life whatsoever.[7]

Interestingly, the solution the virulently anti-French Andrew offers to our national dilemma is exactly the same as that profferred by the Québécois separatist firebrand Pierre Bourgault: separate states, one English, the other French. Otherwise, Andrew wrote in 1977:

It is my guess that within ten years from now, Canada will have gone through *six* [italics mine] stages, each of which I want to deal with separately. The stages are:

    1. Growing resentment.
    2. Open hostility.
    3. Imposition of police state.

4. Civil war.
5. The outcome.[8]

Bilingual Today, French Tomorrow was followed by *Enough! Enough French. Enough Quebec.* in 1988, in which Andrew noted that "English-speaking Canadians in Quebec have no language or political rights whatsoever except the right to vote."[9] Furthermore, he had established that our country was hostage to "a militant and avaricious minority [of Francophones] which is sworn by secret oath to the extermination of English Canada and the English language, province by province, territory by territory, and municipality by municipality."[10]

Gosh.

RESPONDING to the insult to their flag in small-town Ontario, Québécois rowdies in Montreal booed our national anthem at ball games, obviously unaware that "O Canada" had in fact been composed by one of their own, Calixa Lavallée, on his return to Montreal after he had served as a bandsman with the 4th Rhode Island Regiment in the U.S. Civil War. Compounding the irony, it was the St. Jean Baptiste Society, rabidly nationalist today, that commissioned Lavallée to set Judge Adolphe Routhier's poem *"O Canada! Terre de nos aïeux"* to music.

Even as our politicians, out on the hustings, have traditionally promised one thing in French and another in English, so the song that Parliament officially proclaimed our national anthem in 1980 is an exemplar of our national schizophrenia. The French version, except for the first two words, could be belted out in good conscience by the most uncompromising of Québécois separatists:

> *O Canada, terre de nos aïeux,*
> *Ton front est ceint de fleurons glorieux.*
> *Car ton bras sait porter l'épée,*
> *Il sait porter la croix!*
> *Ton histoire est une épopée*
> *Des plus brillants exploits.*

> *Et ta valeur de foi trempée,*
> *Protégera nos foyers et nos droits,*
> *Protégera nos foyers et nos droits.*

A literal translation would read:

> O Canada! Land of our ancestors,
> Your brow is wreathed with glorious garlands.
> For your arm knows how to carry the sword,
> It knows how to carry the Cross!
> Your history is an epic of the most brilliant exploits.
> And your courage, blended with faith,
> Will protect our homes and rights,
> Will protect our homes and rights.

But the official English-language version goes:

> O Canada! Our home our native land!
> True patriot love in all thy sons command.
> With glowing hearts we see thee rise,
> The true North strong and free!
> From far and wide, O Canada, we stand on guard for thee.
> God keep our land glorious and free!
> O Canada, we stand on guard for thee,
> O Canada, we stand on guard for thee.

It should also be noted that in the summer of 1990, CBC-TV's annual soporific, "The Canada Day Special," inexcusably mawkish as ever, surfaced with a sponsor sufficiently patriotic not to worry about the ratings: Toshiba of Canada. And Bryn Smith, a journeyman pitcher who had jumped the Expos to sign with the Cards, found Montreal, its many fine restaurants notwithstanding, a hardship; his wife was obliged to shop across the border, in Plattsburgh, New York, a forty-seven-mile drive, in order to keep the family supplied with Doritos. Then vandals took to the streets spray-painting the inflammatory word STOP on road signs to make it look like "101," as in Bill 101, the French Language Charter. True, nitpickers could argue that "stop" was correct French as well as the internationally recognized designation in France and other French-speaking countries. Never mind. Québécois purists insisted that our street corners must be cleansed of that lingering reminder of the conquest, the STOP/ARRÊT sign. So it was ordained that come January 1, 1993, only one word would be legal on the signs, ARRÊT, even though replacing 11,000 signs would set the City of Montreal back an estimated $600,000.

In the autumn, Ottawa contributed to our linguistic squabbles, creating . . . a candy crisis. A food inspector with the Department of Consumer and Corporate Affairs ruled that jelly babies and fruit pastilles, manufactured by Rowntree PLC of Britain, had to be removed from the shelves of a British souvenir shop in Toronto—the Leicester Square WC2 store—because their names and ingredients were not printed in both official languages. Other provocative British imports pronounced guilty of the same offense included Cadbury's Dairy Milk, Fruit & Nut, Nestlé's Milk Bar, and Fry's Peppermint Cream.[11]

Two

FROM THE VERY BEGINNING Canada's development as a nation, rather than a grudging, constantly bickering coalition of provinces, has been retarded by two seemingly insoluble problems: the language issue, and loyalties that burn brightest regionally. In 1839 Lord Durham, High Commissioner of British North America, published a famous report in London that recommended the shotgun marriage of Upper and Lower Canada—of Ontario and Quebec—and led to the passage of the act of Union by the British parliament the following year. Canada, he ventured, actually comprised two nations warring within the bosom of a single state, and the only thing for it was to anglicize the French. "There can hardly be conceived," he wrote, "a nationality more destitute of all that can invigorate and elevate a people than that which is exhibited by the descendants of the French in Lower Canada, owing to their retaining their peculiar language and manners. They are a people with no history and no literature."[1]

In fact they were the first Europeans to settle on this continent, charting its rivers, probing its hinterland, and the names of their explorers still resonate: Cartier, Champlain, La Salle, Marquette, Jolliet, La Vérendrye. It should also be noted in passing that on at least one occasion when the conquerors were in need, it was the ruffians of the north who were sent for. In 1884, when General Lord Wolseley was preparing to set out to rescue Major General "Chinese" Gordon, who was being held captive by the Mahdi in Khartoum, he asked the Governor-General of Canada, Lord Lansdowne, to "engage 300 good voyageurs from Caughnawaga, Saint Regis, and Manitoba as steersmen in boats for Nile expedition." An account of their exploits by one Sergeant Gaston P. Labat, *Les voyageurs canadiens à l'expédition du Soudan, ou Quatre-vingt-dix jours avec les crocodiles,* made it clear from the outset that military discipline would be difficult for the Canadiens. Even before the *Ocean King* set sail from Montreal, bound for Alexandria, Labat wrote, "On Saturday evening, when almost all the voyageurs were aboard, a squaw appeared wanting to see her man. Having caught sight of her, he leaped over the side and there he was, in the arms of his better half. This better half, let me assure you, was a complete whole . . . weighing at least two hundred pounds. There they are, then, embracing each other like Daphnis and Chloe, these two children of the forest, when, to put an end to this tender scene, a move was made to bring our man back on board. Since he resisted, she did likewise. . . . Finally . . . the husband's hands disappeared into the corset of the squaw, seeking to find . . . what? . . . shocking! . . . the maneuver being poorly executed, one heard next the sound of broken glass—a bottle of whiskey had struck the pavement. The squaw began to weep, and he as well, to melt into tears. . . ."[2]

Lysiane Gagnon, a political columnist for Montreal's *La Presse,* once observed, "Years before the English conquered Canada, the French there had already formed a society with its own institutions and traditions that was quite different from France."[3] A society that was at risk as early as 1842, only two years after the Act of Union, when Lower Canada's Louis-Hippolyte Lafontaine, rising in the Assembly on September 13 of that year, dared to speak in French, earning an immediate rebuke from one of the Upper Canada ministers. Lafontaine replied, "I am asked to pronounce in another language than my mother tongue the first speech that I have to make in this House. But I must inform the honorable members that even if my knowledge of English were as intimate as my knowledge of French, I should nevertheless make my first speech in the language of my French Canadian compatriots, if only to protest against the cruel injustice of the Union Act in trying to proscribe the mother tongue of half the population of Canada. I owe it to my compatriots; I owe it to myself."[4]

Following Lafontaine's speech, French was tolerated by the

Assembly, but it was not officially sanctioned until 1848. Nineteen years later, in 1867, the four Canadian provinces in existence at the time (Nova Scotia, New Brunswick, Quebec, and Ontario) were united as the Dominion of Canada, a largely empty space that within three years—once it had been granted title to its northernmost reaches, Prince Rupert's Land—emerged as the second-largest country in the world. However, that booster's statistic, paraded *ad nauseam* by Canadians ever since, is misleading. The truth is that the bulk of our undeniably vast domain remains uninhabitable, and to this day most of us are snuggled within a hundred miles of the 49th parallel, intimidated by the punishingly cold tundra on one side and American pizzazz on the other.

Confederation was authorized in July 1867 by the British North America Act which was passed by the Parliament in faraway Westminster. The House of Commons, three-quarters empty at the time, filled up immediately afterward for a debate on the dog tax bill.

According to Léandre Bergeron, author of the *Petit manuel d'histoire du Québec*, a best-seller in the province, confederation was imposed by the English exploiters with the primary aim of suppressing the French, who would, with a stroke of the pen, "be reduced to one-third of the population and could not prevent the masters of the country from governing them as they wish."[5] On the other hand, the BNA Act, coddling Quebec as a special case, enshrined its right to its own civil code and the use of French in legislative bodies and in the courts, while also recognizing English as the province's other language. It is important to grasp that Canada, ostensibly self-governing under the terms of the act, could not amend its own constitution in the future without the approval of its nanny, the Parliament of Westminster.

From 1927 through 1971 there were nine attempts to repatriate Canada's constitution, a process almost invariably stymied by obdurate Quebec governments that would settle for nothing less than having their "special status," as well as a veto on any future constitutional amendments, woven into the document.

These endless negotiations, a fascination to our politicians, were an immense bore so far as most Canadians, both English and French, were concerned. All the same, they continued. Then, in 1981, after protracted haggling with ten premiers, most of them provincial in more than name only, Prime Minister Pierre Elliott Trudeau rammed through an amending formula that enabled him to bring the constitution home, a hot potato that has led to so much acrimony ever since.

The Constitution Act of 1982, signed by every Canadian province except Quebec, which protested date-rape, did manage to abolish the embarrassing power of the Parliament of Westminster to legislate for Canada. However its Charter of Rights and Freedoms guaranteed us no more, come to think of it, than we have always taken for granted: the right to "freedom of thought, belief, opinion and expression, including freedom of the press and other media of communication."[6] The charter was also undermined by something like a satisfaction-or-your-money-back guarantee. Over the objections of Prime Minister Trudeau but on the insistence of the western premiers, who otherwise refused to endorse the document, it included the "notwithstanding clause." This clause could be invoked by a provincial legislature to override vital sections of the charter that it didn't like for a period of five years, after which it could vote to renew its use of the clause. There was another kicker. The charter recognized English and French as the official languages of Canada, enjoying equality of status, but Quebec, marching to its own drummer as usual, had already ruled French the only official language of the province. In an appearance before a Joint Committee of the House of Commons and Senate on August 7, 1987, Trudeau, who had retired three years earlier, commented on this contradiction. "I do not think," he said, "one has to stretch one's imagination much to see that [Quebec] officials will be inclined to tell immigrants that they are living in a province where there is only one official language, rather than in a country where there are two; and that the Province of Quebec, which constitutes a distinct society . . . is different. I'm not saying they will be taught nonsense, or that it is a sin; I am simply saying that it seems quite clear that the notion of provincial patriotism will become stronger. The same will apply to Newfoundland and British Columbia, minus the linguistic difference."[7]

Some sixty years earlier, Henri Bourassa, a brilliant parliamentarian and journalist from Quebec, opposed to both lingering colonial ties to Britain and a separate French Canadian state, regretted that there flourished in Canada one distinctive patriotism among people living in Ontario, another in Quebec, and yet another on the prairies. But, he lamented, "There is no Canadian patriotism; and so long as we have no Canadian patriotism, there will be no Canadian nation."

As far as Québécois nationalists are concerned, not much has changed since Bourassa spoke up. Now as then, they are convinced that they are a nation, and that the rest of Canada is comprised of pseudo-American drifters. The case for the Québécois nation was eloquently put by René Lévesque, founder of the Parti québécois, in 1968.

"We are Québécois," he wrote.

"What that means first and foremost—and if it need be, all that it means—is that we are attached to this one corner of the earth where we can be completely ourselves; this Quebec, the only place where we have the unmistakable feeling that 'here we can be really at home.'

"Being ourselves is essentially a matter of keeping and developing a personality that has survived for three and a half centuries.

"At the core of this personality is the fact that we speak French. Everything else depends on this one essential element and follows from it or leads us infallibly back to it.

"In our history, America began with a French look, briefly but gloriously given it by Champlain, Jolliet, La Salle, La Vérendrye. . . . We learned our first lessons in progress and perseverance from Maisonneuve, Jeanne Mance, Jean Talon; and in daring or heroism from Lambert Closse, Brébeuf, Frontenac, d'Iberville. . . .

"Then came the conquest. We were a conquered people, our

hearts set on surviving in some small way on a continent that had become Anglo-Saxon.

"Somehow or other, through countless changes and a variety of regimes, despite difficulties without number (our lack of awareness and even our ignorance serving all too often as our best protection), we succeeded.

"Here again, when we recall the major historical landmarks, we come upon a profusion of names: Etienne Parent and Lafontaine and the Patriotes of '37; Louis Riel and Honoré Mercier, Bourassa, Philippe Hamel; Garneau and Edouard Montpetit and Asselin and Lionel Groulx. . . . For each of them, the main driving force behind every action was the will to continue, and the tenacious hope that they could make it worthwhile.

"Until recently in this difficult process of survival we enjoyed the protection of a certain degree of isolation. We lived a relatively sheltered life in a rural society in which a great measure of unanimity reigned, and in which poverty set its limits on change and aspirations alike.

"We are children of that society, in which the *habitant*, our father or grandfather, was still the key citizen. We also are heirs to that fantastic adventure—that early America that was almost entirely French. We are, even more intimately, heirs to the group obstinacy which has kept alive that portion of French America we call Quebec."[8]

Yes, however the *Québécois pure laine* (not necessarily descendants of the original 8,500 French settlers who established roots in Quebec between 1608 and 1763, but made of the right stuff all the same) were apprehensive. In 1842 half of the people in Canada were of French origin, but by 1990 they had been reduced to something like a quarter of the country's population, and now it was feared that one day they could even become a minority in their own province. The problem is that since the eclipse of the church's influence, there has been a precipitous drop in their birthrate, once the highest in North America, with families of a dozen, even sixteen, children being not uncommon. This punishing level of fertility, which seemed to be based on the assumption that women were sows, was encouraged with impunity from the sidelines by the Abbé Lionel Groulx, whose newspaper *L'Action française*, founded in 1917, preached *la revanche des berceaux*, "the revenge of the cradles," which would enable French Canadians to become a majority in Canada. In 1990, however, the birthrate among Québécois women of childbearing age was 1.5, lowest in the Western world save for West Germany, whereas a 2.1 rate is called for just to replenish the existing population.

Immigration, the alternative method of boosting Quebec's French-speaking population, has only exacerbated the situation.

The majority of Italian, Greek, and Portuguese immigrants have understandably wanted their children educated in English, the language of opportunity in North America. In 1968 the Catholic school board of the Montreal suburb of St-Léonard responded by attempting to deny English education to its largely Italian population. Ugly riots ensued and, a year later, there was temporary respite when the provincial government of the day introduced Bill 63, which allowed parents to educate children in the language of their choice. This, in turn, enraged many of Quebec's increasingly nationalistic intellectuals, spawning a commission of inquiry into language rights, and we were already sinking into that linguistic quagmire that would yield Bills 22, 101, and 178, and a disconcertingly tribal society.

Bill 22, passed by Premier Bourassa's Liberal government in 1974, ruled that the children of immigrants had to be enrolled in French schools. "The only exceptions," wrote the late René Lévesque, who was premier from 1976 to 1985, "were children who could demonstrate 'a sufficient knowledge' of English. So tests were imposed on little shavers of six and seven years old, isolated from parents who were boiling mad. Without going so far, I wasn't very hot on the plan myself."[9]

In 1975, when the quarrel over Bill 22 was at its height, a senior adviser to Premier Bourassa told a reporter that not much could be done about so-called clandestine schools, "short," he said, "of drastically rewriting the law to flatly exclude immigrant children whose mother tongue is not English from

English schools."[10] And in 1977, a year after René Lévesque rode into office, winning 71 out of 110 seats, the PQ introduced Bill 101, the French Language Charter, which went even further than that. Bill 101 ordained that wherever a child came from—another country or even another Canadian province—it had to be educated in French, unless one of its parents had been to an English school in Quebec. It ordered the "francization" of any company with more than fifty employees, ruling that it would soon require a certificate to prove it conducted all internal business in French. It declared that all English, or even bilingual, commercial signs would be illegal by 1981. It established a Commission de toponymie to rename towns, rivers, and mountains that bore English names and so offended the *visage linguistique* of *la belle province*. And it pronounced French the province's only official language, a violation of the British North America Act, killing the two-century-old convention that had endowed French and English with equal legitimacy.

Sure enough, a problem soon developed. According to a clause in the Canadian Charter of Rights and Freedoms, the child of a parent who had been educated in English at primary level anywhere in Canada was entitled to an English-language education in Quebec. This resulted in a suit brought against the government by the Quebec Association of Protestant School Boards. The case went to the Quebec Superior Court, which ruled, on September 8, 1982, that the Charter took precedence over Bill 101. The Quebec government's argument, said Chief Justice Jules Deschênes, "demonstrates a totalitarian concept of society to which the court cannot subscribe . . . other societies put the collectivity above the individual . . . [but] this conception of society has not yet taken root here . . . even if certain political initiatives seem at times to be courting it dangerously. . . . Every individual in Canada and Quebec should enjoy his rights in their entirety, be he alone, or a member of a group; and if the group has one hundred members, the hundredth has as much right to benefit from all his privileges as do the ninety-nine others. . . ."[11]

The PQ government served notice of its intention to appeal.

Then, in 1985, Robert Bourassa, who had been displaced as leader of the Liberal party by Claude Ryan in 1978 and written off at the time as a burnt-out case, was back at his old job and running for premier again.

Above all, the perpetually vacillating Bourassa is a survivor. Suspected of covert separatist views by many English Quebecers but unloved by French Quebecers, mocked as a wimp by both communities, he belongs to that big band of wearisome but enduring politicians, strangers to wit or charm, of whom it is unfailingly said, "Ah, yes, but the private man, if only you knew him, is an absolute delight." He was first thrust into office when he was a mere thirty-six because he was taken for an economic wizard, somebody who could put the shop in order, and there was something in that. Before long, however, he became an object of ridicule, hardly ever seen in public in those days without his gun-toting hairdresser. On the evidence, he had no emotional attachment to Canada, but favored le fédéralisme rentable, "profitable federalism," and wanted Quebec to keep its seat at the Canadian table only so it could feast on its share of the country's immense store of natural resources. For all that, in 1985 he was the only real alternative to a divided and no longer coherent Parti québécois, exhausted after nine turbulent years in office.

If elected, Bourassa promised to amend Bill 101, allowing bilingual commercial signs, provided that the French were predominant. "When I am premier," he said, "I will be able to make tough decisions within a hundred days, whatever the short-term political consequences."[12] However, once returned to power on December 2, 1985, winning 99 out of 122 seats, he had second thoughts. Although he had already told a Montreal Le Devoir reporter that "nowhere in the free world is there a country where the minority is prohibited from using its own language on its signs,"[13] he decided that, before relaxing the sign law, he would wait for a decision on its legality from the Quebec Court of Appeal.

Meanwhile, in the dead of that winter, Gilles Rhéaume, an

ardent *indépendantiste*, infuriated because the PQ had temporarily put its sovereignty policy on the back burner, announced that he would march the 158 miles from Montreal to Quebec City, where he would piss on the statue of the conqueror, General James Wolfe, on the Plains of Abraham. On arrival, he also had second thoughts. He decided it was too cold and pleaded with his small band of followers to consider the act done.

That same winter we were astonished to learn that linguistic strife had penetrated the very inner sanctum of Canada's security and intelligence service, as witness the case of *Yvon R. Gingras, Plaintiff* v. *Henry F. Robicheau, Defendant*, heard in the Superior Court, District of Montreal, Province of Quebec (Court No. 500-05-000436-863) on January 17, 1986.

DECLARATION

PLAINTIFF DECLARES:

1. On January 18, 1985, Defendant was present at R.C.M.P. headquarters, Montreal, at approximately 16:45 p.m.

2. Defendant was Regional Director of the Canadian Security and Intelligence Service.

3. Plaintiff was a member in good standing of the service.

4. Without any provocation and in front of witnesses, Defendant proceeded to call him a "Damn pig," a "maudit cochon," and suggested that a committee headed by him was subversive and trying to destroy the service.

5. He also used the word "asshole" and reiterated the word "pig" many times.

6. He said to the Plaintiff, "you and your f____ French rights make me sick."

7. He threatened to hit him and made aggressive gestures.

8. The action of the Plaintiff [sic] constitutes slander and an unjustified attack on Plaintiff's reputation and dignity, contrary to the Quebec Charter of Rights and Liberties.

9. The attack had nothing to do with work and was entirely gratuitous.

10. The damages caused are
    1) loss of reputation $10,000
    2) loss of enjoyment of life,
       humiliation, distress $10,000
    3) exemplary damages, Quebec Charter $10,000
11. Defendant [sic] attempted to obtain an apology but to no avail.
12. $30,000 is due and owing from Defendant to Plaintiff.
13. This action is well founded in fact and law.
    WHEREFORE it may please this Honourable Court
    TO ALLOW this action
    TO ORDER Defendant to pay Plaintiff $30,000;
    THE WHOLE with interest, and special
    indemnity of $1,078.00

                      MONTREAL, January 17, 1986
                      (signed) Grey Casgrain,
                      Attorney for Plaintiff.

(As I write, no decision has been made.)

Mind you, the RCMP, the very symbol abroad of Canadian rectitude, has a gift for slipping over its own banana peels. Take the fabled case of a certain RCMP machine, for instance. In the late fifties, wrote John Sawatsky in *Men in the Shadows*, a new evil replaced communism as a potential menace to Canadian security—the homosexual. The better to combat this threat, a machine was brought into play, its mission to unmask homosexuals among civil servants.

    . . . While the project was a secret and remained so, word at the time leaked out within the security community and rumors began flying. The RCMP tried to recruit members as guinea pigs but nobody would submit to the test. "I wouldn't go anywhere near it in case they put the electrodes on me and the machine blew a fuse," quips one Security Service officer. Jokes circulated and soon the device was dubbed the Fruit Machine, and the name stuck. "You'd better be careful or they'll put you in the Fruit Machine," was a popular refrain.

    One of the Security Service's homosexual informers voluntarily took the test and reputedly was treated as a madman. "Keep him in the corner, don't let him get away," the machine's operator reportedly said. The bewildered homosexual, one of the few who did not hide his sexual proclivity, replied: "I volunteered for this. What's the matter with this guy? Is he crazy?" While the incident is undoubtedly exaggerated, and possibly wholly untrue, the story nonetheless made the rounds and soon members of the Security Service believed, as one member put it, that subjects would be confronted with flashing lights shrieking: "Fruit, fruit, fruit!"[14]

Actually there were no electrodes or flashing lights, but work on this machine absorbed some senior government officials and scientists for nearly four years. The research, secretly funded by the Defence Research Board, was supervised by a psychologist seconded from the Department of National Defence, with the help of an outside psychiatrist and psychologist with security clearance. Basically, the machine—a dentist's chair above which were rigged cameras and other equipment—was intended to measure a subject's pupillary responses to photographic stimuli. If, surprised by a photograph of a male nude with an outsize dick, the suspect's pupils expanded, *but failed to register appetite in response to a photograph of a yummy female nude*, then the government shrink, consulting the outside psychiatrist and psychologist, just might pronounce him "a fag security risk." Problems. Unobliging, even shifty, suspected sexual deviants were discovered to be of different heights, with different-sized pupils and different distances between their eyeballs, which made it impossible for cameras to measure their sexual responses accurately. Another complication was that as each new pornographic image was flashed, the amount of light altered, the subject's pupils adjusted accordingly, decreasing for bright images and increasing for dark ones. Then, after nearly four years of work, researchers had to allow that the change in pupil size in response to images was in any case so small that it was all but impossible to measure accurately.

In the end, it didn't matter. The Fruit Machine, like the horse and buggy, was superseded by a superior invention. It was a device that could be clipped to a subject's cock, measuring changes in width throughout the long day, rendering an accurate report on exposure to which sex prompted it to perk up with interest. Sawatsky, a discreet observer, fails to say whether this instrument was ever deployed among suspects in our civil service. All the same, to this day whenever I'm visiting the bar of the National Press Club in Ottawa and a civil servant drifts in, I check him out to see if he is walking with difficulty. If that's the case, I will accept a free drink, but certainly not an invitation to a candle-lit dinner.

Three

AT WOODY'S PUB, where we were all devoted followers of the Canadian political carnival, it was agreed that 1986 was a vintage year, the Ottawa monkey house yielding a welcome distraction even as we waited for the Quebec Court of Appeal to rule on Bill 178. The silly season was not yet with us when the Mulroney government, which would eventually be swamped in sleaze, surrendered its first flimflam man: the Hon. Sinclair Stevens.

As an Ontario youngster of nine, Sinc Stevens acquired twenty duck eggs, which he subsequently claimed to have hatched under chickens, and then peddled the ducklings for twenty dollars apiece.[1] Fulfilling his early huckster's promise, he emerged as Minister of Regional Expansion in the Mulroney Cabinet in 1984. Two years later he was obliged to resign, caught out in an embarrassing conflict-of-interest muddle. What fascinated me, however, was the involvement of Stevens and his wife, Noreen, in what came to be celebrated as the "Christ coin," an ingenious scheme that would reward the devout with both profit and tax advantages for their faith in Jesus.

"This type of concept is what we call our hobbies," said Noreen Stevens. "I guess a lot of people like to talk about weather, we like to talk about this kind of thing. We like to talk about concepts, applications of different financial transactions." Then, by way of further explanation, she added, "We read a lot. We are, I suppose, bookworms."[2]

The Christ coin would have allowed investors to fork out three hundred dollars for a shekel dated 1986, backed by a strip bond with a guaranteed redemption value of one thousand dollars in the year 2000, as we entered the third millennium after

the birth of Jesus. Sinc and Noreen, suffering the little capitalists to come unto them, figured they could move a million
coins. Taking the project's religious appeal into consideration,
they decided that the obvious sovereign state to mint the currency was the Vatican. So Sinc called on Emmett Cardinal
Carter, archbishop of Toronto. Cardinal Carter pronounced the
notion "extremely interesting" and wrote to Sebastiano
Cardinal Baggio, president of the Pontifical Commission for
the Vatican City, saying, "[Stevens] is well known to me and is
a fine gentleman. I find his proposal extraordinarily interesting
from many points of view." And, giving Baggio the elbow, he
went on to note that it "might be a contribution to covering
the deficit of the Holy See which I perceive is getting extremely onerous."[3] But the Vatican had to pass, because their
ability to mint coins was restricted by the Italian government.

Next Sinc, unfortunately mixing his pet scheme with government business, submitted his inspiration to the Chase
Manhattan Bank in New York. They couldn't go along with it,
either.

"I should like to point out," said one of my Gentile friends at
Woody's, "that the decision of the Chase Manhattan is not to be
interpreted as a lack of faith in *our* Lord, who still enjoys far
more market appeal than Moses. The problem was that the
Jesus coin didn't offer the same tax advantages in the United
States as it did in Canada."

This led us to reflect on other inspired Canadian products
that had been undone by American protectionism.

The incomparable vintage wines of Southern Ontario.

The novels of Frederick Philip Grove.

The California Golden Seals entry into the National Hockey
League.

Eskimo throat singers.

The RCMP musical horseride.

New Brunswick's Bricklin SV 1 automobile of blessed memory.

Then the language issue was back with us.

On December 22, 1986, to nobody's surprise, the Quebec

Court of Appeal ruled that the ban on languages other than French on commercial signs was a violation of freedom of expression as protected by both the Canadian and Quebec Charters of Rights. In a second ruling, the Appeal Court judges voted 3–2 that Quebec did have the power to prevent the display of unilingual English signs.

Then Premier Robert Bourassa, wetting a finger, testing for intimidating nationalist winds, had third thoughts, saying the sign law couldn't be revoked until the Supreme Court of Canada had ruled. It fell to the affable Herbert Marx then minister of justice, to argue Quebec's appeal to the highest court in the land, although he was already on record as being opposed to it. In his 1978 Corry Lecture at Queen's University in Kingston, Ontario, Marx said, "the provisions of Bill 101 that require, with some exceptions, language signs to be unilingually French . . . clashes with the dignity of the forty percent English-speaking minority of [Montreal]. The unilingual French sign requirement in Bill 101 is, in my view, less a question of freedom of expression than one of hiding evidence of the presence of an English-speaking minority behind a French façade. Freedom of expression in Canada has traditionally meant freedom to espouse political, religious and social ideas. Selling shoes should not be put on an equal footing with the selling of political ideas. And Bill 101 does permit bilingual or multilingual signs in a number of areas, including the political and religious fields. The issue is rather that the presence of a large English-speaking minority in Quebec, particularly in Montreal, shall not be made invisible."[4]

Marx was obliged to present his case at a time when public opinion polls showed that three out of four Quebecers favored bilingual signs. Mind you, nationalists were also making their feelings known to shopkeepers who had challenged the law in court or simply ignored it. Rocks were thrown through the windows of the McKenna Côte-des-Neiges flower store and Nat's Auto Parts. Firebombs were tossed at one of Zeller's chain stores, and bomb threats were called into two downtown department stores, Ogilvy and Simpson.

Don MacPherson, the astute Quebec correspondent of the Montreal *Gazette*, our English-language daily, obtained a copy of the sixty-page factum that Herbert Marx was to be armed with for his appearance before the Supreme Court. The factum argued that "freedom of expression does not protect the right to do commercial advertising" and, in any event, Quebec's National Assembly could exempt the province from the provisions of the Canadian Charter of Rights and Freedoms by invoking the notwithstanding clause. "Ultimately," the factum noted, "it is the survival of the collectivity that is at stake."[5] Next, the father of Bill 101, the obdurate Camille Laurin, was heard from. Dr. Laurin, a psychiatrist who dyes his hair black, had become head of psychiatry at the Institut Albert-Prévost, in Montreal, after his tour of duty as the PQ's minister of cultural development from 1976 through 1980. Dr. Laurin has been a favorite of mine ever since he published *A Cultural Development Policy for Quebec* in 1978. The report, as I noted shortly after it appeared, complained that a crippling Canadian presence imposed upon Quebec "restrictions that become shackles when it attempts to develop its own values and cultural endeavors." This, incongruously enough, at a time when there was hardly a separatist painter, composer, or writer in Quebec who wasn't on a Canada Council grant or fettered to such federally funded cultural institutions as Radio-Canada or the National Film Board. The report, pondered and debated for months by the brightest and best Dr. Laurin could gather in conclave, abounded in banalities and bromides. Both sex and age, we were earnestly told, were the result of natural laws: "We do not choose our sex, we do not choose to grow old." Women, we were assured, "are people." In Quebec, as elsewhere, the report claimed, "children make great demands on adult energy." We were also asked to swallow whole the notion that "adolescents make up a large proportion of the population."[6]

All these "brief yet thought-provoking" *pensées* came in Volume I, the real illuminations being saved for the heftier Volume II, in which it was revealed that "books have been one of the most important vehicles of culture for centuries, and will continue to play this role for some time." Then, after pages of reproaches about the smoking and drinking habits of Quebecers, Dr. Laurin, a thinker who can see around corners and then some, ventured that "alcohol becomes all too often a prop, a stimulant or an escape."[7]

Now Dr. Laurin put all of Anglophone Quebec on the couch and pointed out that the banning of their language was shock therapy, and Quebec's English-speaking community had only been discomfited "because they define themselves above all as Canadians who live in Quebec." Furthermore, he said, Bill 101 ended the "scandal" of free choice, whereby immigrants could actually send their children to English rather than French schools.

Possibly Dr. Laurin was unaware that the immigrant problem was already remedying itself.

In August 1987 Alliance Quebec, an English lobbying group, presented a brief to the National Assembly, as Quebec's provincial legislature has been called since 1969. It revealed that since 1972 there had been a net population loss of 293,987 in the province of Quebec. Between 1976 and 1981, some 106,300 English-speaking Quebecers, 19.5 percent of whom held university degrees, had moved out. "The tendency for young adults of childbearing years to be over-represented in this departure," the Alliance brief declared, "has also diminished the capacity of our community to replenish itself demographically. The result is an aging community with fewer children."[8] But so far as Léon Dion, an influential professor of political science at Laval University in Quebec City was concerned, it was the cultural future of *his* community that was being threatened. "If Montreal is left to so-called bilingualism," he told the National Assembly, "this means in less than ten years a kind of English unilingualism."

Liberal Member of the National Assembly (MNA) Reed Scowen, studying the problem from all angles, summed things up in his farewell speech to the National Assembly that summer. "If I follow the reasoning of both sides to its logical conclusion," he said, "in two generations there won't be a single Anglophone left in Quebec, but everybody will be speaking English."

The following March, Montreal's diminishing English-speaking community learned that the Conseil de la langue française had some hanky-panky in mind. A researcher for the Conseil let slip to the *Gazette* that undercover shoppers were to be sent out to make 4,500 visits to local stores to determine whether salespeople greeted their customers in French or the language of *les autres*.

The proposed study by the Conseil had several objectives:

"To verify if the client is welcomed and ultimately served in French in commercial establishments of certain typical sectors of the island of Montreal," that is to say, *dans les voisinages* where English-speaking Quebecers were in a majority.

"To compare the language of approach and service according to the ethno-linguistic origin of the owners of the business and the employees."[9]

The government snoopers were also to snitch on whether an "employee seems by his accent to be a native Francophone or Quebecer," and if, once service in the language of the collectivity is requested, he was "polite or nice, neutral, curt or disagreeable." After the *Gazette* blew the whistle on the proposed undercover op, however, the Conseil backed away from it. So the *Gazette* conducted its own survey, discovering that many shopkeepers, necessarily wary, welcomed customers in a fail-safe combination of English and French, singing out, "Hi, *bonjour*."

Come spring, as we were waiting for the Supreme Court of Canada to pronounce, dissenters within the French community began to speak up. An editorial writer for *La Presse* pleaded with Premier Bourassa to allow bilingual signs in the name of fundamental justice. A man who had served as an inspector for the Commission de protection de la langue française for nine years retired and wrote letters to the editors of *Le Devoir* and *La Presse* denouncing the sign laws as the mischief of "fanatics" and "fascists." The board of directors of the Conseil du patronat, Quebec's largest employers' group, voted unanimously in favor of bilingual signs with French predominant, once the Supreme Court had ruled. The most stinging rebuke to Quebec came from another one of their own, D'Iberville Fortier, then the federal commissioner of official languages. In his annual report to Parliament, Fortier said that English-speaking Quebecers had been "humiliated" by restrictions on their language in the province. A livid Premier Bourassa denied the accusation, and when the opposition PQ tabled a censure motion he promptly toughened its wording and then the motion was passed unanimously. It read:

"That this National Assembly firmly denounces the statements made by the federal commissioner of official languages in regard to the English-speaking minority in Quebec, and calls upon the official in question to give an explanation.

"That the National Assembly reaffirms having exercised its linguistic powers always in a fully democratic manner so as to ensure the survival of the French collectivity and check the threat of anglicization."

The banner headline on the front page of the next morning's *Gazette* read like a charge sheet:

ALL ANGLOPHONE MNAS VOTE FOR CENSURE
The 21 help to make it unanimous,
despite the urgings of constituents
to rebel or at least abstain[10]

In October 1988 an estimated 25,000 Québécois nationalists, anticipating a Supreme Court decision that would declare the sign law illegal, took to the streets of Montreal to protest, chanting, *"Le Québec aux Québécois!"* and a jittery Premier Bourassa, who could never forget that the nationalists had once burnt him in effigy, began to talk about the need to preserve the "social peace."

At the PQ's convention a month later, the new party leader, Jacques Parizeau, announced that he was resolutely opposed to bilingual signs and, obviously eager to demonstrate that he was made of the right stuff, came out in favor of reducing the number of English radio and television stations in Montreal and of intensifying the "francization" program, making it apply to firms with ten employees or more.

Ironically, the patrician Parizeau, a committed *indépendantiste*, is also a dedicated Anglophile: he is a graduate of the London School of Economics and an admirer of Queen Elizabeth. On record as an uncompromising opponent of a bilingual Montreal, he insisted on an English-speaking governess for his own children. He is a son of the Québécois bourgeoisie, a sixth-generation Montrealer, his father having stitched together the city's biggest insurance brokerage. A sybarite of considerable girth, Parizeau seems to have sprung larger than life out of a P. G. Wodehouse novel, his English liberally sprinkled with exclamations of "by Jove" and "jolly good." An inventive economic adviser to several Quebec governments before he ran for office himself, he was instrumental in the creation of the immensely powerful Quebec pension fund, the Caisse de dépôt et placement. In 1985, he resigned as PQ minister of finance and walked out on the party along with other hard-liners, among them Camille Laurin, when the then leader René Lévesque, anticipating an election, swept their suddenly inconvenient independence platform under a rug. Now Parizeau was back, this time as party leader. "The Parti québécois should be sovereigntist before the election," he said, "during the election, and after the election."

Camille Laurin, returned to the fold, also addressed the PQ's November convention, reminding the faithful that before he had been to the mountaintop and brought down Bill 101 in 1977, Quebec was "still dominated by a foreign power,"[11] that is to say Ottawa, where, at the time, several of our most important Cabinet ministers were Quebecers, as were 75 MPs out of a total of 292, as well as three out of the nine Supreme Court justices, the governor-general, some 35,000 civil servants, and Prime Minister Pierre Elliott Trudeau. Thirteen years earlier Trudeau, along with six other French Canadian intellectuals calling themselves the Committee for Political Realism, had published a "Canadian Manifesto" in the magazine *Cité libre*. It called for social justice, a fairer distribution of the wealth, a revised penal code, and an end to nationalism:

> To use nationalism as a yardstick for deciding policies and priorities is both sterile and retrograde. Overflowing nationalism distorts one's vision of reality, prevents one from seeing problems in their true perspective, falsifies solutions and constitutes a classic diversionary tactic for politicians caught by facts. Our comments in this regard apply equally to Canadian or French Canadian nationalism. . . .
> Separatism in Quebec appears to us not only a waste of time but a step backwards. . . . We refuse to let ourselves be locked into a constitutional frame smaller than Canada. . . . We do not attach to its existence any sacred or eternal meaning, but it is an historical fact. To take it apart would require an enormous expenditure of energy and gain no proven advantage. . . .[12]

When Camille Laurin delivered his sermon to the PQ convention in 1978, Canada appeared to be in no danger of being taken apart. The PQ, seemingly moribund, was badly in need of funds and running low in the polls, the choice of a mere 28 percent of the electorate.

Four

EARLY IN DECEMBER 1988, almost two years after the Quebec Court of Appeal had ruled on the sign law, the Supreme Court announced it would deliver its judgment on Section 58 of Bill 101 on the fifteenth of the month, ruling on two different cases against the attorney general of Quebec, those of Chaussures Brown and Allan Singer. The Chaussures Brown case would deal with the Quebec government's prosecution of a number of Montreal merchants who displayed bilingual signs, while the Singer case would cope with the righteous stationer who insisted on displaying an English-only sign.

While waiting for the court's judgment, the Quebec government brought Operation 58 into play. It called for Cabinet ministers' homes to be placed under police surveillance until the court decision was being analyzed, lest *indépendantiste* extremists, known to bomb and kidnap and murder, or the fabled Anglophone resistance fighters of Westmount (Montreal's most affluent suburb), the most crazed of whom were actually threatening to delay payment of their Hydro-Québec bills, went on a rampage. A document outlining Operation 58 stated that once the court's judgment came down, "the navigator holds the course despite tempests or turbulence."[1]

Premier Bourassa had already let it be known that the solution he fancied was to allow bilingual signs inside but only unilingual French signs outside. It was rumored that if this proposal were adopted, two Cabinet ministers, both representing largely English-speaking ridings, would resign. Anglophone ministers and backbenchers, Bourassa ordained, would not be accommodated by a free vote in the National Assembly; they would have to hold their noses and support the government's response to the court's decision, a response that our navigator, who had procrastinated over the problem for three years, promised would be "calm, lucid, and serene."[2] Meanwhile, in the days leading up to the court decision, Montreal's Urban Community Police warned Anglophone merchants to make sure that their shops were well lit, to clear away garbage pails to discourage arsonists, and to keep their shop interiors visible to patrolling cops by removing signs from storefront windows. Then, as anticipated, the Supreme Court ruled the sign law illegal. Actually, there were two court judgments. The first answered the challenge to Section 58 of Bill 101 by five businesses—Chaussures Brown Inc., McKenna Inc., Masson Tailors and Cleaners, National Cheese Co. Ltd., and Valerie Ford—all of whom questioned that commercial signs in Quebec had to be in French only. The second judgment dealt with the case of Allan Singer and the legality of English signs only.

In the first case the court ruled unanimously, "Language is so intimately related to the form and content of expression that there cannot be true freedom of expression if one is prohibited from using the language of one's choice."[3] Then, leaning on Quebec's very own Charter of Human Rights, the court declared the sign law a clear violation of freedom of expression and stated that a ban on other languages was not needed to defend the French language. Finding against Allan Singer in the second case, the court endorsed Quebec's right to legislate the promotion of French in order to protect the province's *visage linguistique*. While, in the court's opinion, exclusivity for the French language did not reflect the reality of Quebec, the judges did rule that the province was entitled to pass a law requiring the predomininant display of the French language: "The predominant language [of Quebec] is French. This reality should be communicated to all citizens and non-citizens alike, irrespective of their mother tongue."[4]

Allan Singer, the truculent seventy-six-year-old stationer who had appeared in court forty-five times since 1978, spending $120,000 of his own and supporters' money, threatened to take his case to the United Nations. "No damned government is going to tell me to take down my English sign," he said.

On Monday, Premier Bourassa invoked the notwithstanding clause and then introduced a bill in the National Assembly that would ban English on outdoor signs but allow it and other languages on indoor signs, providing the French was predominant. He knew, he said, that this was difficult for the English-speaking minority to accept, but he implored them to look at the sunny side of Bill 178. After all, they had gained the right to post indoor bilingual signs, providing that the French was predominant.

Premier Bourassa's inside/outside solution managed to alienate just about everybody in the province. Alliance Quebec warned that his decision, unspeakably repressive, could lead to another English exodus and thousands of aroused Québécois nationalists filled the Paul Sauvé Arena to protest what they interpreted as his retreat. The PQ opposition leader denounced the proposed law, claiming that the pusillanimous premier had chosen the "most pernicious and hypocritical route to anglicization."⁵ So far as he was concerned, "social peace was finished."

The prime minister of Canada, Brian Mulroney, took his own inside/outside approach to the problem. Speaking in French outside the House of Commons, he said, "It is important to emphasise that Quebec has no lessons to learn from anyone regarding its way of treating its language minorities. . . . I think Quebec is a leader in this field."⁶ But once inside the House, speaking in English, he claimed that he had asked Premier Bourassa not to invoke the notwithstanding clause.

One of the regulars at Woody's Pub, an old friend of the prime minister's, once told me that when the young Mulroney settled in Montreal, after he had graduated from Laval Law School, he was readily accepted by French Canadians and Jews, but not by his WASP establishment contemporaries, none of whose fathers had ever gone golfing in Bermuda or salmon fishing in the Gaspé with Mulroney's dad, a North Shore electrician. Mulroney had come out of Baie Comeau, the blackfly-ridden backwoods, and was a graduate of a no-account university, St. Francis Xavier in Nova Scotia. "Brian never forgot how some people snubbed him here," said his old friend, "and in this quarrel over language rights I'd say he identifies with French Canadians and is not exactly displeased to see them shoving it to the WASPs in Westmount."

I first met Mulroney in the early spring of 1980, a couple of months before Quebec was to vote in a referendum, its unbelievably coy question set by a fainthearted PQ government:

"The Government of Quebec has made public its proposal to negotiate a new agreement with the rest of Canada, based on the equality of nations; this agreement would enable Quebec to acquire the exclusive power to make its laws, levy its taxes and establish relations abroad—in other words, sovereignty—and at the same time, to maintain with Canada economic association including a common currency; no change in the political status resulting from these negotiations will be effected without approval by the people through another referendum; on these terms, do you give the Government of Quebec the mandate to negotiate the proposed agreement between Quebec and Canada? Yes. No."[7]

Mulroney had already lost a Tory leadership convention to Joe Clark, who went on to become prime minister. Clark, whose minority government had lasted less than seven months, was now leader of the opposition, Trudeau having been restored to office in February, and Mulroney was president of the Iron Ore Company of Canada. Although ostensibly he had returned to private life for good, it was no secret that he was already scheming to displace Clark. I invited Mulroney to lunch at the Ritz, because I was researching an article on Quebec and mutual friends had assured me that he knew where the horses were buried. I was not disappointed. At a time when most political observers expected the referendum result to be uncomfortably close or even saw it as a toss-up, the street-smart Mulroney predicted without hesitation that the vote would come in 60–40 in favor of the No side, and he turned out to be absolutely right. He was also a highly entertaining companion, charged with appetite and armed with a grab-bag of indiscreet political anecdotes. He smiled too eagerly and was a shameless flatterer.

Something else. Incongrously, this small-town Quebecer, the third-born son of six children, wearing a suit that looked too expensive by far and Gucci shoes, glib in both English and French, struck me as the quintessential South Boston pol, a more likely congressman than MP.

When Mulroney and I met for lunch again several months later, it was at the Mount Royal Club, a favored haunt of insufferably boring WASP tycoons that was designed by Stanford White and had refused Sam Bronfman membership twice but later condescended to accept his son Charles, as well as a number of toilet-trained French Canadians. Mulroney had arranged for us to eat in a private dining room, and after we got into the cognac I saw something of his dark side. Scornful of Joe Clark, he obviously felt he could handle him, but the graduate of St. F.X., his background blue-collar, was intimidated by Pierre Trudeau, the arrogant rich brat who had been ferried to Montreal's Jesuit-run Collège Jean de Brébeuf in a chauffeured car and had gone on from there to the Université de Montréal, the London School of Economics, and Harvard. All the same, I was left in no doubt that he was going to reach for the roses.

One afternoon a week later I was in New York, sitting in the *New York Times* editorial offices, drinking with A. M. Rosenthal, then executive editor, and Sidney Gruson, a member of the board of directors. Both of them were Canadian-born. And so, for their benefit, I expounded at length, I'm afraid, on the Canadian political zeitgeist. I suggested that the *Times* Ottawa man, if they had one, ought to do a story on Mulroney, because he might very well be the next prime minister of Canada and—only peripherally aware that Gruson had wandered over to the window and that Rosenthal's eyes were glazing over—I went on to explain how this could come about.

"Aw, what does it matter?" said Rosenthal, changing the subject.

Working on a piece for the *Atlantic Monthly*, I went to the Tory convention in Winnipeg in January 1982, and there I caught up with Mulroney again. Ostensibly a staunch supporter of Joe Clark, it seemed unlikely that Mulroney shed a tear when his rival—supported by two-thirds of the 2,406 delegates in a secret ballot, the other third thirsting for a leadership review—foolishly announced that he was resigning and called for a leadership convention to be convened as soon as possible. Clark would, he said, be a candidate himself and fully expected to win. Later that night I dropped into Mulroney's hotel suite and found the sitting room already filling with old supporters and new supplicants, while the leader-in-waiting was receiving in the bedroom.

"Look at this," said an outraged Mulroney, thrusting at me a printed endorsement of Clark by a noted British Columbia socialite. "Did you know that she was a vicious anti-Semite?"

"Oh, come on, Brian. I just came by to say hello and wish you luck, that's all."

During the leadership convention in Ottawa that summer I happened to be in the National Press Club when a Clark honcho and a Mulroney organizer, both of whom had possibly been standing at the bar for too long, almost came to blows.

"I don't care what you've been reading in the fucking *Globe*," said the Clark man, "the fact is we have been guaranteed the support of at least sixty percent of the Quebec caucus."

"Like shit," said Mulroney's organizer. "I happen to be sure of the votes of a clear majority of those delegates."

"Listen, you prick. We know. I paid to bring them here, and I'm handling their hotel bills."

"So am I!"

"Son of a bitch."

"Yeah."

Going into the leadership contest, which he would win on the fourth ballot, Mulroney was irrevocably committed to Trudeau's "patriation" of the constitution, totally opposed to a free-trade deal with the United States, and scornful of Clark for playing footsie with Québécois nationalists, an act of folly, he assured Canadians, that he would never stoop to. Yes, certainly. But in the federal election of 1984, Mulroney counted heavily on PQ support in Quebec, and then rewarded Québécois nationalists with seats in his Cabinet. And in 1988, he fought another election on the free-trade deal with the United States, which he had come to strongly advocate. Furthermore, he had now come to realize that Trudeau's "patriation" of the constitution had been shameful, because it had excluded Quebec from the Canadian family. There were only two ways of looking at our prime minister. Either he had been a barefaced liar to begin with or he grew in office.

The morning after Premier Bourassa invoked the notwithstanding clause, three of his English-speaking ministers—Clifford Lincoln, Herbert Marx, and Richard French—resigned from the Cabinet and announced they would vote against Bill 178. Lincoln's speech in the National Assembly moved some of his Francophone colleagues to tears. "In my belief rights are rights are rights," he said. "There is no such thing as inside rights and outside rights. . . . There are no partial rights. . . . Rights are links in a chain of fundamental values that bind all individuals in the society; they must be inalienable, just and fair."[8]

Responding to the resignations, Premier Bourassa risked obloquy and made a rare speech in English in the National Assembly. Addressing himself to Quebec's English-speaking community, he insisted that, as political leader of a collectivity representing less than 2 percent of the population of North America, he had no choice in the matter. He pleaded with *les autres* to be understanding. Bourassa found an unlikely ally in D'Iberville Fortier, the official language commissioner who, in 1987, had maintained that Bill 101 humiliated Quebec's English-speaking minority, but on reflection, a year later, now stated in his annual report to Parliament that it was French, not English, that was the threatened language. "Quebec," he wrote, "has traditionally shown more generosity toward its Anglophone minority than was required of it by constitutional or legislative documents."[9]

Then Prime Minister Mulroney, who had been battered by the parliamentary opposition for his fancy footwork, made another pass at Bill 178. Speaking outside the House of Commons, he said that he disapproved of Quebec's invoking the notwithstanding clause to suspend minority rights. "How can a parliament say," he told reporters, "'We have legislated your inalienable rights, and by the way I forgot to tell you these rights can be overridden by a premier.'"[10] Once inside the House of Commons, however, he added that he would not demand that Premier Bourassa revoke Bill 178. If anyone was to blame, he charged, it was the former Liberal government of Pierre Trudeau, which had allowed the notwithstanding clause to slip into the constitution in the first place.

The same day Premier Bourassa amended Bill 178, tightening the screws. It was now ruled that franchise outlets with more than five employees would not be allowed to post indoor bilingual signs. Even so, he was attacked by the PQ for backsliding on the strictures of Bill 101. In response, the premier protested that he had gone further than the PQ ever had to impose French on the province, and he vowed that Montreal, 20 percent of its population English-speaking, would never look like a bilingual city. But when his government tried to explain how it would enforce "markedly predominant" French in those stores where inside bilingual signs would still be tolerated, it was greeted with laughter from the opposition and from its own backbenchers. The minister then in charge of the French Language Charter said, "It's not the size of the letters. It's not the color of the letters. It's not their placement higher or lower, to the left or to the right of French compared with English. It's not the number of the signs. It's all of that."[11]

Pondering Bill 178, *Gazette* columnist Don MacPherson asked, "If French unilingualism is necessary to protect the French language, why is it only necessary outdoors? And if freedom of expression is a fundamental freedom, why must it be respected only indoors?"[12]

A former Quebec civil servant I met with, who requested that he not be identified by name, allowed that the new law was fatuous, but, he added, *les Anglais* had only themselves to blame. "From the very introduction of Bill 101, eleven years ago, they surprised us by being timorous beyond belief. When Eaton's, Ogilvy's and Steinberg's [large Montreal commercial establishments] and the rest were asked to shed their apostrophes, why didn't they just stand together, denounce the law as lunatic, and refuse to comply?"

Because, I pointed out, Anglophones tended to be law-abiding to a fault.

"Do you think," he said, "their directors would have been hanged or imprisoned for life? Bullshit. Rather than risk ridicule abroad, the PQ would have retreated and that would have been that."

NINETEEN EIGHTY-EIGHT ENDED BADLY. Fires were set in English-language schools in St-Jean-sur-Richelieu and Quebec City. Then, on December 30, somebody put the torch to the downtown Montreal offices of Alliance Quebec, causing an estimated $200,000 in damages. A detective sergeant of the Montreal Urban Community criminal investigations squad was quickly on the spot, sizing things up. "From our point of view," he said, "there is something to investigate."[13]

At the time the alliance claimed 40,000 members, but its demands were so mild that irritated members of what should have been its natural constituency had already dubbed it Compliance Quebec. Suddenly, however, the lobby group was talking tough. Alliance president Royal Orr warned that a number of English-speaking Quebecers were thinking of taking to the streets or forming new political protest parties. "I'm not convinced that . . . civil disobedience is the answer," he said, "but I'm not going to condemn anybody who takes that route."[14]

Early in the new year, as the language wars continued to escalate, a mind-boggling Gallup Poll revealed that, on the one hand, 61 percent of Quebecers believed that bilingual signs should be tolerated in the province, but on the other, 77 percent felt that it was more important for French-speaking Quebecers to preserve their culture than to honor the freedom of speech of English-speaking Quebecers. Then, on January 20, the tabloid *Journal de Montréal* ran an explosive headline:

TOUT NOUS CONDUIT A ROYAL ORR

Quoting an anonymous police source, the *Journal* accused Orr of having set fire to his own offices in order to discredit Quebec nationalists. Orr promptly denounced the story as a "deliberate and vicious attempt to defame"[15] him and filed suit for $400,000 in damages. The case against Quebecor Inc., publishers of the *Journal*, has yet to be heard.

Five

WHEN BONNIE PRINCE CHARLES was on the lam, following his defeat at Culloden, he could be certain he was approaching a country inn that would offer him shelter if the publican grew yellow roses, the emblem of the Jacobite sympathizer, in his garden. Similarly, in the winter of 1989, Montreal's besieged Anglophones could be assured of a warm welcome in any downtown watering hole that dared to advertise on its outside steps:

TODAY'S SPECIAL
Lancashire Hot Pot

Happily, at Woody's Pub, our safe house, there was a good deal to divert us that winter, beginning early in January with the celebrated case of *les grosses maudites Anglaises*.

I should explain, first of all, that for years now one of the most deeply felt complaints of French-speaking Montrealers has been that the sales staff of the department store chains located downtown, a district where English is the norm, have been unable or even unwilling to serve them in French. A conspicuous offender, according to legend, has been the Ontario-owned T. Eaton Company, which didn't establish its downtown Montreal department store until 1920, but back in 1901 published a mail-order catalog that included the following injunction: "To all our French-speaking customers—Please Place Your Orders in English." Eaton's was delinquent yet again as recently as 1982, when Claude Charron, then a Cabinet minister in the PQ government, was nabbed by one of the store's security agents as he attempted to flee with a stolen sports jacket. After Charron was found guilty and fined $300, seething nationalists called in to radio hot-line shows to charge that he had been "an obvious victim of English vengeance," his disgrace the dirty work of "Toronto racists," and some of the callers cut up their Eaton's credit cards and mailed them back to the store. Never mind that even earlier, in 1977, Eaton's had been born again as Eaton in all of its Quebec outlets, as a consequence of Bill 101, under which just about every Anglophone commercial establishment in Montreal acquiesced without a peep to the loss of its incriminating apostrophe. In January 1989 the long-cherished resentment against the T. Eaton Company erupted in the case of *les grosses maudites Anglaises.*

In an interview with *La Presse*, Pierre MacDonald, then minister of industry and commerce in Quebec's Liberal government, said that his chums in the National Assembly had told him that they were "fed up with going to Eaton and being served by a big fat damned English lady who couldn't speak a word of French."[1] MacDonald's want of chivalry managed to enrage both French and English women's groups. La Fédération des femmes du Québec, not all of them svelte, denounced the minister's remark as "sexist and extremely offensive." An ad hoc group of Englishwomen, calling themselves the Big Fat Damned English Ladies, demanded that the Liberal caucus apologize. Then the Conseil was heard from. According to the most recent survey undertaken by their agents, the staff of downtown department stores addressed their customers in French 83 percent of the time.

"I'm glad to see progress has been achieved," MacDonald said, "but there's still work to do." He was, he added, fed up with the language issue. "I think that most people want to get on with the business of making money."[2] Then, noting that the dibs in politics were far from munificent, this people's tribune revealed that he would really like to buy a new cottage in the Laurentians as well as replace his twenty-five-year-old Beechcraft with a new airplane. Six months later the former banker would announce his imminent return to private life.

In February former provincial communications minister Richard French, addressing an Alliance Quebec rally, surfaced with an original solution to the language impasse. Bilingual signs, he said, should be restored in French *and any language but English.*[3]

Urdu? we wondered?

Esperanto?

Then British newspaper tycoon Robert Maxwell turned up in Quebec City on a flying visit.

IN A CANADA JUSTIFIABLY better known for its spaces rather than the places we have built, Quebec City is a shining exception to the rule. Rising out of Cape Diamant, an eight-mile-long plateau of solid rock, North America's only walled city soars over the narrows of the St. Lawrence, its Citadel and Château Frontenac—perched 200 feet above the shore—commanding the river and its approaches. Gazing down from its heights more than a hundred years ago, Charles Dickens noted the motley crowd of gables, roofs, and chimney tops and the St. Lawrence sparkling and flashing in the sunlight. "It formed," he concluded, "one of the brightest and most enchanting pictures the eye can rest upon."[4]

Quebec City, originally an Indian village called Stadacona, was discovered by a happy fluke. When Jacques Cartier, the seafarer from St-Malo in Brittany, landed in 1534, it was a direct water route to India and Cathay he was seeking, not beaver pelts. The city proper was founded in 1608, a fur-trading post established by Samuel de Champlain, and from here—and later Montreal—the fabled voyageurs ventured north by canoe as far as Hudson Bay, the great Mackenzie River beyond the prairies and the shores of the Arctic, in search of beaver pelts, and south, through Illinois, riding the Mississippi to New Orleans. Another official, Jean-Baptiste Talon, first intendant of the colony, conceived the idea of importing shiploads of orphaned girls from France for the settlers, *les filles du roi.*

"After the regiment of Carignan was disbanded," a French officer wrote home, "ships were sent out freighted with girls of indifferent virtue, under the direction of a few pious duennas, who divided them into three classes. These vestals were, so to speak, piled into three different halls, where the bridegroom chose his bride as a butcher chooses his sheep out of a flock. There was wherewith to content the most fastidious; for here were to be seen the tall and the short, the blonde and the brown, the plump and the lean; everybody, in short, found a shoe to fit him. The next day the governor caused the couple to be presented with an ox, a cow, a pair of swine, a pair of fowls, two barrels of salted meat and 11 crowns in money."[5]

Je me souviens (I remember), the melancholy motto of the province, is inscribed in flowers in Quebec City in the gardens of the Place d'Armes. And what the Québécois remember above all else is the conquest of 1759 and the struggle on the Plains of Abraham, their Wailing Wall. After a two-month siege, but a battle that lasted only twenty minutes on those windy plains on September 13, 1759, General James Wolfe's army, having scaled the cliffs under the shelter of darkness, took the city for the British, settling a country's fate for at least 126 years minimum.

Both Montcalm, the French commander, and Wolfe were slain in the battle and now share a common monument in the Jardins des gouverneurs, just below the Château Frontenac. Its inscription reads: "Valour gave them a common death, history a common fame, posterity a common monument."

Quebec City's skyline is dominated by the green copper roof, the spires, the portcullis, dormer windows, castlelike turrets, and uncertain plumbing of the Château Frontenac. Before the turn of the century the hotel was built on the site of the Château Saint-Louis, once the residence of the governors of New France, among them Louis de Buade, the fiery Comte de Frontenac.

Poor Frontenac. He abandoned the pleasures of the court of Louis XIV at the age of sixty-two once his beautiful wife, a grudgy type, denied him access to her bed. After he died, at the age of seventy-eight, his heart was carved out and sent back to Madame la comtesse. But she spurned the little silver casket, saying she had never had her husband's heart when he was living and didn't want it now that he was dead.

"The impression," wrote Charles Dickens of Quebec City,

"made upon the visitor by this Gibraltar of North America, its giddy heights, its citadel suspended, as it were, in the air; its picturesque steep streets and frowning gateways; and the splendid views which burst upon the eye at every turn, is at once unique and lasting."[6]

An earlier traveler, the American Joseph Sansom, ventured into Lower Canada in 1820 to report to his countrymen on its future prospects. "We know not," he wrote, "whether the French, in Canada, are to be dreaded as enemies, or to be conciliated as friends."[7]

Sansom's charming little book, *Travels in Lower Canada*, is introduced by a disclaimer from his London publisher, Sir Richard Phillips & Co.:

> The Editor of this London Journal has preferred to allow Mr. Sansom to speak for himself in his own words, conceiving that this would be more just towards him; and that, as a specimen of Americanisms, used by a man of good education, the work would thus be a greater curiosity to those English Readers, who are not aware of the deterioration which the language is suffering in the United States. For analogous reasons, many opinions of the Republican Author are retained, because they will add to the interest of the work, though they may sometimes offend by their coarseness, and evident want of discrimination. If, however, an individual, or a people would correct errors, the exposition of them must be borne, from whatever quarter or country it proceeds."[8]

Sansom, in fact, turned out to be a shrewd if cheeky observer, maybe even prophetic:

> I left Quebec with a confirmed opinion, that, although its citadel, reputed the strongest fortification in America, with its hundreds of heavy cannon, and its thousands of well-disciplined troops, might possibly, in future wars between the two countries (which Heaven avert), fall prey to American enterprise and intrepidity; yet the conquest would cost infinitely more than it could be worth; and must be with difficulty maintained against the re-action of the greatest naval power on earth, to those whose approaches by sea must ever remain accessible.

I say not the same of Upper Canada, whose population is, or will be, essentially American; and whose attachment to the government of Great Britain must inevitably yield to the habits and opinions of their continental neighbours. In short, I may venture to predict, with little apprehension of controversy, that by the next competition between England and America, if it be not hastily brought on, Upper Canada will be nearly Americanised. Montreal itself will have become to all efficient purposes an American town; the French population there will gradually assimilate, or disappear; unless, indeed, French Canada should be consolidated by national independence; and the eventual boundary of Lower Canada will probably be Sorel on one side, and the St. Maurice on the other; leaving to his Majesty of Great Britain and his successors the sterile and inhospitable shores that stretch. . . .

To farthest Lapland and the frozen main.

Canada is as costly a feather in the royal cap as any other of the imperial trappings; and why should republicans volunteer their services to prevent its being paid for beyond its value.[9]

Elsewhere, Sansom proves to be a decent inquiring reporter. In Pointe-aux-Trembles, he asked the postilion who conducted him over the Jacques Cartier River about the state of the country.

"Monsieur, c'est le pays le plus aimable pour la misère, que vous trouverez nulle part. On travaille beaucoup pour gagner peu. Oh! c'est une occupation que la vie, ici, je vous assure. Nous avons un petit bout d'été et donc, tout de suite, la gelée, qui vient toujours à la St-Michel. Quelquefois pendant la Récolte même. Toujours avant la Toussaint."

"Sir, this is the most charming country for misery that you'll find anywhere. We work a great deal to earn little. Oh, life is an occupation here, I assure you. We have a little bit of summer and then, all of a sudden, the frost, which always comes by St. Michael's Day. Sometimes even during the harvest. Always before All Saints."

Sansom asked the postilion his age, thinking he might be about sixty.

"Monsieur, j'ai quarante ans, juste."

"Sir, I'm just forty years old."

Next he wanted to know how the French liked the English.

"Comme ça! Messieurs les Anglois" were very brave, generous, and so forth. *"Mais ils ne sont pas polis, comme les François. Quelquefois aussi ils ne sont pas de bonne humeur. Ils se mettent en colère souvent sans savoir pourquoi."*

"Pretty well. . . . But they're not polite, like the French. Sometimes they're not in a good mood. They often get angry without knowing why."

And finally, anticipating umpteen royal commissions to come over the next century, Sansom asked if *les Canadiens* were content under British rule. After obliging with the required polite noises, the postilion inquired, *"Y-a-t-il loin, Monsieur, d'ici à Philadelphie?"*[10]

"Is it far, sir, from here to Philadelphia?"

ON HIS FLYING VISIT TO QUEBEC CITY, where he had come to negotiate the purchase of a pulp and paper giant owned by the provincial government, the late Robert Maxwell did at least manage to ingratiate himself with a thousand Québécois businessmen at a winter carnival luncheon. Without language protection, he said, Quebecers could lose their identity and scatter around the world as the Jews had 2,000 years ago.

Quebec City's annual winter carnival was enlivened by more than the menace of another Diaspora. An organization out there in California called Team Celebrity had shipped twenty of its glittering clients to the party, among them Carrie Fisher, Margot Kidder, Woody Harrelson, Gregory Harrison, Eugene Levy, Margaux Hemingway, Brooke Shields, Mary Wilson, and Fawn Hall. Sponsored by Pepsi Cola, the stars were granted a free holiday for themselves and a companion as well as free skiing outfits and equipment. Alas, there was a problem at the traditional carnival ball. Quebec City's newspapers complained that their very own carnival queen, Mlle Isabelle Boutin, had been upstaged by the dishy Brooke Shields and quit the festivities in tears, "visibly upset by a ball that wasn't hers." Furthermore, *Le*

Journal de Québec noted with a certain asperity that the entertainment was "entirely by anglophones or foreign dancers."[11]

The next day guests who had forked out $150 to attend the dinner ball—or $250 if they were to be seated next to Carrie Fisher or Fawn Hall—protested about the English entertainment at such a quintessentially Québécois event. "Look," responded the carnival chairman, "we couldn't welcome Hollywood celebrities with pea soup and a show by [chansonnier] Félix Leclerc. We'd been advertising a Hollywood-style show for three months."[12]

Six

PREMIER BOURASSA, still trying to work out Bill 178 guidelines, promised new sign rules on March 14. Meanwhile, the Mouvement Québec français organized a march of 10,000 in Montreal to demonstrate against the dire threat of bilingual signs inside stores. Then a fringe nationalist group published a pamphlet calling for a total halt to immigration, warning that newcomers were stealing jobs from better-qualified real Québécois, whose only sin was that they were not black, yellow, or red: "The first foreigners to establish themselves in our country—the English—entered by force and they haven't stopped bringing in immigrants ever since who, as a general rule, side with them at every opportunity."[1]

An even larger peril for the French was predicted by a television documentary shown on Radio-Canada, *"Disparaître: Le sort inévitable de la nation française d'Amérique?"* ("Disappearance: The Inevitable Fate of the French Nation in America?")

As the opening credits rolled, the camera focused on a reunion of the Tremblay clan of Chicoutimi, all of them *Québécois de vieille souche*, that is to say, white, Catholic, and French-speaking, with roots that ran back many generations. A family spokesman, addressing his fellow Tremblays, exhorted them to "wake up and multiply!" Then Lise Payette, the former PQ Cabinet minister who narrated the film, broke in ominously, *"Les Tremblay sont menacés! La nation, aussi!"* ("The Tremblays are in danger! The nation also!") Ms. Payette, who now writes the prime-time soap opera for Radio-Canada, warned that racial problems will occur in any city once a minority grows to 14 percent of the population, and in Montreal the racially impure, including myself and my loved ones no doubt, already accounted for 18 percent. "We are living dangerously," she said.

We perceived exactly how dangerously when the film shifted to Marseilles, where the North African minority was a problem, and then on to racially tainted England, where we were shown a British mum who has yanked her kid out of school because, she said, "He started to sing nursery rhymes in Punjabi and Urdu." The most fascinating statistic in "Disparaître"—understandably passed over on the fly—was that of the 516,000 immigrants who had come to Quebec since 1969 some 312,000 took a good look around and skedaddled. Even so, a Jesuit priest interviewed in the film anticipated Montreal becoming another Beirut and urged that immigration be restricted to countries compatible with Quebec's culture. And Gilles Vigneault, the popular nationalist poet and folk-singer, took it as self-evident that French would be reduced to a residual culture in Quebec by the year 2000.

In that case, it was possible that the rest of Canada would ride to the rescue. Or, put another way, what "Disparaître" failed to take into account was the burgeoning popularity of French studies among enlightened middle-class families in English-speaking Canada. In 1977–1978, only 37,865 English-speaking children had been registered for French immersion (school classes conducted almost totally in French) but twelve years later that figure had escalated to 265,579, and in some schools there were waiting lists.[2] Unfortunately, the newfound enthusiasm for all things French has occasionally backfired in some quarters. Consider the case, for instance, of the rich man's son who opened Voilà in Halifax, a restaurant whose opulence was enhanced by white silk draperies and a white grand piano. When a waiter brought a diner the platter bearing his entrée, assiette anglaise or whatever, it was sheltered under a silver dome that was whipped off just as the waiter sang out, "Voilà!"

The Voilà survived no longer than eighteen months, its owner rebuking Haligonians for being insufficiently cosmopolitan and deficient in "discerning taste."[3]

Following Radio-Canada's documentary, La Presse ran a seven-part series, "Franciser ou Disparaître" ("Francisize or Disappear"), in which it was argued that it wasn't sufficient for immigrants to learn French: "It is relatively easy to teach immigrants French. It is much harder to integrate them into the francophone majority, to bring them to adopt our culture and our values, to make them Québécois as the children we won't have would have been."[4]

Next, the host of a radio talk show, stopping just short of soliciting, put a decidedly saucy question to his phone-in audience: "To avoid our disappearance, would you be willing to have a baby out of patriotism?"[5]

There was soon another spur to fecundity. Money. Come spring the voice of Robert Bourassa was heard in the land, bringing in a "cash for kids" policy, the government offering a $500 bonus for the first child, $1,000 for the second, and $6,000 for each additional child.

While we waited for Bill 178 guidelines, Premier Bourassa, responding to PQ heat, announced that there would definitely be no more amendments. Rumors to the contrary, department and chain stores would not be allowed to post any bilingual signs inside and the government would be "very, very vigilant" about imposing this restriction. As a safety measure, however, he would tolerate bilingual signs on ski hills, pointing out SHEER DROP and other hazards rather than risk losing American tourists, but there was no substance to a *Le Devoir* report that bilingual highway signs would also be sanctioned. For example, a warning indicating DYNAMITING AHEAD was out.[6]

Even as he protected his nationalist flank, Premier Bourassa found himself in hot water with the other side. The Anglophone president of Ingersoll-Rand Canada Inc. announced that instead of building a plant in Valleyfield, Quebec, which would have created a hundred new jobs, he would invest $30,000,000 in a new facility in Downsview, Ontario. "If the government can eliminate individual rights just like that," he said in an interview, "they can eliminate something else in the future. Who knows what this province is capable of doing?"[7]

Bourassa denounced Ingersoll-Rand's stance as insulting, even "crazy," but then the president of the Conseil du patronat allowed that he knew of "some Anglophone leaders in the business community who are thinking like Ingersoll-Rand." He also cautioned the premier against the proposed "francization" program, which would extend the French-language laws to firms employing ten to fifty people, citing how expensive it would be for some 25,000 small businessmen. "The use of English," he said, "is very important [in Quebec] to be competitive."[8]

On Sunday, March 12, nationalists took to the streets of Montreal again, this time some 60,000 of them marching to protest Bourassa's decision to allow bilingual signs inside some Quebec stores. Among the demonstrators were the Québécois pop singers René and Natalie Simard, sometimes described as the Donny and Marie Osmond of Quebec. "We were raised in French," René burbled to a television interviewer, "and I want my children to suffer the same fate." Then, realizing what he had said, he hastily added, "The same beautiful fate, if I may say so."[9]

Fifteen hundred jeering French-language activists greeted Bourassa outside the National Assembly when it reconvened a couple of days later. Once inside, the premier, who three years earlier had pronounced the banning of English on public signs as "totally unacceptable," boasted that his government, showing its courage, had outdone the PQ in putting it to *les autres*. "Never before in the history of Quebec," he said, "has a government suspended fundamental liberties to protect the French language and culture."[10]

By this time we already knew some of the long-awaited details of the sign law. Under the new directives, an official of the Commission de protection de la langue française had declared:

"French letters must be bigger than English letters.

"The space around the French letters must be larger than the space around the English letters.

"The French message must be placed to the left of the English one, or on top.

"The color of the French and English lettering should be the same. If it's not, the color of the French should be stronger. The language inspector will decide what color is stronger.

"If the French and English are given equal prominence on

any signs, then there must be twice as many French signs as English ones."[11]

Then Claude Ryan assumed Cabinet responsibility for the language portfolio. Ryan, the once highly regarded intellectual who had been publisher of *Le Devoir* for fifteen years, had grown accustomed, while filling that post, to having Quebec premiers consult him before daring a giant or even a baby step. "I've been used to governments who would have a great respect for the paper," he once told a reporter, "and myself in particular, who would heed my opinions to a large extent."[12]

After the Lévesque-led PQ routed the Liberals in the 1976 election and a humiliated Bourassa resigned, Ryan ordained that what the Liberal Party required was a new leader "known for his reputation for integrity, and respected by his fellow citizens,"[13] Looking into the mirror, caught a gleam of recognition in his reflection's eye. Hello, hello. Claude fit the bill. Hailed as a savior by the Liberal Party establishment, Ryan's waltz to the leadership was threatened only briefly by a potential convention scandal. The scarf scandal. The scarves in question, wrote L. Ian MacDonald in *From Bourassa to Bourassa*, were red and worn by all of Ryan's supporters in the Quebec Coliseum, and there was a problem:

> They were clearly marked "Made in Japan." Which was sure to offend Quebec's struggling textile industry, not to mention the possibility of the press putting it out that Ryan had unilingual English scarves . . . a group of volunteers stayed up all through one night taking the labels off thousands and thousands of scarves.[14]

Thrust into the leadership in 1978, Ryan stumbled badly in the 1981 election, losing to the PQ, possibly because there was something about the man, notoriously frugal as he was, which suggested that if he were elected there would be no more cakes and ale. Shorn of the leadership in 1982, he settled for becoming the most important minister in Bourassa's Cabinet and in December 1988 threatened to resign unless the premier, vacillating at the time, invoked the notwithstanding clause and brought in Bill 178. And now Ryan confirmed that "for the foreseeable future" no bilingual signs would be allowed inside franchises and large stores.

Ryan's stance astonished English-speaking Quebecers, who recalled that in 1977, while editor of *Le Devoir*, he had denigrated the proposed French Language Charter for creating "the disturbing impression that in the present government's eyes, there are two classes of citizens in Quebec: Francophones, and others,"[15] a view of the province, he wrote, that was unacceptable to any democrat. In another editorial he denounced the bill for the "harsh, dogmatic . . . and authoritarian manner with which it attempts to decree the exclusive use of French . . . the government [having] nimbly crossed over from a policy which protects the majority's rights to one which quite simply negates the rights of the most important minority group in Quebec."[16] A year later, speaking during a Montreal by-election, he observed, "Once you have alienated your individual rights, they never come back, they never come back."[17]

The unapologetic Ryan rationalized his about-face by saying that he had come to realize that the management of linguistic rights was not a question of fundamental rights. "It's not like free speech or freedom of religion. That's sacred," he told the *Gazette*. "Language rights are a function of concrete arrangements that will vary according to the circumstances." Commercial signs, in his opinion, were merely advertising. "We regulate advertising in all sorts of ways. That's not a question of free speech. That's the freedom of the dollar, and it's not my bag."[18]

Soon Ryan was back with another announcement, this time in his office as minister of education. Responding to a Supreme Court decision that the province, and not the individual school board, had the power to set curriculum, he declared that he would now deny provincial grants to French schools that taught English as a second language prior to grade four because "we've long understood that premature exposure to English might not be compatible with the best development of the child."[19] Happily, he was not bothered by a similar concern about the possible ill effects of premature French instruction in schools where an increasing number of English-speaking kids began French immersion in kindergarten.

Quebec's strictures on education, so gratifying to nationalists, were beginning to annoy many French parents. As things stood, not only were their children denied instruction in English before the fourth grade and then restricted to three hours' instruction a week, they could not be legally transferred to an English-language school in order to broaden their knowledge as well as enhance their future job opportunities; only parents who could afford to educate their children in other provinces could circumvent the law. An English-speaking businessman I know told me, "Years ago, if we placed an ad in the papers looking for a bilingual employee, a good many of the applicants were Francophones. Now they are for the most part Anglophones, Italians, or Greeks. The young Francophones are being forced to revert to unilingualism, which will deny them the most jobs whether this province separates, drifts out to sea, or whatever."

Quebec's passion for the preservation of a language that has evolved somewhat differently from the French spoken in France—the culture having been separated from the motherland for more than 300 years—has bestowed upon us "hambourgeois" as the only acceptable alternative to "hamburger." The determination to purge the language of intrusive anglicisms has yielded several indigenous dictionaries, among them *Dictionnaire des difficultés de la langue française au Canada* by Gérard Dagenais and *Le Dictionnaire des petites ignorances de la langue française au Canada* by Camille-H. Mailhot. Mailhot, a purist, objects to any group of musicians being designated *une bande*. Instead, he argues, they should be called *un corps de musique, une harmonie*, or *une fanfare*. Québécois concern for the integrity of French has also reached across the seas to the transgressions of France itself. The venerable Pasteur Institute of Paris, it was discovered, conducted most of its seminars in English and had recently taken to publishing the bulk of its scientific papers in English out of fear that they might otherwise go unread by the international community. A scandalized chairman of the Conseil de la langue française lodged a complaint with his French counterpart. The initial French reaction was limited to radio, bemused commentators teasing Quebec for its touchiness, but then France's general commissioner for the French language either welcomed an opportunity to pepper the pot or was maddeningly ill-informed. Never mind that Quebec had its own civil code and guaranteed language rights, in his opinion its collectivity had been under perpetual attack by the English for more than two centuries and therefore had to be vigilant. Fortunately, the more sophisticated motherland did not require anything like Bill 101. The people of France, the commissioner said, "would find intervention by the government to be pointless, fanatical, and chauvinistic."[20] Yes, possibly, but it must also be said that many of them did not take kindly to words plucked from *la langue du Coca-Cola* contaminating their own idiom, say, *le snack-bar, le drugstore,* or *le playboy.* According to Robert McCrum, William Cran, and Robert MacNeil, the authors of *The Story of English,* "it is estimated that in a newspaper like *Le Monde,* one word in a hundred and sixty-six will be in English." Another calculation has one-twentieth of the workaday French vocabulary composed of *anglicismes.*

Quebecers—cut off from multilingual Europe, adrift in a monolithic Anglo sea, but determined to preserve French as the language of home and workplace—are inundated daily by American television channels, both network and cable, and American films, magazines, and pop music. So if they have grown increasingly chippy, even paranoid, the truth is that they feel they are manning a vulnerable dike in their attempt to hold back a surging wave. "The rise of English is a remarkable success story," write the authors of *The Story of English:*

> When Julius Caesar landed in Britain nearly two thousand years ago, English did not exist. Five hundred years later, *Englisc,* incomprehensible to modern ears, was probably spoken by as few people as currently speak Cherokee—and with about as little influence. Nearly a thousand years later, at the end of the

sixteenth century, when William Shakespeare was in his prime, English was the native speech of between five and seven million Englishmen and it was, in the words of a contemporary, "of small reatch, it stretcheth no further than this iland of ours, naie not there over all."

Four hundred years later, the contrast is extraordinary. Between 1600 and the present, in armies, navies, companies and expeditions, the speakers of English—including Scots, Irish, Welsh, American and many more—travelled into every corner of the globe, carrying their language and culture with them. Today, English is used by at least 750 million people, and barely half of those speak it as a mother tongue. Some estimates have put the total closer to one billion. Whatever the total, English at the end of the twentieth century is more widely scattered, more widely spoken and written, than any other language has ever been. It has become *the* language of the planet, the first truly global language.

The statistics of English are astonishing. . . . About 350 million people use the English vocabulary as a mother tongue: about one-tenth of the world's population, scattered across every continent and surpassed, in numbers, though not in distribution, only by the speakers of the many varieties of Chinese. Three-quarters of the world's mail, and its telexes and cables, are in English. So are more than half the world's technical and scientific periodicals: it is the language of technology from Silicon Valley to Shanghai. English is the medium for 80 per cent of the information stored in the world's computers . . . [it] is the official voice of the air, of the sea, and of Christianity: it is the ecumenical language of the World Council of Churches. . . .[21]

Early in May Claude Ryan, who had once complained in *Le Devoir* that what the Liberal Party suffered from was a lack of *le leadership*, delivered the latest refinement of Bill 178. It introduced his "two-for-one" rule on indoor bilingual signs, which meant that French signs had to be twice as large or twice as numerous as English ones. His ruling, which would affect some 100,000 Quebec businesses with four or fewer employees, had to be complied with by December 1990. It was, Ryan insisted, the simplest possible application of the markedly predominant principle. Variations on the theme, he said, would be dealt with individually. If, for instance, a store's French signs were neon green and the English ones plain beige, but there weren't twice as many French signs as English ones, an inspector from the language commission would file a detailed report, and the commissioners would eventually decide whether French signs had a "much greater impact."[22]

Of course, Ryan's interpretation of the law, which could involve bringing in color charts as well as the expert testimony of interior decorators, was immediately attacked by Québécois language zealots and outraged Anglophones.

The president of the St. Jean Baptiste Society said, "The message to Quebecers is that now we have two languages in the province and one is somehow bigger than the other so we should feel secure."[23] And the new president of Alliance Quebec denounced Bill 178 as a colossal absurdity. "It is incredible," he said, "that people of a supposedly reasonable degree of intelligence should have spent three seconds dealing with this kind of issue." But he doubted that the law was vulnerable to a court challenge. "Frankly," he said, "it's too silly to dignify by contesting it."[24]

At Woody's Pub, it was ordained that the law, as set forth by Ryan, did not go far enough, and we immediately formed something called the Twice As Much Society. The society, it was decided, would lobby for an amendment to Bill 178 that would call for French to be spoken twice as loud as English inside and outside. Inspectors from the language commission would be armed with sound meters to detect Anglophones who spoke above a whisper, sending offenders to the slammer. A Francophone hockey player scoring a goal for le Club de hockey canadien would have to be cheered twice as loud as a minority group teammate. A member of the collectivity, ordering a meal in a restaurant, would have to be served a double portion, and so forth and so on. We also drafted a letter to Premier Bourassa demanding that his fertility payola be made available only to *Québécois de vieille souche*, lest garlicky Allophones, driven by avarice, take to polluting the province with racially impure families of a dozen kids or more.

Then, awash on another round of drinks, we tried to imagine how English would be impoverished if, in order to oblige linguistic zealots, it was shorn of all its French words. One of our number, a middle-aged clothing manufacturer, started things off by recalling how in his first year of puberty the very sight of the word "brassiere," never mind a photograph of a girl actually modeling one—just the word itself—was sufficient to propel him into the bathroom to run cold water over his head. Next we tried to improvise a story, which ordinarily could lean on gallicisms here and there, but now had to make do with Anglo-Saxon substitutes. It began:

"Clarissa and I got together for a head-to-head later that morning. Ah, but how attractive she appeared, seated on her long chair, wearing a linen article from her woman's wardrobe, through which I could just catch a glimpse of her mammary-gland hanger. We had filtered coffee and crescents for breakfast. Then she asked me if we could also have dinner together.

'Of course I could manage it,' I replied. 'Excellent,' she said, 'because I have heard of a public eating place that happily does not specialize in the new kitchen. In fact, the cook has studied at the school of the blue rope.'"

Seven

FOR SOME TIME my meetings with chums at Woody's Pub had necessarily been limited to once a week, because since 1986 my wife and I have been rooted in our cottage on Lake Memphremagog in Quebec's Eastern Townships. We drive to Montreal, where we still maintain an apartment, only once a week, usually staying overnight. Providing we haven't been hit by blowing snow or freezing rain, it's an easy run of an hour and twenty minutes and, in the other direction, it's just a short spin across the border into Vermont, a trip often made by the locals to gas up and buy milk, chickens, and other groceries, all of which are much cheaper Stateside.

Quebec's history, it should be understood, is far from entirely French, the Townships being a case in point. Something like a third of our thirty-two-mile-long Lake Memphremagog lies in Vermont, and our little *soi-disant* Québécois village of Austin, which has so far escaped being renamed by the Commission de toponymie, was in fact named after one Nicholas Austin, of Somersworth, New Hampshire, who came here in 1791 and two years later became the first white settler on the lake. Mr. Austin emigrated to Canada, wrote Mrs. C. M. Day in *Pioneers of the Eastern Townships, a Work Containing Official and Reliable Information Respecting the Formation of Settlements with Incidents in Their Early History and Details of Adventures, Perils and Deliverances*, because "in consequence of his firm allegiance to his Royal Master during the troublous time in which he lived, he was persecuted by the government that came into power."[1]

When Nicholas Austin reached the head of the lake in 1791, he bought a canoe from some Indians who were camping there, and set out across the water.

"Could we but roll back the years to the summer morning of

1791," wrote a regional historian in the Georgeville *Settlement* in 1922, "and view with him the landscape as it unfolded in his progress down the lake, what a scene would be revealed! The broad expanse of the virgin forest, many-tinted and undulating over hill and valley, unscarred and perfect as when formed by the Great Creator: Its dim aisles resonant with the song of birds, the drumming of partridge, the call of the stag, the screech of the panther and all the varied sounds of its teeming avenues; the emerald islands scattered in profusion upon the cerulean expanse of lake; the jutting points and promontories; the sylvan bays lined with pebbled beaches; the receding vistas of headlands, shores and mountains, bathed in the soft glow of the summer sunshine; the distant cry of the loon; the sudden noise of the startled ducks escaping from before the intruder, and the splash of the 'longe' rising to the surface on every hand. Such would have formed some of the sights to captivate the senses of the occupant of the boat as he plied his industrious blade that eventful morning."[2]

Unfortunately, soon after Mr. Austin settled on the lake, clearing ninety-five acres, he became involved in a good deal of litigation and, wrote Mrs. Day, "from being a man of opulence and influence, he became reduced in means and limited in resources."[3] There were also family problems. His wife, Mrs. Day continued, "having suffered for years from a partial derangement of her mental faculties, which was probably induced by a (to her distasteful) change from a home of luxury and refinement, to the hardships and self-denials of life in the woods, involving, as it did, the loss of all moral or intellectual culture. She had been delicately and tenderly reared; and, till her removal to Canada, had been used to occupy a position in society in accordance with her taste and capabilities; is spoken of as having been naturally a person of high spirits, of reserved and uncommunicative nature, but of elevated moral sentiments."[4]

Mr. Austin, who died in 1821 ("ruined in fortune," wrote Mrs. Day, "and disappointed in hope"),[5] was only one of an estimated 45,000 Tories, loyal to King George III, who had emigrated to Canada.

In 1789, two years before Nicholas Austin paddled across Lake Memphremagog, Sir Guy Carleton, Lord Dorchester, governor-in-chief of the (remaining) British North American provinces, requested the Council of Quebec "to put the mark of honour upon the families who adhered to the unity of Empire and joined the Royal Standard in America before the Treaty of Separation in the year 1783."[6] Thereafter, all Loyalists were to be distinguished by the letters "UE," for "Unity of Empire," affixed to their names.

Many of the Loyalists who sought refuge in Canada, wrote Mrs. Day, were prominent and influential men: "Warmly and sincerely attached to the Royal cause, it was with mingled excitement, indignation, and disgust, that they beheld people demanding redress for wrongs which seemed to them more imaginary than real, and enforcing those demands with threatening manifestations."[7] The Loyalists risked not only indignities but also imprisonment as a consequence of their principles: "after prolonged attempts to subdue a power already too strong for them, they were forced to yield to inevitable necessity, and resign house and lands, home and friends, wealth and station, all that men desire in this life, aside from that precious boon itself."

Mrs. Day, a writer of considerable integrity as well as elegance, felt obliged to add:

> But it cannot be denied that many were brought in by the exigencies of the times, who could only be regarded in the light of unavoidable evils, being of that irresponsible, ill-regulated class that accumulates and thrives amid scenes of tumult and commotion, and constitutes a disturbing element in any community.
>
> It is well understood that for many years before the revolution reached a culminating point, a numerous floating population representing many different nationalities had been accumulating in those Colonies which offered not only an asylum for the oppressed of all grades and distinctions but a hiding place for the refugee from justice. This class of people, without fixed principles, or permanent interests in the country, on the breaking out of the war, at once sided with the party which could offer the most tempting inducements. Some were drawn into it by a morbid taste for exciting adventure; others may have

had some private pique to be gratified, or some personal quarrel to be avenged, and but waited the opportunity for giving vent to a long nursed wrath; while others still, who were but designing and unscrupulous adventurers, rushed into the conflict with the mere hope of gaining some advantage.[8]

The United Empire Loyalists, the society of Anglophones *de vieille souche*, still exists today. It has a membership of 3,500, all of whom are obliged to provide documentary proof of their descent from the original Loyalists. A necessary precaution, this, considering that land-hungry Yankees, some of whom didn't cross the new border until 1800, had the gall to promote themselves as "late Loyalists."[9] So the association's credentials society is necessarily strict. According to Vanessa Bacola, UE, one of its genealogists, "Our requirements need to be as strict as the Daughters of the American Revolution and the Mayflower Society."[10]

In the summer of 1989, Quebec on the boil, the United Empire Loyalists' Association nevertheless decided to hold a convention celebrating the two-hundredth anniversary of Lord Dorchester's order in council in Lennoxville, in the very heart of the Eastern Townships. Their guest of honor and keynote speaker was His Royal Highness Prince Philip, Duke of Edinburgh.

Actually, the Loyalists did have some title to the Townships. An early settler, the "Loyal American" Captain Henry Ruiter, formed the Philipsburg King's Rangers to join the British at Ticonderoga in 1783. Then, in 1792, after the prohibition against Loyalists settling so close to the border was lifted, thousands of Americans set down roots in the region. The Loyalists, wrote Walter Stewart in *True Blue, The Loyalist Legend*, were settled in their military units even after these units were disbanded. The truth is, like Israeli settlers positioned on the West Bank almost 200 years later, they were set in place to discourage unfriendly activity, in this case by adventurers out of Vermont and New Hampshire. Stewart noted:

> The Townships were divided into equal lots between parallel concessions roads, and every man, whatever his rank had been,

drew for a lot on a random basis. . . . Although the location of farms was set by lot, the size allotted was determined by the recipient's rank. Civilians received fifty acres, if single; one hundred if the head of a family. Privates got the same allotment, while non-commissioned officers received two hundred acres, and so on up the scale to field officers—colonel and above—who got one thousand acres.[11]

By the mid-nineteenth century there were almost 90,000 Anglophones of British or American descent in the Townships, making it the largest English-speaking community in the province, but today the 34,020 Anglophone Townshippers account for no more than 9 percent of the population, most of them aging, many of them on welfare. Mind you, the Townships was also the birthplace of several men of distinction. Mack Sennett, the King of Comedy, whose silent one-reelers launched the film careers of Charlie Chaplin, W. C. Fields, and the Keystone Kops, was a Townshipper born and bred. Né Michael Sinnott, he was raised on his father's 150-acre spread near Danville and later attended school in Mégantic. Reminiscing about those early days from the safety of California, stretching things a little, he once said, "We often had to walk six or eight miles in ice and snow [to school] in below-zero temperature. Usually it was forty below. People who could afford it banked their houses with manure to keep warm. We were bundled in furs and bogged down with leggings and heavy shoes. To sustain us, Mother always dosed us with a soupçon of the 186 proof."[12] The man who cleaned up Dodge City, Bat Masterson, was also a Townshipper, born Bartholomew Masterson in Henryville in 1853. Another Townshipper, Dr. Joseph Henry Barnard, turned out to have been one of Sam Houston's riders, a hero of the Texan War of Independence. He was buried in Richmond until his body was exhumed by the State of Texas in 1981, the Texans carrying him back to be buried again with honors, a hero of the battle of Goliad, about a hundred miles downstream from the Alamo. The distinguished literary scholar Northrop Frye was born in Sherbrooke, the only full-blown city in the Townships. And the Sherbrooke *Record* was once owned by another Townshipper, Conrad Black, who has since acquired the London *Daily Telegraph*, *The Spectator*, *The Jerusalem Post*, and *Saturday Night* magazine, among other publications. The *Record*, which once boasted a circulation of 30,000, now serves a much-diminished Anglophone community and has to get by with a daily sale of approximately 6,000 copies.

The Townships bar I favor late in the afternoon, the Owl's Nest out on the 243, only a fifteen-minute drive from our cottage on the lake, squats on the edge of a territory known as the Lost Nation. Although most of the regulars at the Owl's Nest are the progeny of families that have been in the Townships for generations, none of them could tell me how the territory came by this name. I discovered the answer in Pearl Mailloux Grenier's *The Lost Nation*, published by the Brome County Historical Society. To begin with, the territory in question went by the innocuous name of Pleasant Valley. Then, sometime in the mid-nineteenth century, missionaries began to appear, summoning the locals to prayer meetings in the local schoolhouse every night of the week. "It is safe to say," wrote Mrs. Grenier, "everyone accepted because it was something to do." But after a week of nightly warnings of the fire and brimstone to come, the preachers asked all those present to come forward for Christ. Nobody made a move. Furthermore, the preachers were told to clear out of town at once or risk being tarred and feathered and ridden out on a rail. Packing their belongings hastily, the preachers seemed disposed to flee, but then one of them was heard to cry out, "O Lord, have mercy on these wretched people for they are truly a lost nation!"[13] And ever since the territory has worn that appellation as a badge of honor.

The regulars at the Owl's Nest are a compatible mix of house painters, carpenters, snow-removal men, and handymen, their wives of both French and English origin, intermarriage commonplace. For the most part, they are the children of farmers who lost their land long ago, selling the "useless" Lake Memphremagog frontage first, off-loading maybe a thousand feet of choice shoreline in 1951 to some dumb city slicker with a hard-on for nature for 25,000 green ones (har, har, har), the same land now worth a cool million, maybe more. Once the French Language Charter was set in place, many of the English-speaking regulars, even the road workers, were obliged to pass a French proficiency test. One of the men, a Hydro-Québec line-man for more than twenty years, told me, "I don't even speak English that good. You know, like with grammar. So why the fuck are they throwing this French shit at me at my age?"

PRINCE PHILIP, SPEAKING in Lennoxville, reminded his au-dience that the original Loyalists had not all been British. Far from it. The most numerous, he said, had been the Germans, accounting for 28 percent, and the next-largest bunch had been the Scots, who made up 23 percent of the Loyalists. Among those loyal to the crown there had also been Mohawk Indians and Africans, some of the latter runaway slaves and others the property of fleeing slave owners. In fact, according to historian Dorothy Williams, author of *Blacks in Montreal, 1628–1986: An Urban Demography*,[14] some 12 percent of the original 45,000 Loyalists had been black.

"I think it would be foolish," Prince Philip told the Loyalists, "to take Canada's future for granted. You have to work for it. You have to have a vision of a civilized and harmonious commu-nity and consciously work toward achieving it. This I believe is what the Loyalists would expect from their descendants."[15]

Less than two months later, some Townshippers, obviously sunshine patriots, began to work against Canada's future. Emboldened by a *Maclean's* magazine poll that revealed 23 per-cent of Quebecers would like to see the province join the United States, André Perron, an unemployed salesman, an-nounced, in Sherbrooke, the formation of Parti Québec-51, its mission to make the province the fifty-first state.

"What about the survival of French culture?" he was asked.

"What good is the mother tongue," he replied, "if you haven't got any food to put on your tongue? . . . Money is the universal language and Americans are very open."[16]

A month later, the party's name changed to Parti-51, Perron called a press conference. He wanted Quebecers to benefit from the low prices of American goods, he said. "The people in border towns like Stanstead know what I'm talking about. They're always lined up at U.S. customs going across to buy their gas."

Then Perron introduced his candidate for Anjou, Michel Gauthier, a truck driver. Gauthier pronounced the French language doomed in Canada. "The way it goes," he said, "[it] is going to disappear anyway in twenty-five or thirty years, if we stay in Canada. With all the immigrants coming in all the time, they'll go with the English people. So in twenty-five or thirty years we're going to assimilate with them. So if we want to get assimilated, I would like the choice to get assimilated with people I like. I would like to get assimilated with the people of the United States."[17]

Eight

PREMIER BOURASSA, riding high in the polls, called an election for September 25, 1989. Michel Gratton, a Cabinet minister and veteran of seventeen years in the National Assembly who had been against Bill 178, announced that he would not run again. He told a reporter that the government, immediately following its landslide victory in 1985, had bungled in not honoring its promise to permit bilingual signs. "I would have preferred," he said, "that we did what we said in our party platform. With hindsight, I think everybody, including Mr. Bourassa, would agree with that."[1]

The Liberals and the PQ aside, twenty-seven other parties decided that they would contest the election, among them the Marxist-Leninist Party, Parti citron, Mouvement socialiste, Parti communiste du Québec, United Social Credit, Parti des travailleurs du Québec, Parti indépendantiste, Party for the Commonwealth of Canada, Parti vert du Québec, and an Anglophone protest group, the Equality Party, which had been formed only a few months earlier. The Equality Party's star candidate, who would be running in the affluent, largely Anglophone suburb of Westmount, a Liberal fortress traditionally rewarded with a Cabinet seat, was a Woody's Pub stalwart: Richard Holden, QC.

If the ostensibly affable but often acerbic Holden, a longstanding maverick and an old chum of Prime Minister Mulroney, had a fault, it was that he never met a reporter he wasn't eager to stroke with a quote, especially if it presented him with the opportunity to violate a confidence. In fact, friends of Holden, myself included, have long since come to assume that any deprecating remark about them published in the press must have originated with him—unless the reporter insists that he has quoted "a reliable source."

Holden had stood for election twice before, once as an independent in a provincial contest and again as a Tory in a federal election. The first time out, in 1962, he endeared himself to everybody by fainting just after he rose to make his nomination speech. A headline in the next morning's *La Presse*, appearing over a photograph of Mrs. Holden fanning her supine husband on the platform, ran:

> *Il déclare la guerre à René Lévesque;*
> *et il s'évanouit.*[2]
> (He declares war on René Lévesque—and then swoons).

The irreverent Holden, much given to quixotic gestures, came to public notice again when, in the late seventies, he tilted his lance against that 107-year-old bastion of WASP rectitude and financial clout, the Sun Life Assurance Company. What happened is that on November 15, 1976, the very day the PQ came to power in Quebec, Sun Life announced that, as a consequence, it would be shifting its head office to Toronto. To grasp what that meant, it is necessary to appreciate that a generation of English-speaking Montrealers, Richard Holden's and mine, was raised on the stirring boast that the massive Sun Life head office rooted in Dominion Square, a handsome granite building enriched by fluted Corinthian columns was, by George, the biggest building in the whole bloody British Empire! Yes, indeed, but so far as Francophones were concerned, it was actually a symbol of Scotch Presbyterian arrogance. They had a point. Although a third of the company's business was done in Quebec, its investment in the province was negligible, and only 200 of its 2,000 employees and two of its twenty-one directors were Francophones. (Since I first published what I took to be the facts in *The New Yorker*, I have heard from John D. McNeil, CEO and Chaiman of the Sun Life Assurance Company of Canada. He wrote to say that since the late seventies, the Sun Life investment in Quebec has grown to be "in excess of $2.0 billion." He also disputed the claim that "a third of the company's business was done in Quebec." He protested, "The facts are that over the years in broad brush terms, Canada has accounted for close to one-half of our total worldwide business while Quebec, not surprisingly, has accounted for around a quarter of our Canadian business.) Holden, arguing that the company's use of policy holders' proxies to endorse the move of its head office was illegal, challenged the directors at a general meeting in Toronto. To nobody's surprise, he lost his case, but he did succeed in slowing down the move. Sadly, Sun Life's departure emboldened many another business in Montreal to follow suit. Since 1976, it is estimated that 14,000 of Montreal's management jobs have been lost to Toronto.

Another Equality Party candidate was a brash seventy-year-old retired radio sportscaster, Gordon Atkinson. Atkinson, a decorated veteran of World War II and the Korean War, was nominated in Montreal's Notre-Dame-de-Grâce constituency while he was on vacation in Europe. On his return, he fed already-amused Francophone reporters by hailing his painfully naïve leader, young Robert Libman, as "the Lech Walesa of Quebec today."[3]

Atkinson wasn't the only equalitarian given to hyperbole. Party president Gerald Klein, an inexperienced youngster, obviously unable to distinguish between farce and tragedy, earned justifiable ridicule in both the French- and the English-language press by comparing the human rights deprivations of Anglophone Quebecers with those of the blacks in South Africa.[4]

Libman, a squeaky-clean twenty-eight-year-old architect whose only previous community involvements had been as coach of a Little League baseball team and as a B'nai B'rith summer camp counselor, told me that he became politicized after he had sat down with some friends in 1988 and grasped that half of their McGill graduating class had moved to Toronto and that many of the others were thinking seriously about it. "I invited eight friends to that first session in my office," he said, "but only three turned up. That was on March 21, 1988, and the next time we got together—after D'Iberville Fortier had complained about the Anglophones being humiliated—there were eight or nine of us. We found out that in order to be recognized as a political party we needed sixty signatures from each of ten different ridings, and early in December we started going door-to-door to collect them. Some people thought we were crazy. 'Good luck, buddy, but you'll never get anywhere.' Then the Supreme Court ruled, Bourassa invoked the notwithstanding clause and brought in Bill 178, and suddenly it was easier to get signatures. By this time maybe forty to fifty people were coming to our meetings. Some of my friends wanted us to call ourselves the Freedom or Liberty party, but I convinced them to go with Equality. Three hundred people attended our first public meeting late in March and, with the necessary number of signatures in hand, we were officially accepted as a political party on April 7, 1989. So I began to look for candidates. I had heard a lot about Holden. Some people like him, others told me he was a *putz*. We met and he said, no, he wouldn't consider running, and then he called me back and suggested we go out for lunch and I knew I had him."

For all that the Equality Party was still considered a non-starter by the politically informed, a bit of a prank, it was also an immediate embarrassment to the anxious pillars of a traditionally timorous Jewish community. After all, Libman was a graduate of Herzliah High School, and almost all of his associates in the Equality Party were also ostensibly nice Jewish boys. He had declared himself a candidate in the D'Arcy McGee riding, just about 80 percent Jewish, its former MNA Herbert Marx now a Superior Court justice. If Libman were elected, what would the Francophones say?

One after another, alarmed Jewish establishment heavies threw their support behind a compliant Liberal candidate, who hinted darkly that if the electors of D'Arcy McGee misbehaved, rocking the collectivity's boat, they would be putting government-pledged funds for Jewish public health and cultural institutions at risk.

Some members of the Jewish community were outraged by such blatant blackmail, but even more, remembering recent incidents in the Montreal suburb of Outremont, were apprehensive.

Nine

CANADIAN MYTHOLOGY has it that until very recently the true movers and shakers in this country were the dour Scotch Presbyterians of the incomparably affluent Montreal suburb of Westmount. If this was in fact once the case, it hasn't been true for years. All the same, a popular French Canadian variation on this theme is enriched by the conviction that, even today, the quintessential Westmount man—a banker—is chauffeured each morning to his office on St. James Street, where, in need of a daily hee-haw, he will foreclose on an impecunious habitant and then hurry home to mount the ravishing but innocent Francophone maid, throwing her off the roof if she gets preggers. The women shop at Holt Renfrew and then repair to the neighboring Ritz-Carlton Hotel for drinks and, providing they are not hopelessly frigid, assignations as well. And once a year the Westmount men and women convene at the Ritz in their tribal finery for St. Andrew's Ball, their champagne-laden tables attended by the white niggers of North America, *Québécois pure laine*, whose parents live in an unheated East End flat, owned by a short fat Jew slumlord, the mother suffering from consumption and the father bound to die without ever once wintering in Hollywood, Florida, a lifelong dream.

Problems.

Today there are probably more French Canadians and Jews rooted in the mansions of Upper Westmount than there are Scots Presbyterian bankers, which suits me just fine, incidentally. And not one of these bankers enjoys anything like the clout of an executive of the Caisse de dépôt et placement du Québec, a.k.a. *La Machine à milliards*, with an estimated bundle of thirty-five billion bucks to play with. And if the banker is still being chauffeur-driven each morning, it is surely to his

French lessons and only later to his office on the street that has long since been born again as rue Saint-Jacques. And your average habitant, though certainly not rich, is doing very nicely these days, thanks to a federally imposed milk quota that entitles Quebec's farmers to produce 48 percent of Canada's industrial milk, needed for the production of yogurt, cheese, and other products. Something else. That legendary bastion of WASP privilege, the Ritz-Carlton Hotel, is now managed by French Canadians, and any day of the week you will hear more French than English being spoken in the bar, which is as it should be.

Even when Westmount was still a true Calvinist power base, some French Canadian historians got it wrong. In Professor Léandre Bergeron's *The History of Quebec, A Patriote's Handbook*, published in 1971, he deals with the World War II political crisis created by the plebiscite. I should explain, for the benefit of non-Canadian readers, that as late as 1942, more than two years into a war that was going badly for the Allies, Prime Minister Mackenzie King's government, fearful of Quebec, conscripted the country's young men for military service within Canada only. Then, in the spring of 1942, King seeking a mandate to send his soldiers overseas to fight, put a question to Canadians. Commenting on the result of the plebiscite, Bergeron wrote:

> In Quebec, 71.2 percent answer NO. The Québécois (the population of Quebec minus the English in Westmount and the Eastern Townships) in fact vote 85 percent NO.[1]

In one sentence, as it were, Bergeron managed to perpetuate not one but two racial clichés popular with Quebec's tribalists:

1. Contrary to the repeated reassurances of PQ leaders, the only genuine Québécois are the French, and the others, even if their families have been living in the province for generations, remain foreigners. *Les autres*. Mind you, even such xenophobia is subject to revision when dictated by economic considerations, as witness the case of the Steinberg supermarket chain, founded by a Jewish immigrant in Montreal, but claimed as a bona fide Québécois institution by the Caisse, prodded by

Premier Bourassa, when it was in danger of being acquired by an Ontario company.

2. The canard that Quebec's Anglophones are roosted only in Westmount opulence or Eastern Townships estates, when the truth is that the vast majority live either in working-class Point St. Charles, Griffintown, and Snowdon or middle-class Montreal West, Notre-Dame-de-Grâce, the West Island, and other suburbs. And, speaking as a latter-day Townshipper myself, I can vouch for the fact that most of the remaining Anglophones out here winter on welfare.

For all that, Westmount is still the cynosure of Francophone wrath. As recently as 1980, René Lévesque, happy to play the demagogue when circumstances called for it, raged in public against what he called "the Westmount Rhodesians."

Actually, Canada *has* been held hostage for at least twenty years by a quarrel endemic to a Montreal suburb. But that suburb is Outremont, not Westmount; Outremont, where the following political figures were either raised or are still resident: Pierre Elliott Trudeau, Robert Bourassa, Jacques Parizeau, Claude Ryan, Camille Laurin.

Today Outremont, rich in parks, tree-lined streets, elegant homes, and modish boutiques and cafés, is where many Francophone artists, intellectuals, and professionals are rooted, but once it also enjoyed a large Jewish component as well.

When I was a boy, living four streets below Park Avenue, a dividing line of sorts, Outremont, blessed Outremont, starting one street above Park, on the west side of Hutchison, was where our doctors and dentists and lawyers and businessmen lived in heated apartments or duplexes or detached fieldstone cottages. Their daughters, so far as we were concerned, were always in season, and we pursued them with vigor if only because they could entertain us in furnished basements with wet bars. The neighborhood, in those days, was well served by a number of synagogues, a YMHA, a Talmud Torah parochial school, the Jewish Public Library, and a variety of delicatessens and bakeries, which have long since followed after the Jewish middle class to other suburbs.

The commercial streets of my boyhood, streets that once catered to the appetites of both Outremont and St. Urbain, have been transmogrified. Take Laurier Avenue, for instance. Schachter's Cigar & Soda, where my father used to retreat some nights for a game of gin rummy, half a cent a point, in the back room, is now a pricey antique shop. Elsewhere, up and down once nondescript, even depressing Laurier, Francophone élan have converted dingy little groceries and shoe repair and barber shops into a bright street of gourmets delights: there's a Le Nôtre, and a splendid butcher shop and other fine food stores, a bookshop and boutiques and several good restaurants. Only a couple of blocks away, on Bernard Avenue, there are more decent restaurants and cafés with sidewalk tables . . . and there are also those obdurate Jews who did not move on with the rest. The Hasidim.

In 1986 Francophone Outremont discovered, to the chagrin of some of its residents, that its Hasidic community, once a negligible part of a population of 23,000, had grown to 3,000, large families commonplace, even as they had been among French Canadians themselves forty years earlier. The trouble surfaced when the Vishnizer Hasidim, one of the twelve sects extant in Montreal, sought a routine change in a zoning law that would enable them to build a synagogue on a vacant lot on St. Viateur Street. The Outremont city council voted 6–3 against the request, the opposition led by Gérard Pelletier, a one-time Front de libération du Québec terrorist who had copped a seven-year jail sentence in 1972 for his role in an armed robbery. "We don't want Outremont to become a Hasidic city," he said. "This minority is not respectful of bylaws."[2]

Then, in August 1988, the monthly *Journal d'Outremont* published a letter by a television personality complaining that the Hasidim were "disturbing, encroaching, bothersome."[3] This, in turn, led to an article in *La Presse*, *"Outremont se découvre un 'problème juif"* ("A 'Jewish Problem' Crops up in Outremont"), in which the Hasidim were described as a "bizarre minority," with the men "in 'pigtails,' all in black, like 'bogeymen,'" and the women and children "dressed like onions."[4] The article, noting the high fertility rate of a religious sect that, just like the Catholic church, forbids birth control, went on to say, "Outremont is discovering its minority had children." Spokesmen for the Canadian Jewish Congress and the B'nai B'rith's League for Human Rights issued a statement of protest. A week later, on Yom Kippur, *La Presse* responded with a two-page spread on the *problème juif,* including a column by Gérard LeBlanc that suggested Anglophone Jews could do penance on their holy day by reading his column. LeBlanc protested that he had nothing against the Jews in general, only against those who were Anglophone. "Jews," he wrote, "are often found in the highest reaches of Anglophone organizations like Alliance Quebec and certain Anglophone media which did everything to make it difficult for Francophones to ensure the survival and promotion of French society in North America,"[5] and then he repeated the familiar charge that Jews had long ago integrated into the province's Anglophone minority rather than its French majority.

Most of the letters in *La Presse,* including one from Claude Ryan and another from the newspaper's very own Lysiane Gagnon, defended the Hasidim, but there was another letter from a man who complained about what he called the self-imposed isolation of Jews and asked, "Is there a single country in the world where the majority of the *native* [italics mine] population really likes the Jews?"[6] The jocular editorial cartoon, titled "Le Problème Franco-Québécois," showed a mournful Hasidic father instructing his three children to pointedly ignore a cheerful family of Francophones, one of whose children is waving warmly as they pass. The Hasidic father says, *"ces gens-là, ne s'intégreront jamais!"* ("these people will never integrate!")[7] Obviously the Hasidic father, surprisingly well versed in secular matters, was echoing an old prejudice against French Canadians once held by Franklin Delano Roosevelt. On May 18, 1942, Roosevelt wrote to then prime minister Mackenzie King:

When I was a boy in the "nineties" I used to see a good many French Canadians who had rather recently come into the New Bedford area near the old Delano place at Fair Haven. They seemed very much out of place in what was still an old New England community. They segregated themselves in the mill towns and had little to do with their neighbors. I can remember that the old generation shook their heads and used to say, "This is a new element which will never be assimilated. . . ."[8]

The *La Presse* editorial writer ventured that Jews had protested the newspaper's original article because they failed to understand French language and culture or they would have recognized, as if that were the heart of the matter, that "dressed like onions" was a colloquialism of the province's St. Jean region that meant "bundled up to the neck."[9] Finally, he suggested that possibly the only people who should be reading *La Presse* were *Québécois pure laine*, who at least understood the nuances of regional expressions.

The following winter another *La Presse* columnist wrote, "Jews have always intrigued me. They are a very complicated people and even, I believe, a bit twisted. . . ." As evidence, he quoted a story from *The Jerusalem Post* that told of a Tiberias hotel owner who had enlivened a New Year's party for his guests by having a helicopter appear overhead, a couple inside simulating intercourse. "Strange people, as I said," he wrote. "Very religious among themselves, they don't eat pig meat, which doesn't stop them, as we noted, from screwing naked in helicopters above swimming pools."[10]

Since then Irving Abella, a professor of history at York University in Toronto and coauthor of *None Is Too Many*, a damning indictment of Canadian policy toward Jewish immigration during World War II, has made public a survey, undertaken at York's Institute for Social Research, that measured anti-Semitic attitudes. Twenty-eight percent of Anglophone Canadians, but 42 percent of Francophones, also thought that Jews were more willing than others to use shady practices to get ahead. The survey, based on interviews with 3,500 Canadians, the work of University of Toronto professor Joseph

Fletcher, confirmed that anti-Semitism was far more prevalent in Quebec than elsewhere in Canada, some 70 percent of his respondents in *la belle province* falling into that category.

Montreal's Jewish community, once the largest and most vibrant in Canada, 120,000 strong twenty years ago, had diminished to 95,000 by 1989, two-thirds of that figure more than fifty years old. Actually, even more Montreal Jews than these statistics indicate have quit the city, but over the past thirty years the community has also been replenished by the immigration of French-speaking Sephardic Jews from North Africa, who now account for approximately a quarter of the city's Jewish population. Jews who have remained behind in Montreal feel that Premier Bourassa betrayed them with Bill 178, and they are wary of the tribalism that has taken hold here. René Lévesque was not an anti-Semite. Neither is Jacques Parizeau. All the same, Jews who have been Quebecers for generations understand only too well that when thousands of flag-waving nationalists march through the streets roaring *"Le Québec aux Québécois!"* they do not have in mind anybody named Ginsburg. Or MacGregor, come to think of it.

Ten

I WAS BROUGHT UP in a Quebec that was reactionary, church-ridden, and notoriously corrupt—a stagnant backwater—its *chef* for most of that time, Premier Maurice Duplessis, a political thug—and even its intellectuals sickeningly anti-Semitic for the most part. However, when I was first registered for school (at the age of six in 1937), within the sheltering confines of a largely self-contained working-class Jewish community, I was of course unaware that *Le Devoir* had advocated that Jews be denied civil rights or that one Anatole Vanier had already written in the influential *L'Action nationale*, "By their dispersion and their persistent habit of elbowing others out of the way, [Jews] are the authors of their own misfortune. . . . What is happening in the new Germany is germinating everywhere where Jews are considered as intruders. And where, one may well ask, are they considered otherwise?"[1]

We did not yet have a Canadian national anthem, and so our school day began with the singing of "God Save the King" or that then ubiquitous song, since adjudged politically incorrect for obvious reasons, that began:

> In days of yore, from Britain's shore,
> Wolfe, the dauntless hero, came,
> And planted firm Britannia's flag
> On Canada's fair domain.
>
> Here may it wave, our boast and pride,
> And joined in love together
> The Thistle, Shamrock, Rose entwine
> The Maple Leaf forever!
>
> The Maple Leaf, our emblem dear
> The Maple Leaf forever;
> God save our King, and Heaven bless
> The Maple Leaf forever!

In *The History of Quebec, A Patriote's Handbook*, Léandre Bergeron has written that in the thirties and forties many in Quebec saw the Jews of Montreal as their worst enemy.

At the beginning of the twentieth century, Jewish immigrants from Russia, Poland, almost everywhere in Europe, found themselves like most other immigrants at the bottom of the social ladder. However, by playing the capitalist game, a few of them managed to escape from the exploited class to become the owners of small businesses, factories, shops and grocery stores—copying the life style of the Montreal English bourgeoisie. They adopted the exploiter's language, English, using the French only to give orders to their employees in their shops and to their maids at home.

So to some people, the exploiters of the Québécois no longer seem to be the English who are pulling the hidden strings of high finance and big business, but the Jews of St. Lawrence and Craig Streets and the Jewish shoe and clothing manufacturers who operate more openly.[2]

The Jews of Craig Street, I should explain, though few in number, were pawnshop proprietors, and our section of St. Lawrence, or The Main, as we called it, was triumphantly Jewish. It was where working-class Jewish families went to buy their food, haberdashery, and furniture. And in my experience none of these families, my own included, could afford French Canadian maids or other employees. In fact, if my brother did become fluent in French, it was because, in the forties, he was a student at the Université de Montréal. My own initial experience of French Canadians was far from unpleasant. I had, along with a couple of school friends, acquired a chemistry set, and once a week the three of us went to visit a French Canadian pharmacist to present him with a list of our requirements. I can no longer remember the man's name, but he ran a drugstore at the corner of Park Avenue and St. Viateur, in the very heart of the city's Jewish quarter, and he could not have treated a Nobel laureate with more courtesy, nicely commingled with *gravitas,* than he did three scruffy kids determined to create the ultimate stink bomb. He would unfailingly invite us into a back room, where chemicals were stored in large jars, weighing our purchases on a delicate scale, contriving never to charge us more than a token thirty-five or fifty cents for whatever we needed. Come summer, our families would rent what I can only describe as shacks from French Canadians in the Laurentians, usually in Shawbridge, or down the hill, across the North River, in Prévost. None of these cottages had electricity, but each boasted its own bumble bee-ridden outhouse. One summer we rented from a Monsieur Blondin, a Shawbridge blacksmith, and I spent a good deal of time watching him at his anvil, hammering away at red-hot horseshoes, indifferent to the cascading sparks. Blondin's kids were familiar with the best fishing holes and knew where the wild raspberries grew in abundance. On our field trips together, sniffing out differences, we exchanged useful sociological data, such as "Do your father and mother still sleep together?"

Though I was never directly confronted by hostility in either Shawbridge or Prévost, the highway was rich in reminders that there were clearly those who resented us. Swastikas had been daubed on some overhanging rocks, and I remember a boulder on which somebody had painted:

A BAS LES JUIFS

Miriam Chapin wrote in *Quebec Now*, which she published in 1955, that in the years leading up to World War II, one of the most outrageous "accusations evolved by the anti-Semitic fringe of the nationalist movement was that Jews gained control of the clothing business in order to force modest French Canadian maidens to wear improper gowns modelled in New York styles."[3] Once war broke out, wrote Chapin, the charges grew more serious. Laurent Barré, the Quebec minister of agriculture, informed the Assembly

that his son, on entering the army, had been subjected to the indignity of a medical examination by a Jewish doctor, and had been ill as a consequence. "Our children were thrown into the hands of infamous Jewish examiners who regaled themselves on naked Canadian flesh." L'Abbé Gravel of Boischatel, near

Quebec City, explained the fall of France to his parishioners by telling them that France was dechristianizing itself. "If it lost the war, it was because in the years preceding it had that dirty Jew Blum at its head."[4]

From the beginning, French Canadian nationalism has been badly tainted by racism. The patron saint of the *indépendantistes*, the Abbé Lionel Groulx, was not only a virulent anti-Semite but also a nascent fascist, an unabashed admirer in the thirties of Mussolini, Dollfuss, and Salazar. In 1935 Groulx wrote that he longed for the appearance of *un chef* who would lead Quebec into "the new order which is evolving, in which the theories by which we live today appear perhaps to have expired." Even earlier, Groulx's quest for an indigenous superman led him to revive the story of Dollard des Ormeaux, a French officer who was sent out to New France in 1657, where he was posted to the garrison of Ville-Marie, as Montreal was then known. Three years later Dollard led sixteen companions into battle against three hundred Iroquois not far from Long Sault, in defense of Ville-Marie, according to some historians. After holding out for eight days against all odds, Dollard and his party were overwhelmed and killed, but the Iroquois abandoned their plan of attacking the settlement. In another version of the story, favored by other historians, the Iroquois had no intention of attacking Ville-Marie but were bound for the settlement to trade their furs. Dollard and his party, actually bushwhackers, set out to rob them and died in the attempt.

Burnishing the myth of Dollard for the benefit of young nationalists, Groulx held him up as an inspiring example of the hero who was willing to sacrifice his life in defense of French Canadian culture. On occasion the abbé's enthusiasm for the cult of Dollard radiated something like adolescent sexual heat. Certainly his conclusion to the lecture *"Si Dollard revenait . . ."* delivered at the Monument National Theatre in Montreal in 1919, was a veritable rhapsody:

O Commander of the old Fort of Ville-Marie, it is time you were among us! We have such pressing need of a young leader like you, a leader of men. Look, on the frontier where you fell a barbarous throng as menacing as the old threatens our French soul. The work we must now undertake is one of total reconstruction and restoration. Arise, Dollard, and live on your granite pedestal. Summon us, with virile charm, with hero's accents. We lift toward you our hands quivering like palm leaves, ardent with ambition to serve. Together we shall work for the reconstruction of our family's house. And should you command it, O Dollard, O powerful leader, we are ready to follow you to the supreme holocaust for the defense of our French tongue and faith.[5]

Lionel-Adolphe Groulx, who was born on a farm not far from Montreal in 1878, was sent off to study for the priesthood at the age of thirteen. Five years later he wrote in his diary that he was eager to do battle with Jews, Freemasons, "and the fanaticism of other races which cannot forgive us for remaining French." With this in mind, he founded L'Action catholique in 1901, a nationalist movement that evolved into the Association catholique de la Jeunesse canadienne-française (ACJC) by 1917, also the year in which Groulx was blessed with the insight that Canada's soul was menaced by "cosmopolitan European immigration," that is to say, Jews. Deeply influenced by the French fascist writer Charles Maurras, who had already formed the party L'Action française in France, Groulx founded a newspaper of the same name in Quebec to advertise his conviction that race "determines the political, economic, social and intellectual life of a nation." Elaborating on the theme of race, he published a novel under a pseudonym in 1922: *L'Appel de la Race*. The sins of the novel's protagonist, a hugely successful lawyer named Jules de Lantagnac, were threefold: he had become bilingual, moved to Ottawa, and taken an English Protestant wife, who converted to Catholicism. Happily, a sagacious priest eventually straightened out the errant lawyer. Whatever Abbé Groulx's merits as a writer of polemics, his verse anticipated Hallmark cards and he was an appalling novelist, cursed with a tin ear among other failings. But he was an effective propagandist. Following the scene of de Lantagnac's epiphany, which comes after a visit to the cemetery where many of his ancestors are buried:

Lantagnac's voice faltered as he uttered the last words in a moved and solemn tone. Then he went on in a firmer voice: "Thanks to your guidance, Father Fabien, my intellectual being was made whole again by my contact with the great masters of French thought; now my emotional being has been fulfilled by the countryside around Saint-Michel, the people, the things, the sweep of the horizon, the memories of my paternal house. On the Lantagnac tombs I was reconciled with my ancestors and my race. I realized then, indeed I felt it as a palpable reality, that the Lantagnac I had become was a doomed and anarchic force. I could not help thinking, as I strolled among the tombs, that here on this earth whatever value we have can only be achieved through tradition and continuity. One generation must rise on the shoulders of the previous one. Just as great works of art cannot be created with isolated sentences or disjointed fragments so two great races cannot be created with disconnected families. I can hear the voice of my dead ancestors whispering to me: 'A long time ago Gailhard de Lantagnac inherited the second farm on Chenaux Lane in Saint-Michel from Roland de Lantagnac, then later [Roland de Lantagnac, called Lamontagne inherited it] from Paul Lamontagne; because of them all, because of the successive and cumulative work of all these generations, a corner of the homeland was cleared and made habitable; proficiency in agriculture was gradually learned; successive generations of Lamontagnes took possession of a large portion of the parish of Saint-Michel and in their homes was preserved the moral force which has brought you back to your original integrity.'"

The priest's face increasingly radiated happiness: "Your words are pure gold, my friend."

Lantagnac got up. His hands resting lightly on his hips, his shoulders squared, he stood erect in an attitude which he often adopted when strongly moved: "That is not all, Father. There in the cemetery at Saint-Michel, upon my family's tombs, I made a solemn resolution. Shall I tell you what it was?"

"Yes, do," quickly replied Father Fabien, hoping to hear the ultimate decision.

"I promised my ancestors that I would restore my children to them."

"Good for you!"

"My sons and daughters," Lantagnac continued, "have some English blood in their veins because of their mother; but through me they have inherited above all the ancient blood of the Lantagnacs, of our Canadian ancestors to begin with, and of the French Lantagnacs from Monteil and Grignan—forty generations. I have vowed that this is the side to which they must turn."

"Good for you!" repeated Father Fabien.[6]

A contemporary of Abbé Groulx's, a French Canadian patriot cut from much finer cloth, the far more cultivated Henri Bourassa—born in Montreal in 1868, elected to Parliament in 1896, a founder of *Le Devoir* in 1910—was unfortunately for many years also tainted by anti-Semitism. In 1906, when Parliament was pondering a resolution of sympathy for victims of Russian pogroms, Bourassa contributed to the debate, saying, "Russian peasants have been sucked for centuries by Jewish usurers . . . it is not surprising that they are now acting terribly in dealing with them." Then, during a debate on the Lord's Day Act, he pronounced again: "The experience of every civilized country is that Jews are the most undesirable class of people any country can have."[7] He also came out against an immigration policy for the West that, he claimed, would people the prairies with foreigners, that is to say, Jews from Poland and Russia, rather than French or Belgian colonists. In 1915, however, he had a change of heart of sorts and wrote to a constituent, "Perhaps I am mistaken, but the tendency [of certain Catholics to explain everything as the action of Freemasonry] and International Jewry has always seemed false to me. . . . In many cases, the enemies of the Church and the Fatherland have done without Jews and Freemasons nicely in achieving their work of destruction. I hope you will not be scandalized if I tell you that repeated reading of the works of Drumont has cured me of anti-Semitism."[8]

In his indispensable *The French Canadians*, Mason Wade describes Bourassa as "keenly intelligent, idealistic, widely read in both French and English and a powerful speaker in either tongue, unimpeachable in character, deeply religious, highly cultured, and charming in manner. . . ."[9] Opposed to Canadian participation in both the Boer War and World War I, Bourassa set out his views on British imperialism in a lecture delivered at the Théâtre national in Montreal in 1901 that was published as a pamphlet a year later:

> British imperialism—as opposed to British democracy, to British traditions, to British grandeur—is a lust for landgrabbing and military dominion. Born of the overgrowth of British power, bred by that blatant and stupid sense of pride known as *Jingoism*, it delights in high-sounding formulas:—*"Britannia rules the waves"*. . . . *"Britons never shall be slaves"*. . . . *"Trade follows the Flag"*. . . .[10]

If Henri Bourassa was not immune to the racial prejudice that was a plague in his time, he was nonetheless something of a visionary. Speaking at the first Congress of the French Language in Quebec in 1913, he stated, "The conservation of the language is absolutely necessary for the conservation of the race, its genius, its character and its temperament" and went on to argue that if French Canadians lost their language, "We would perhaps be mediocre Englishmen, passable Scots, or bad Irishmen, but we would not be true Canadians." And then, anticipating the policies Pierre Trudeau would set in place some sixty years later, he insisted on the right of French Canadians to use their mother tongue from Halifax to Vancouver. If the two languages were official in Canada, he declared, both had the right to exist in every aspect of Canadian public life.

IN 1933, IN DEFENSE OF HIS NOTION of racial purity set out in *L'Appel de la Race*, Abbé Groulx's review, now called *L'Action nationale*, declared that it would be necessary to deny Jews full civil and political rights as well as cut off their immigration from Germany. "Happy are the peoples who have found dictators," he wrote a year later under a pseudonym, at a time when the busy abbé was also involved in the Achat chez nous movement. This was a campaign, sponsored by church officials, to persuade Québécois to avoid Jewish shopkeepers, who, according to *Le Devoir*, had "cheating and corruption in their bloodstream."[11]

As I was born and bred in Quebec in the years when the dominant political party was the Union nationale, I was of course used to corruption in high and low places, some of it tolerable. Driving out to join us for summer weekends in Shawbridge, for instance, our fathers always kept a folded two-dollar bill in the same celluloid case as their license, just in case they were stopped by a provincial speed cop. Come an election, university students were enlisted to stuff the ballot boxes, paid to vote for the Union nationale candidate as often as twenty times, having been thoughtfully provided beforehand with the names of those who were housebound or had died since the last census. Tooling about the countryside, we never had any doubt which riding had voted for *le chef* and which had been delinquent. Those ridings that had been politically correct enjoyed paved roads, and those that hadn't, didn't. Out on the hustings, Duplessis didn't mince words. He threatened townships blatantly. "Do you want a new hospital? A new bridge? A new school? Then vote Union nationale. I would hate to force gifts on you that wouldn't be appreciated."

Maurice Duplessis, founder of the Union nationale, was premier of Quebec from 1936 to 1939. Returned to power in 1944, he served as premier as well as his own attorney general until his death in 1959, his party surviving in office for another year. If Duplessis's band of bandits cannot be credited with the invention of corruption in Quebec politics, they can certainly claim that, inspired by unshackled greed, they were incomparably proficient in its practice. During the Union nationale's last period of uninterrupted rule, liquor licenses for Montreal nightclubs sold for as much as $30,000, whereas later, under the Liberal government that had displaced it, they could be obtained for $100. In 1961, a Royal Commission, reviewing the Union nationale record, estimated that kickbacks paid out by companies doing business with the provincial government over a sixteen-year period came to about a hundred million dollars, or roughly a billion in today's bucks.

A shrewd but cruel man, Duplessis, while in office, delighted in humiliating his Cabinet members in the Assembly, yelling *"Assieds-toi!"* at any one of them who rose to speak without his permission. Acting as his own attorney general, he often sent out his notoriously brutal provincial cops to club acquiescence into men in the picket lines. The years in power of this Québécois variation of the banana republic strongman were later dubbed the time of *la grande noirceur*, "the great darkness," by the intrepid intellectuals who opposed him, among them René Lévesque, Pierre Trudeau, Jean Marchand, Gérard Pelletier, and André Laurendeau. It was Laurendeau—appointed editor in chief of *Le Devoir* in 1958—who developed the theory of *le roi nègre*, that is to say, that it was the real rulers of Quebec (the English) who manipulated a French Canadian (Duplessis), allowing him to govern the province, just as colonial powers appointed African puppets to keep their tribes in order.

In 1958, after Duplessis had ordered his provincial police to throw a *Le Devoir* reporter out of a press conference being held in his office, Laurendeau responded in an editorial. With two exceptions, he noted, Quebec's other newspapers had not protested the outrage. He was surprised, in particular, by the silence of the English-language press, which, he observed, was usually "more sensitive than we are to any infringement of their liberties." He continued:

> . . . The English papers in Quebec act like British administrators in an African colony. Wise in the arts of political science, the British rarely destroy the political institutions of a conquered country. They keep a close check on the nigger-king but they wink at his whims. On occasion they permit him to chop off a few heads; it's just part of the local folklore. But one thing would never occur to them: to expect the nigger-king to conform to the high moral and political standards of the British.
>
> The main thing is to get the nigger-king to support and protect British interests. Once this collaboration is assured, the rest is less important. Does the princeling violate democratic principles? What else can you expect of the natives? . . .
>
> I am not attributing these attitudes to the English minority in Quebec. But it is as though some of their leaders have subscribed to the theory and practice of the nigger-king hypothesis.

They pardon in M. Duplessis, chief of the native people of Quebec, things they would not tolerate in one of their own kind.

You can see it in the Legislative Assembly. We saw it in the last municipal election. We have just seen it demonstrated again in Quebec.

The result is . . . constant collusion between Anglo-Quebec financial interests and the rottenest elements in provincial politics.[12]

True, there was collusion. Certainly some odium should be reserved for those ostensibly fastidious Montreal WASPs in high finance who found Duplessis and his band convenient to deal with, if uncouth. But, even so, Laurendeau's face-saving *roi nègre* analogy won't wash. It is too clever by half. After all, in Quebec, unlike in the African colonies, the "natives" had the vote. And, as I argued some years back in the pages of the *Atlantic Monthly*, if Duplessis ran the province out of his pocket for twenty years, enriching his cronies, it was the French-speaking majority that thrust him into office again and again and again. The shame, such as it is, is theirs, not mine.

Another attempt to blame *les autres* for a failing of many *Québécois pure laine* appears in Bergeron's *History of Quebec*, in which he wrote:

But anti-semitism in Quebec existed largely in the minds of the English who were only too happy to stir it up on occasion and bring it forward as more "evidence" that the Québécois are inescapably fascist and reactionary, and not to be trusted to govern themselves. The English rejoiced all the more when the Québécois *could be persuaded* [italics mine] to blame the Jew as his chief exploiter. Hiding behind the big enterprises and institutions of high finance, the English and American capitalists cynically played off Jews against Québécois. In fact, the real anti-semite was the English imperialist colonizer, who kept the Jewish bourgeois out of his social clubs and shuddered to see Jews buying property in Westmount.[13]

Once again we are dealing in half-truths. Yes, anti-Semitism was rife among the WASP bourgeoisie, which did bar Jews from its clubs, established quotas against them in universities, and did its best to prevent them from buying property in Westmount or the Town of Mount Royal, but they most certainly didn't have to persuade French Canadians to adopt a cause advocated from just about every one of their church pulpits. It is worth noting that in Bergeron's history, subtitled *A Patriote's Handbook*, he fails to point out that one of the stated aims of the Patriotes' rebellion of 1837–38 was that all Jews in Upper and Lower Canada be strangled and their goods confiscated. Abbé Groulx, Bergeron tells us, was an early leader of Quebec nationalists, who dreamed of a French state that might be called Laurentie, but the closest he comes to acknowledging that this vile little cleric was also a fascist is to say, *en passant*, "[he] had praise for Mussolini," and he never once mentions that Groulx was also a fervent and hardworking Jew-baiter.

Another nationalist hero, André Laurendeau, wrote in *Les Cahiers des Jeune-Canada* in 1933, "*Les Israélites aspirent—tout le monde sait cela—au jour heureux où leur race dominera le monde. Ils ne sont d'aucun peuple, mais ils sont de tous pays; partout par la puissance que communique l'argent.*"[14] ("The Jews aspire—everyone knows this—to that happy day when their race will rule the world. They are of no people, but they are of every country; everywhere, by that power that money bestows.")

According to Mason Wade and others, Laurendeau changed his mind about Jews after a two-year sojourn in Europe, including a passage through Hitler's Germany, before he returned to Montreal in 1937 to become editor of *L'Action Nationale*. But on his watch, the magazine continued to publish anti-Semitic bilge. As late as 1939, Roger Duhamel, president of the St. Jean Baptiste Society and a director of *Le Devoir*, wrote, "*Le Juif, à travers le monde, exerce une activité parasitaire . . . abaisse le niveau de la moralité, etc. etc.*"[15] ("The Jew, throughout the world, engages in parasitical activities, lowers the level of morality, etc., etc.")

In June 1941 Canada, already at war for three years, proclaimed compulsory military service, but only for the defense of the country. A good thing, too, according to Léandre Bergeron, who wrote that, after the fall of France, the Québécois had "no desire to get killed defending the interests of imperialist powers," but "they were ready to fight to the death against an eventual German invasion of Quebec."[16] On the other hand, more than 50,000 Québécois enlisted for overseas service in 1941, and some were among the 2,752 Canadians who died in the botched 1942 raid on Dieppe.

In April 1942, Prime Minister Mackenzie King, reneging on a promise, ordered a plebiscite to be held. It put the following question to Canadians: "Do you agree to free the government from all obligations resulting from previous promises restricting the methods of mobilization for military service?"

In response to the plebiscite, Jean Drapeau, the future mayor of Montreal, organized the Ligue pour la défense du Canada, with the help of André Laurendeau, among others, to bolster the No side in Quebec. A rally organized by the Ligue in February, its speakers urged on with shouts of "Down with the Toronto Two Hundred!" and "Down with international Jewish finance!" ended with a mob charging down The Main, smashing the plate-glass windows of Jewish shops, yelling, "Kill them! Kill them!"

Recalling the event, Laurendeau wrote:

Our audiences had perhaps inherited the vague anti-Semitism of the Depression years. It was a feeling that came naturally to shopkeepers going broke who were furious against merchants who were smarter than they were and reputedly less scrupulous. It was kind of astonishment and revulsion directed *against foreigners* [italics mine] whose habits were disconcerting and who had the reputation of getting rich quick. It was a kind of pseudo-religious emotion working against the people who had crucified the Savior, against the race who had shouted, "May his blood fall on the heads of our children and our children's children." In short, it was the whole apparatus of anti-Semitism which was popular in the western world.

For that matter French Canadians had no monopoly on this prejudice, but they expressed it more noisily than others. I must admit its existence among some of us.[17]

The overall Canadian reply to Mackenzie King's question was Yes 63.7 percent, No 36.3 percent.

Commenting on the Québécois' large vote against, the ever-logical Léandre Bergeron wrote: "The Québécois are opposed to fascism but refuse to have a uniform put on their backs to be sent overseas and used as cannon fodder for the English."[18]

The Ligue pour la défense du Canada evolved into a political party, the Bloc populaire, strongly nationalist in tone, disposed to look with favor on Salazar, Franco, and Marshal Pétain, but split over whether its worst enemy was international socialism or the Jews. According to an April 1943 Gallup Poll, the Bloc was favored by 37 percent of Quebec voters. So in the federal election that summer the Bloc—André Laurendeau now established as its provincial leader—decided to field candidates in Cartier, my own working-class Jewish neighborhood in Montreal, and the Eastern Townships riding of Stanstead, which included the largely French Canadian mill town of Magog as well as a considerable Anglophone component.

The Bloc's candidate had to contend with four rivals—Fred Rose, a Communist, the most prominent of them. Of these four *Le Devoir* reported that the Bloc candidate had "commented with humor" that "there isn't very much Canadian about those guys. They sound more like Jerusalem Canadians."

Cartier, noted Brian McKenna and Susan Purcell in their splendid biography of Jean Drapeau, was something special, election day a time of "brass-knuckle fights in polling booths between rival gangs of telegraphers wheeling from poll to poll to vote in other people's names and arriving simultaneously, others voting from long lists of fictitious people registered at fictitious addresses."[19]

In any event, Fred Rose won by 150 votes and became the first and only Communist ever to sit in Parliament, but the Bloc's man was triumphant in Stanstead.

As of December 1944 Canada's Reserve Army draftees—or the "zombies," as we had come to call them—were no longer safe, but could actually be sent overseas to fight. Not all of them, wrote Léandre Bergeron, responded favorably to the opportunity.

> As for the soldiers themselves, of the 10,000 due to leave for Europe on January 3rd, 1945, 7,800 go AWOL. Of a total of 18,943 deserters, Quebec contributes close to 10,000. These Québécois, all in uniform and ready to defend their country to the death if attacked, refuse to get butchered in Europe for the benefit of England, France and the United States. These patriots whom the English treat as cowards and traitors are opposed to fascism, but also have the courage to fight the colonialism of Ottawa, London and Washington by this individual action, and to face the consequences.[20]

Once again, Bergeron is peddling bilge water. He needn't be so defensive about French Canadian valor. Many *Québécois pure laine* did grasp that World War II was about rather more than colonialism and fought with honor in the Canadian armed forces overseas, but to suggest that those who took to the woods—French or English—were propelled by ideological considerations is utter nonsense. With very few exceptions, they were understandably determined to save their pale white asses, and that's all there was to it.

IN 1958, ANDRÉ LAURENDEAU became editor of *Le Devoir*. Five years later, Prime Minister Lester Pearson appointed him co-chairman of the Royal Commission on Bilingualism and Biculturalism, a position he filled until his death in 1968. He was an interesting man—intelligent, troubled—a perplexed observer of the Canadian scene. In 1991, the diaries he kept during the years he served with the B & B Commission were published in an English translation by Patricia Smart and Dorothy Howard, with an encomium from Lise Bissonnette, the present publisher of *Le Devoir*, on the back cover. Reviewing the *Diary* in *The Globe and Mail*, Ms. Bissonnette adjudged Laurendeau to be a "great" writer, which makes one wonder, in passing, what adjective she might have held in reserve to describe Proust, Balzac, or Flaubert.

Laurendeau did in fact become an able and likable journalist, alert to Canadian conundrums. "I often have the impression," he wrote in 1964, "that there is a fatigue that comes from being Canadian—an almost impossible undertaking and a heavy responsibility, given the proximity of the United States."

That same year, justifiably irritated by the ignorance regarding Quebec he encountered again and again on his tours with the B & B Commission, he complained at some length about this pervasive provincialism.

> Most of them are afraid we want to force them to speak French, and that explains their hostility. Everywhere it's necessary to insist that that is not the case. . . . In the big cities we are constantly being told how hard it is to get used to speaking or understanding French when there's never any chance to use it. I admit that the more often I hear this argument, the less convincing I find it, especially when we're in the presence of intellectuals and when it's simply a question of being able to read French. In Halifax I began to refer to the number of French who know German without ever having set foot in Germany, or of British who know French, and who can therefore communicate with the works of that country even if they can't carry on a conversation in the other language. In other words, there is a real intellectual laziness—doubtless a North American phenomenon—which has quite serious consequences, as it prevents hundreds of academics from communicating directly with French Canada, at least by means of its newspapers, magazines and books. Their error seems to me twofold: both in relation to their level of culture, and to that of a country in which a third of the population is French-speaking.[21]

On February 22, 1964, he put succinctly a feeling common to many Quebecers—myself included—on travels through the western provinces:

> Faced with certain Anglophones, I feel an inner urge towards separatism: "They're too deaf, they won't listen to anything but force." But when I get home, the separatists make me a Canadian again: they're too naïve, too unaware of political reality—or else strangely fickle and superficial. . . .[22]

The same night he also stated precisely the unsolved problem that is still confounding Canadians of good will:

> How to achieve an arrangement in which the minimum of what is being demanded by French Canadians today would be combined with the maximum of what Anglophones judge acceptable?[23]

Unfortunately, Laurendeau, commendably quick to react to any insult to French Canadian sensibilities, was totally blind to the affront Abbé Groulx represented to the Jews. On April 18, 1964, he wrote in his diary:

> Today the *Montreal Star* published an article (in my opinion a stupid one) on the racism of Abbé Groulx. I believe it was directly inspired by Mason Wade's book *The French Canadians*. The following extract gives an idea of its tone:
>
> "He has indeed almost elevated racism to the dignity of a dogma, a strange conclusion to come to by a Christian. . . . If this be treason, let its terms be set. The terms are racist. . . . The values he cherishes are racist and must be maintained. The call of the blood transcends all others and when he calls the English Canadian 'racist,' it is because he profoundly believes that there can be no compromise and that poison must be placed at the roots of the very revival and enlightenment upon which French Canada has staked its future."
>
> All this is all the more strange because in the last few years the *Montreal Star* has been making a real effort to understand what's going on in Quebec. And now, here is a flaming up again of the old points of view: all of a sudden the *Star* is incapable of distinguishing between racism and cultural nationalism. . . .[24]

It was unjust, Laurendeau concluded, to attack Groulx for things he was not guilty of. But surely it was Laurendeau, among others, who could not distinguish between racism and cultural nationalism. As late as 1954, Abbé Groulx, still pondering the Jewish question, wrote to a Mr. Lamoureux,

> *Mal enraciné partout où il se trouve, se refusant à toute assimilation, l'ordre politique et social autour de lui, lui est indifférent. C'est la raison,*

sans doute, qui le fait se trouver mêlé à toutes les révolutions quand il n'est pas l'un des principaux agents. Il faut compter tout autant avec sa passion innée de l'argent. Passion souvent monstrueuse qui enlève tous les scrupules. De l'argent, il est prêt à en faire de tous bois. Ici encore, comme il arrive de trouver le Juif au fond de toutes les affaires, affaires louches, de toutes les entreprises de pornographie: livres, cinéma, théâtres, etc. Ce même souci d'argent lui fait enjamber, dans les affaires, dans les professions, tout scrupule moral.[25]

The Jew never puts down roots anywhere, refuses to assimilate, and is indifferent to the political and social order around him. No doubt that is why he gets involved in all the revolutions— when he isn't one of the main instigators. His natural passion for money must also be reckoned with. A passion that is often monstrous and which makes him lose all his scruples. He is ready to make money from anything. Jews can be found behind all businesses, all shady enterprises, all the pornography opera- tions: books, cinema, theatre, etc. This same concern for money makes him put aside all moral scruples.

Bigoted clerics were not uncommon during Groulx's halcyon days, which I take to be the thirties, a decade when that notori- ously anti-Semitic radio priest, Father Charles Coughlin, founder of the National Union for Social Justice, flourished, in the United States. What is astonishing is that given the nature of the racist claptrap that was Groulx's stock-in-trade he did not fade away, like Coughlin, a blight limited to his times, but went on to become a major influence on some of Quebec's lead- ing intellectuals and politicians, among them Laurendeau, Claude Ryan, and Jean Drapeau. "We loved him dearly," wrote Laurendeau after the eighty-nine-year-old abbé died in 1967. "He was," wrote Claude Ryan, "the spiritual father of modern Quebec. Everything noteworthy, everything novel on the Quebec scene has carried the imprint of Groulx's thought."

Jean Drapeau, Montreal's ebullient mayor for twenty-three years, the promoter who brought us Expo 67 and the 1976 Olympic Games, was not only a disciple of Groulx but also an admirer of the fascist writer Charles Maurras. In 1940 Drapeau wrote in the Université de Montréal's newspaper, *Le quartier latin*, that the streets where I was brought up, in Montreal's old

Jewish quarter, were in fact "a filthy carnival where rotten meat sits stacked beside stale crusts of bread, and where the sidewalks too often serve as garbage pails for decomposing fruits and vegetables." The city's East European Jews, he continued, bestowed "on our metropolis repulsive neighborhoods we cannot pass without our stomachs turning" and, furthermore, were "ruining French Canadian business by disloyal competition, based on immoral if not openly dishonest tactics."

In his salad days Drapeau was also a member of the ludicrous but once enormously powerful Order of Jacques Cartier, its Montreal branch known to insiders as "La Patente" (The Thing). The order, a response to the equally malign, Catholic-hating Loyal Order of the Orange Lodge, was started in 1926 by a bunch of French Canadian civil servants who were denied access to top-level federal jobs in Ottawa because of English Canadian prejudice. Blessed by Quebec's bishops, the order longed for an independent fascist Catholic state, its inspiration Franco's Spain: in 1940, it supported Marshal Pétain's government in France and its cry of "Family, Fatherland, and Work." At home, it supported the Union nationale and its *chef*, Premier Maurice Duplessis, who, in 1943, claimed he had evidence of an international Jewish conspiracy, its aim to bribe Ottawa into inviting 100,000 Jewish refugees to settle on Quebec farmlands.

The order, whose members included the late, revered Cardinal Paul-Emile Léger, published two journals—one official, *La Boussole*, the other secret, *L'Emerillon*—both raging against the perfidy of Anglophones and of course Jews. The names of the grand commander of the order and the twenty-five members who comprised the supreme council were only available on a need-to-know basis. However, Brian McKenna and Susan Purcell, the resourceful authors of *Drapeau*, were able to describe the initiation process in their biography of the mayor:

> The ritual initiation was called VAPDA—*le Voyage au pays des ancêtres*, the Voyage to the Land of Our Ancestors—a harkening back to the roots of Quebec. The initiate was ushered into a temple, or room serving as such, by his sponsor, who knocked at

an inner door and asked permission to enter. Inside, the Grand Commander presiding over the rite signalled his consent with a rap of a gavel. Blindfolded, the initiate was ushered into the inner sanctum as an old French-Canadian folk tune was played in the background. In the presence of silent brothers on all sides, he was then put to a series of symbolic tests, first drinking a cup of bitters. Then guided by a brother on each side, he was led stumbling through an obstacle course. At the end, he faced the water test, his hand thrust into a jar of water with a mild electrical current passed through it; the air test, his face whipped by a turbulent wind from an electric fan; the fire test, his hand heated gently by the flame of an alcohol lamp. Finally he swore solemnly to guard the secrets of the order.

His blindfold was then removed and the master of the rite approached and officially inducted him into the sect by knighting him on each shoulder with the blade of a shimmering sword. After the revelation of a sign (the pressing of the index finger on the inside of the palm of the hand), the Grand Commander pointed out the symbolic meaning of each test. Then the brothers lined up according to their rank in the order, arms upraised at an angle, and cried out emphatically: "Secrecy! Secrecy! Secrecy!" Members were forbidden to reveal membership even to their wives.[26]

Eleven

For years now many sophisticated French Canadians have maintained that their Jewish problem stems from the fact that we integrated long ago into the province's Anglophone minority—insofar as this was tolerated—rather than its French majority. The standard Jewish response to this complaint is that we were not welcome in the French Catholic school system. An answer that is certainly true, but also disingenuous. We would have identified with the English-speaking community in any event. We were the progeny of hardworking, sometimes even driven, immigrants, who were counting on us, the first Canadian-born generation, to catapult them into a better life, and the glory road to self-improvement was clearly paved with English, French an obvious cul-de-sac. Look at it this way. Back there on St. Urbain Street, during World War II, we were poor, but the French were poorer. I still carry with me the image of a spunky French Canadian kid, maybe ten years old, who was often seen on St. Urbain Street, searching the gutter for cigarette butts, pulling a wagon in which sat his even scrawnier older brother, a victim of rickets, a disease that I expect is unheard of today, except in the Third World.

My parents were divorced in 1944, and after the war my mother, obliged to support herself, ran a succession of small summer boarding-houses in Ste-Agathe-des-Monts. During the Depression years we had to make do in summer with Shawbridge or Prévost, swimming in the murky little North River that was officially off limits each August, the traditional month of the polio scare, but wartime prosperity propelled us further down the Laurentian highway into Ste-Agathe-des-Monts, hugging the Lac des Sables shoreline.

The Québécois novelist Harry Bernard wrote disapprovingly

of this latest Jewish migration in his novel *Dolorès:*

> *Des lacs clapotent, remplis de Juifs en vacances. Des familles entières trempent dans l'eau. Un chien allemand, oreilles droites, jappe en courant après une balle. Baigneuses en maillot serré, les seins offerts, suivant le bord de la route. Elles rient aux éclats, se bousculent, saluent de la main une auto crème et verte. Chalets invraisemblables loués pour la belle saison, derrière lesquels sèchent des pyjamas rouges et des chemisettes de soie artificielle. De beaux arbres jettent leur ombre sur ces laideurs. La villégiature moderne, allonge partout ses tentacules. Que dirait le curé Labelle, le bon gros curé Labelle, devant ces transformations de son empire du Nord? Que penserait-il de ces Laurentides données par lui à la civilisation, devenues le parc d'amusements d'une province?*[1]

The lakes are choppy, full of Jews on vacation and whole families lie soaking in the water. An excited German Shepherd barks as he runs after a ball. Young women in bathing suits walk along the road, showing off their figures. They giggle, jostle each other and wave at a passing creme and green car. The most unbelievable cottages are being rented for the holidays, with red pyjamas and fake silk blouses hanging to dry in the backyards. Tall, handsome trees cast their shade over all this ugliness as modern tourism spreads its tentacles in every direction. What would Cure Labelle, good old Cure Labelle, think of what has become of his northern domain? What would he think of his Laurentians which he opened up to civilization, that have now been turned into a provincial amusement park?

I can well imagine what the Curé Labelle would have thought, because in the immediate postwar years Ste-Agathe became a veritable Jewish paradise. A minor-league Catskills. Indigenous comics played a flourishing hotel circuit that included Greenberg's, the Castle des Monts, Levine's, the Hotel Vermont, Rabiner's, the Chalet, and many others. Children's camps proliferated on small neighboring lakes: Camp Hiawatha, Pripstein's, Pine Valley. A Jewish baker set up in town, and there was of course a synagogue and a kosher butcher. On Saturdays in July the rue Principale and the rue Tour de Lac swelled with noisy Jewish families parading in their finery, tooting the horns of their newly acquired Buicks, lining up for a midnight medium-fat smoked meat on rye at the local deli. At the time, it occurred to me that it was surprising that French Canadians and Jews did not get on better. Certainly we had a good deal in common. A lust for life. A love of display. A fear for the survival of the *mame-loshn*, French or Yiddish, and an inner conviction that only our society was truly distinctive. Sadly, however, abrasiveness continued to be the rule.

From the balcony of my mother's modest little inn the old men in their yarmulkes, gossiping in Yiddish, could just make out the sign on the outside wall of the Hôtel Chez Maurice, immediately across the dirt road. It read:

RESTRICTED CLIENTELE ONLY

Three blocks away, equally boorish WASPs played lawn bowls behind the sheltering cedar hedge of the Laurentide Inn, which was also restricted to Gentiles only. At the time, I was a hot-blooded teenager—a *New Statesman* reader who actually believed justice would be served in this world—so these twin signposts of the gut feelings of our "two founding races" outraged me. With hindsight, however, I am bound to admire the goofy stance of these two doomed hotel proprietors, determined to protect their Alamos of bigotry, refusing to acknowledge that they were already surrounded by cavorting, cigar-chewing men, pinochle mavens in Hawaiian shirts, and fat ladies plopping into the lake, squealing, "It's a *mechaiah*, Bessie! I swear it's a *mechaiah!*" And neighboring hotel loudspeakers that crackled before bellowing, "Long-distance call for Moishe Tannenbaum," or "Mrs. Bishinsky, your niece Jewel from Turrono is at the train station and needs a lift."

Looking back, it is now clear to me that Ste-Agathe-des-Monts, like Oxford, was once a champion of lost causes and, furthermore, what happened there in the late forties is a metaphor for what ails Canada now.

Examined closely, what really exercises our two founding races today is the recent intrusion into this privileged and still largely empty land of so many southern Europeans and wogs from Asia, Central and South America, the West Indies, and North Africa. In Montreal, where the French are officially eager for more French-speaking immigrants, their bourgeoisie is unofficially fleeing the city—its schools contaminated by the children of Moroccans, Haitians, Lebanese, and Vietnamese—for the etiolated suburbs, say Laval, which is still purportedly racially pure. And out there in Vancouver the indolent natives, who once tied Chinese coolies together by their queues and tossed them over cliffs into the sea, are scared stiff of the many new and obviously astute arrivals from Hong Kong, certain to run circles around them before breakfast. And when the middle classes of both our founding races open their newspapers in June and see that most of the high school scholarship students have Asian faces, they tend to feel a chill, even as they once winced at the photographs of all those hot-to-trot Jewish prize winners with unpronounceable names. Hence the plaintive racial cry in the streets of Montreal of *"Le Québec aux Québécois!"* and out west the revolt of the nerds, that is to say, the sudden rise of the equally xenophobic Reform Party, and the emergence in Orangeman's Ontario of APEC and screwy, paranoid books like *Bilingual Today, French Tomorrow*, claiming sales of 110,000 copies. Put plainly, the most insecure members of our two founding races—failed, according to Conrad Black, by their elites—have seen the Canadian future and grasped that it won't work as well as the past for them.

As things stand now, 40 percent of Canadians are of neither English nor French extraction. Surely within the next thirty, maybe even twenty years, they will form a majority of our population, and our children will not think it out of the ordinary to see Canadians of Chinese, Sikh, African, and Central American descent seated in Parliament alongside those of Polish, Greek, Ukrainian, and Italian origin already in place. Surely, too, these people will demand an end to the wasting tribal quarrel between the English and the French. Resentment was evident as early as 1964, when André Laurendeau was traveling the country with the B & B Commission, taking the pulse. Out at Fort William and Port Arthur (now Thunder

Bay), on the north shore of Lake Superior, a Ukrainian activist in his forties spoke out. "The other day," he said, "I heard a French Canadian from Quebec on television. He was saying that the *New Canadians* [italics mine], and he specifically mentioned the Ukrainians, couldn't expect to obtain the same privileges as the French Canadians, who developed a large part of the country. Well, we were pioneers too, in other parts of the country which we settled before anyone else arrived. . . ."[2]

I expect that sooner, rather than later, Canadians who are of neither English nor French extraction will point out the obvious. Except for our First Nations, we are all immigrants here . . . and, come to think of it, damn few of us with a claim to have come out of the top drawer, as it were.

Look at it this way. Some of the *Québécois pure laine* or *de vieille souche* are in fact the progeny of *les filles du roi*, or hookers, imported to New France by Jean-Baptiste Talon to satisfy the appetites of his mostly functionally illiterate soldiers. And many of those United Empire Loyalists—from whom, Walter Stewart has written, one out of six English-speaking Canadians is descended[3]—were either obdurate reactionaries or—*pace* Mrs. C. M. Day—refugees from justice, men without fixed principles, or designing and unscrupulous adventurers. Mind you, we didn't even get the top-of-the-line conmen and thieves or whores. Those were shipped to Van Diemen's Land in shackles, culturally enriching Australia, not us.

Once they have taken over the wheel room, the Canadians who are of neither English nor French origin are bound to be outraged by the mess they have inherited from our two foundering races. "What [their elites] delivered," wrote Conrad Black in 1991, "was an uncompetitive, slothful, self-righteous, spiteful, and envious nanny-state, now hovering on the verge of bankruptcy."[4]

It is true that there is now a considerable industrial base in Ontario, which was given rather more than a jump start by the U.S.-Canada Auto Pact signed in 1965. I know that Quebec can legitimately boast of its massive James Bay Hydro project. I have been assured that we are leaders in the field of telecommunications. Yes, yes, but all the same, it must be allowed that for the most part Canadians, a notoriously lazy bunch, still live off the riches we were fortunate enough to stumble on here in the first place. Our prosperity, such as it is, is based on what we can dig or pump out of the ground or harvest from its surface or the surrounding seas. On my weekly drive into Montreal I regularly pass a considerable number of Volvos and Saabs on the road, cars specifically designed to cope with our unforgiving climate. Sadly, with four times the market base of Sweden, we have failed to develop anything comparable here. Instead we are grateful for the Auto Pact, which guarantees us work producing American cars and, more recently, assembling some for the Koreans. The Koreans, I should point out, are here only because, sheltering under the terms of the Auto Pact, they can sneak their product into the U.S. market without worrying about import quotas. A case in point is the Hyundai automobile plant that is now in place, if not exactly flourishing, in the Eastern Townships town of Bromont. In order to attract this plant to Quebec, with its promise of a thousand jobs, our provincial and federal governments threw hundreds of millions of dollars and the promise of a tax holiday at the far-from-needy Koreans. And now that they are here, they allow our natives (*Québécois pure laine*, UEL descendants) not to manufacture but merely to assemble their vehicles, and only under the supervision of Korean foremen. This has led to some sour comment from one of the wags who used to frequent Woody's Pub. "Possibly," he said, "in the near future—and of course providing our profligate governments fling millions at them—possibly then the Moroccans will be sufficiently thoughtful to ship us their oranges and lemons to crate for the American market. Our future, I think, is as the Third World's Third World."

A FRENCH CANADIAN complaint, directed not specifically against Jews but towards all English-speaking Quebecers, is that we suffer from a nostalgia for the fifties, when Anglophones ruled the economic roost and the *Québécois pure laine* felt themselves to be second-class citizens at home, the hewers of wood and drawers of water. And certainly there is something in that: something that led to the election of Jean Lesage's Liberal government in 1960 and Quebec's so-called Quiet Revolution, its slogan *Maîtres chez nous* ("Masters in our own house").

In 1963 the publisher of the Montreal *Star* organized a seminar, his contribution to a better Canadian understanding of "The French Fact," to be conducted at the Queen! Elizabeth!! Hotel in Montreal.

Oh-oh.

Seven years earlier, in 1956, Mayor Jean Drapeau appeared in a demonstration calling for the name of the Queen Elizabeth Hotel to be changed to Château Maisonneuve. Drapeau also wrote an open letter to Donald Gordon, president of Canadian National Railways, which owned the hotel. "How would you like it," he asked, "if in Toronto the CNR established a hotel called the Dollard-des-Ormeaux or Louis-Joseph Papineau?"[5]

For the benefit of non-Canadian readers I should explain that Louis-Joseph Papineau, born in Montreal in 1786, was a militia officer during the War of 1812, speaker of the House of Assembly of Lower Canada from 1815 to 1822, and again, beginning in 1828, a leader of the Patriotes' rebellion in 1837—and Donald Gordon was something else again.

In 1962 the arrogant Gordon declared that he had never appointed any French Canadians vice presidents to CNR because they lacked the essential university training. As a consequence, he was burned in effigy in Montreal's Place Ville-Marie. Then an enterprising Toronto reporter discovered that of the thirty vice presidents employed by Canada's two railway systems (the other one being the Canadian Pacific), only seven had actually been to university and, lo and behold, Donald Gordon was not among them.

Participants in the Montreal *Star*'s seminar included Gérard Pelletier, then editor in chief of *La Presse*; the Honorable René Lévesque, then minister of natural resources in the Lesage government; and André Laurendeau, then editor in chief of *Le Devoir*.

Laurendeau laid out the causes of the Quiet Revolution:

"We are unhappy with education, politicians, patronage, the role of the clergy in lay affairs; unhappy with the newspapers and with the intellectuals, with our own small importance in the economic life of the province, with the lack of interest in our underdeveloped areas; unhappy again with the doctors, the civil servants, and unhappy with our English Canadian partners. We're starting over. Many old taboos have disappeared. Passions are aroused by questions which, yesterday, would have left us cold."[6]

Actually, Laurendeau was the first speaker called upon by the chair, and he began by saying, "Inevitably, this meeting is being held in the artifical locale of a large hotel, in a district of Montreal from which French Canada is apparently, and often in fact, somewhat removed. Save for the skyline you will see from the windows and a few words of French, you could be in Halifax, Toronto, Vancouver or even Chicago. One can cross Montreal at a clip without an inkling that two-thirds of the city's population are French Canadians. As for the French Canadians, they know the setup well. They accept or endure it, but the minute they realize what strangers they are in the heart of the city, they feel humiliation. Thus they realize that Montreal is not so much their city as a North American metropolis, and that their economic role is a small one in a city where they number one million inhabitants."[7]

The Queen Elizabeth Hotel has long since been reconsecrated, reborn as Hôtel Le Reine Elizabeth, and even more recently its address was changed from Dorchester Boulevard to Boulevard René-Lévesque, just as other streets in Montreal have been renamed, denying their history but feeding the appetite to conform to the city's suddenly one and only *visage linguistique*. At the same time, in the province at large, the zealots who run the Commission de toponymie have been rushing about renaming towns, mountains, rivers, and lakes. The financial levers of the province's government and public institutions are now also largely in the hands of *Québécois pure laine*. This is not to complain, but only to make it clear that were André

Laurendeau alive today, looking out of a Hôtel Le Reine Elizabeth window, he would find that it is the English language that has been somewhat removed and that it is now the Anglophones who feel humiliated in a city that was once theirs, too. My point, briefly, is that our nostalgia for the 1950s is far exceeded by an exasperating Francophone failure to grasp that the era in question skidded to an abrupt end thirty years ago: instead, locked into a time warp, Francophones are still doggedly fighting against injustices that no longer exist.

Something else.

Anglophone nostalgia for an earlier Montreal is not necessarily based on a longing for economic dominance but rather for a time when English, as well as French, thrived there and the two cultures enriched rather than excoriated one another. Those, those were the days when Montreal, beyond a doubt, was the most enjoyable and cosmopolitan city in a still picayune country. Those, those were the days when the most significant English-language literary magazine in Canada, *Northern Review,* was published in Montreal, its editor, John Sutherland, bringing out a first short story by Mavis Gallant, then a reporter for the Montreal *Standard,* the Saturday edition of the *Star.* Those, those were the days when Christopher Plummer was still acting in the Mountain Playhouse and Oscar Peterson was—as our ineffable entertainment columnists had it in the idiom of the day—"tickling the keyboards" in the Alberta Lounge. And Rupert Caplan was directing compelling radio plays, adaptations and originals, for the CBC's first-rate "Stage" series, which Andrew Allan produced out of Toronto on Sunday nights from 1944 through 1955. Hugh MacLennan, a Montrealer by adoption, had already published his novel about the unresolved tensions between the city's two communities, and its title would enter the language: *Two Solitudes.* We also read novels by French Canadians (in my case, in translation), among them *The Tin Flute* by Gabrielle Roy and *The Plouffe Family* by Roger Lemelin.

At the time, Montreal's English-speaking community was

able to support three daily newspapers: the *Star*, the *Herald*, and the *Gazette*. However, the demise of the *Herald* in 1957 and the *Star* in 1979 cannot be laid at the feet of Quebec nationalists but was part of a pattern true of most North American cities, where one afternoon newspaper after another has expired. It would also be unfair to hold the Parti québécois solely responsible for Montreal's decline. The electoral triumph of the PQ in 1976 certainly accelerated the city's tumble, but it did not inaugurate it. Once the St. Lawrence Seaway was in place, diminishing the importance of our port, and the Toronto stock market was doing more business than St. James Street, Montreal's slippage was inevitable. What I do blame the Parti québécois for, unreservedly, is that if I grew up in a city where an Anglophone young man or woman could feel at home and anticipate settling into a future commensurate with his or her ability, that is clearly no longer the case. Just about everything has been done to make the Anglophone youth, even those who are fluently bilingual, feel unwelcome in Quebec.

Twelve

As CANADA TEETERS on the verge of fracturing, I am sometimes subject to fits of sentiment about this cockeyed country I grew up in and still call home. Impatient with our two founding races, I wonder why, instead of constantly picking at the scabs of their differences, they couldn't learn to celebrate what binds them together. On that necessarily short list I would unhesitatingly place as the number-one adhesive, the true common denominator, bad taste.

André Laurendeau, traveling with the B & B Commission in the spring of 1964, sentenced to a short stay in a hotel in Winnipeg, wrote in his diary, "I wish I were somewhere else. From my window I see a discordant urban landscape, with absolutely no beauty: a few modern buildings, some flat roofs, a tiny badly fenced patch of green."[1]

Canadians, blessed with a natural landscape of incredible beauty and variety, have managed to entrench ugliness just about everywhere they have built. Our cities tend to be functional but nondescript, anchored against the wind, with nothing to please the eye. Quebec City is an exception and so was Montreal, until Mayor Jean Drapeau, hungering for a larger tax base, untroubled by any appreciation for aesthetics, turned the vandals loose. In their indecent haste to make money out of parking lots, they were allowed, noted Luc d'Iberville-Moreau in *Lost Montreal*, to destroy one old building after another, some of the demolitions positively criminal. One example, quoted by the author, was actually perpetrated by McGill University—the tearing down of the Prince of Wales Terrace on Sherbrooke Street in 1973 and its replacement by a building of the utmost banality.

In his introduction to *Lost Montreal*, d'Iberville-Moreau wrote:

> Over twenty years ago Gérard Morisset cautioned that "There are two ways to spoil a country. Either get rid of its monuments one by one, those that are worthy of interest, its crown, or bury them amid a mass of architectural mediocrity to hide them from view; or detract from their architectural qualities by cluttering up their surroundings." In choosing the first of these approaches to our environment—destruction—Montreal has irresponsibly achieved some kind of immortality. It once possessed architecture that was among the oldest and richest in North America. Now that many outstanding treasures of our past have been torn down in the name of "progress," we can enjoy them only in photographs, while bitterly regretting their loss. For such vandalism there is no rational explanation other than our own ignorance or—worse—stupidity: the blind indifference of the city fathers we ourselves elected, the vanity of priests with an "edifice complex," the self-righteous contempt that so many people have for the arts and culture of any period other than their own. To them our old buildings are nothing but piles of rubbish devoid of interest, hindrances to modern development.[2]

The problem with Magog, the largest town on the Canadian shores of Lake Memphremagog, is something else again. A missed opportunity. Nestled in an enviably appealing site, on the shores of a lovely lake, sheltered by low-lying hills, it is—like so many other Québécois or English Canadian small towns—a catch-all for almost unrelieved ugliness. Garish. Crude. Ill-featured. Replete with all the cultural needs of small-town Canada, English or French. A Colonel Sanders. A McDonald's. A video rental shop rich in porn and all-star wrestling films. A Legion Hall. A restaurant that offers Chinese-Canadian cuisine, whatever that may be, and another that specializes in pastas stuck together in a lump, its sauce leaning heavily on a ketchup base. In winter, obviously in protest against prevailing gray skies, snow, and ice, many of the houses between Austin and Magog are suddenly framed by constantly lit multicolored bulbs, giving them the appearance of giant, mislaid pinball machines.

On September 25, 1989, I was seated in the Owl's Nest, the bar I favored not far from our lakeside cottage, watching television as the first provincial election results began to trickle in. Most of my good companions in the Owl's Nest had grown up on farms lost long since, managing without electricity until the early fifties. Now they worked during the summer for the affluent Montrealers with cottages on the lake, paid under the table to housepaint or build a new deck or retile a roof, and then cut their own firewood and hunkered down to winter on welfare. Among them there was a friend of mine I'll call Ed, who mowed lawns all summer long but absolutely refused to take on mine. "Jeez," he said, "no hard feelings, eh, Mort, but I already got like three days' work a week."

Once it became obvious that Robert Bourassa was riding back into office, one of the men, a foreman at the Clairol plant in Knowlton, pronounced. "As they say in Roman," he said, "he came, he seen, he conquered."

Studying the detailed results in the *Gazette* the next morning, I was pleased to see that the Jews of Montreal's D'Arcy McGee riding had not been intimidated. They had elected the far-from-charismatic Robert Libman to the traditional Liberal seat with a stunning majority of 6,600 votes of the 28,648 cast. Even more surprising, 126,000 Montrealers, voting in nineteen ridings, supported the Equality Party, electing three more of its candidates, five others qualifying as runners-up. The Four Equals, as they were inevitably dubbed, were Libman, Gordon Atkinson, Richard Holden who squeaked through in Westmount with a plurality of 508 votes out of 21,611 cast, and Neil Cameron, a history teacher at a junior college. Neither Atkinson, resident in Quebec for thirty years, nor Cameron, a westerner, spoke adequate French. Holden had studied for a year at the University of Grenoble and was fluently bilingual. So was Libman, who was married to a Moroccan-born woman, one of many French-speaking Sephardic Jews who had settled in Montreal.

Libman, suddenly thrust into the limelight, was all too obviously nourished by it. Unfortunately, he did not score high on sensibility in his first big splash in the *Gazette*. "I've always wanted to be a rich and famous architect-developer," he said. "It's the wheeling and dealing and the sign of success—the need to show you've been successful that is very important to me."[3]

Bourassa's Liberal government had been returned to power with ninety-two seats, but the big election story was the unexpected rise of the Equality Party. "If we can do this in five months," Libman said, "imagine what we can do in four years."[4]

On second glance, observers noted that the PQ, adjudged comatose only eighteen months earlier and weighing in with a hard line on independence this time out, had taken twenty-nine seats, ten more than it had held when the legislature was dissolved, and had won 40 percent of the popular vote, slightly better than it had managed in 1985. Party leader Jacques Parizeau, who had given up his seat in 1984 and walked out on the PQ a year later, had been returned to the National Assembly by his old riding of L'Assomption. Bolstered by a poll, taken only a week before the election, showing that 29 percent of Quebecers were for outright sovereignty, a gain of 14 percent since 1985, he proclaimed, "The idea of sovereignty, they said it was dead. It's alive."[5]

So, incidentally, was anti-Semitism.

In April 1990 Pierre Péladeau, bumptious publisher of the tabloid *Journal de Montréal* and something of a folk hero here, a regular on television talk shows, was accused by an interviewer from *L'actualité* magazine of rebuking his newspaper's staff when it ran articles praising Jews. He was quoted as saying, "I have a lot of respect for Jews, but they take up too much space. I want to help our people first, we need it more."[6]

Péladeau claimed to be a victim of a smear job. "I never reproached the *Journal* for devoting an article to a Jew because he was a Jew, but because he was not a Francophone." He had, he said, written a memo to his staff when the newspaper launched a fashion section: "In the city here—the city in which the *Journal de Montréal* runs—there is no doubt that the fashion industry is controlled by the Jewish people, English-speaking. It so happens that they are Jewish, but they speak English. If they were to speak French it would be a different story."[7]

Péladeau insisted that he had done nothing wrong and had no intention of apologizing, and the next day, when he repeated his charges on a popular radio show about the Jews taking up too much space, most of the call-in public supported him warmly. Not so an association representing fifty journalists and photographers at the *Journal*, which promptly issued a statement: "The association condemns such chauvinistic declarations and considers that the pluralism that runs through the whole of Quebec society must be accepted."[8]

Péladeau, one of Quebec's highly touted new entrepreneurs, is founding president and controlling shareholder of Québecor Inc., its annual revenue an estimated $500,000,000. He not only publishes the trashy *Journal* but also two other dailies— one in Quebec City and another in Winnipeg—as well as forty-three weeklies and seven magazines, among them a number of supermarket tabloid standards: *Nouvelles et Potins, Journal des Vedettes* and *Le Nouveau Samedi*. Privately, however, he professes to read Balzac, Dostoyevsky, and Plato, and to consider Beethoven "the most important man ever on earth."[9] A child of penury, he cherishes his upstart image as a *p'tit Québécois* who has risen to become a member of the exclusive Club St. Denis as well as a fund-raiser for the Orchestre métropolitain du Grand Montréal. He is a very short, owlish-looking man with a receding chin. A former alcoholic and boastful womanizer ("I've had all the women I wanted, when I wanted them,"[10] he once told a Toronto *Globe and Mail* reporter), he has been born again as a believer and expects one day to be led into heaven to the strains of the choral movement of Beethoven's Ninth Symphony. While he waits, Péladeau, who drives to his office every weekday from his ten-acre estate in the Laurentians, favoring his Rolls-Royce in summer and a Mercedes in winter, explains his newfound faith by saying, "I needed the spirituality."[11]

Responding to Péladeau's interview in *L'actualité*, the president of Crazy Ted Cellular threatened to withdraw $250,000 worth of annual advertising from the *Journal* unless the publisher apologized. Pepe Canada Clothing Inc. canceled its advertising in *Clin d'Oeil*, a fashion magazine owned by Québecor, and urged other Jewish businessmen to follow suit. Then Lysiane Gagnon, writing in *La Presse*, revealed that Péladeau was to be awarded an honorary degree by the Université de Montréal. "[His] xenophobic nationalism" she wrote, "recalls the Quebec of the 30s, when our fascist-leaning elites denounced the supposed omnipresence of Jews in the economy in absolutely similar terms in the name of the same nationalism."[12] Next, a union, representing 3,000 teaching assistants and lecturers at the Université de Montréal, protested and the publisher's name was dropped from the awards list. Finally, Péladeau, obviously brooding over advertising accounts at risk, delivered a mealy-mouthed apology which was quickly accepted by Crazy Ted, Pepe Canada Clothing, and the rest.

April also yielded a blow to Canadian unity from an unexpected quarter. Premier John Buchanan of Nova Scotia said that if Quebec left Canada, then the Atlantic provinces, suddenly reduced to a severed limb, would have no choice but to apply for American statehood. "What are we going to do?" he asked. "Form our own country? That's absurd. Stay as a fractured part of Canada? A good possibility, but that's all. Or be a part of the United States? There's no choice."[13]

Only a day later Buchanan learned that if there was no choice, there would also be no welcome wagon. An aide to the District of Columbia's congressional delegate, Walter Fauntroy, a leading advocate of statehood for the district, warned that Canadian provinces opting for statehood would just have to wait in line behind the District of Columbia and Puerto Rico. Nova Scotia, the aide said, would first have to declare itself independent of Canada, and then become either a territory or a commonwealth, as Alaska had for almost a century, before it could even ask for statehood.

A couple of months later there were more anti-Semitic incidents in Montreal. Vandals spray-painted swastikas and other graffiti ("Heil Hitler," "Death to the Jews," "KKK") on the outside walls of the Yeshiva Gedola on Van Horne Avenue. The same night a fire gutted the children's school of the Congregation Toldos Yakov Yosef in Outremont. Headstones in Jewish cemeteries were defaced or overturned.[14]

It was in this climate that I finally caught up with Morton Brownstein, the man who had taken his case against the sign law (Section 58 of Bill 101) all the way to the Supreme Court of Canada. I met Brownstein, president and CEO of Chaussures Brown/Brown Shoes Inc., at his office in Ville St. Laurent, a suburb of Montreal. The company, founded by Brownstein's father, is a retail chain with twenty-three stores across Canada, fourteen of them in Quebec. For all his objections to the sign law, Brownstein did not fit the Québécois stereotype of the arrogant "Westmount Rhodesian," determined to keep the French in their place as *les nègres blancs d'Amérique*; on the contrary, he was convinced that the Anglophones' best chance of having their rights restored was within a Quebec that had achieved sovereignty-association. But there was a problem. Like just about everybody else in the province, he wasn't sure what sovereignty-association actually meant.

Brownstein is fluently bilingual, as are his children, one of whom studied in France for three years and another has a master's degree in French from McGill. He was, it turned out, so supportive of the French Fact that he would be in favor of English-speaking students being obliged to write their McGill entrance exams in French. He also welcomed the new Francophone entrepreneurs, who had taken the province's economic reins into their own hands at last. "There's been a dramatic change here," he said. "Ten, twelve years ago Francophone businessmen dreaded the thought of sovereignty-association, but now most of them have moved over to the separatist side." He had the greatest respect, he went on to say, for the PQ's leaders, whom he took to be refreshingly honest.

What, then, I asked, was his problem?

"The sign law. They trampled on my rights. In order to establish the supremacy of French here, I do not feel it was necessary to deny Anglophones their individual rights."

A past president of Montreal's Jewish General Hospital,

Brownstein also lamented the fact that so many English-speaking doctors and nurses had pulled out of Quebec over the past fifteen years. "Lots of my friends have left," he said, "and the young graduate from McGill and they are almost totally going, gone."

A week later I had lunch with Mrs. Ludmilla de Fougerolles, head of the Commission de protection de la langue française. Expecting a linguistic Madame Defarge, the fearsome overseer of the province's dreaded tongue-troopers, I found myself in the company of a cultivated lady who was far from doctrinaire. She told me that she and her family, led by her father, had walked out of Czechoslovakia in 1949, when she was only seven years old, crossing the border illegally by night. After three years in France, they emigrated to Quebec. A graduate of McGill Law School, she had been appointed to her $75,000-a-year job in 1987. Increasingly busy, she said her language cops had investigated 2,277 alleged infractions of Bill 101 in 1988 as opposed to a mere 539 in 1985. Mrs. de Fougerolles also had to cope with a deluge of complaints from self-appointed vigilantes, like the middle-aged man with the camera I had encountered outside Woody's Pub. A hard core of these vigilantes, some 200 strong, had accounted for roughly 10,000 complaints against 1,744 commercial establishments in 1988.

A so-called Allophone, filling a controversial office, Mrs. de Fougerolles now runs into flak from Québécois underlings, who feel she is not sufficiently severe, and English-speaking friends, who accuse her of serving the enemy, a *vendue*. Her inspectors, she told me, far from being zealots, apply the law with a soupçon of tolerance. There was, for instance, the celebrated case of the lady who runs the Westmount Bead Emporium and had been hounded for years because she displayed bilingual signs. Finally, a perspicacious inspector established that the lady gave English-language courses in batik and the history of beads. He ruled that the emporium was in fact a cultural institution and therefore exempt from the sign law, and she was pestered no more.

Did the commission's inspectors, I asked, imposing an

unpopular law on shopkeepers, ever meet with a violent reception? Say, a baseball bat?

"As a matter of fact," she said, "they run into more abuse from Francophones—say, a motel owner or the proprietor of a souvenir shop, both dependent on the tourist trade—than they do from Anglophones."

Thirteen

In May 1990 the Parti québécois published its long-awaited forty-six-page manifesto, *La Souveraineté: Pourquoi? Comment?* "We must," it said, "break the iron collar of a federal system which serves us badly, which will always subordinate our national interests to those of another majority."[1] As expected, the pamphlet fudged the hard questions, but it did set out some of the party's plans for independence, which was to be negotiated "properly and intelligently."[2] There would be a free circulation of people and goods between the new republic and English Canada, which was clearly more than we had now. Take, for instance, the day that the civic officials of Aylmer—a town that lies in Quebec, but is actually a rich residential suburb of Ottawa, which sits immediately across the Ottawa River in Ontario—ruled that newly laid sidewalks had to be uprooted because they had been built with Ontario-made bricks. At the time, approximately 40 percent of the construction jobs in Ottawa were being filled by Quebec workers, but Ontario laborers required a permit to function in Quebec.[3] Then, in 1989, the Steinberg supermarket chain and real estate holding company, wasting in a family feud, came up for sale. Steinberg's, which had been founded by the late Sam Steinberg, who had started out as a clerk in his mother's small grocery store in the heart of Montreal's old Jewish quarter, now employed over 30,000 people. The takeover offer favored by both Steinberg employees and shareholders came from Oxden, an Ontario conglomerate with experience in food marketing, but, following a phone call from Premier Bourassa, the Caisse de dépôt et placement du Québec stepped in to prevent this Québécois institution, the achievement of a Jewish immigrant, from falling into the hands of *les autres*.

It is to be hoped the Steinberg family was gratified to have Sam's inspiration qualify as québécois at last. Clearly, it was not yet the case in 1954. At that time, the ubiquitous Abbé Groulx wrote to a M. Lamoureux:

". . . There is no need for me to tell you about the problems created by the Jews in our economic life. Their passion, or rather their ambition to dominate in this area gives them an extraordinary appetite for monopoly. They are not content simply to compete. Their lack of judgement makes them brutal in success. One example is the recent establishment of the chain of grocery stores that are in the process of ruining small French-Canadian business."[4]

In any event, in tandem with the Société de développement du Québec, the Caisse bought $140,000,000 worth of debentures, enabling Socanav, a shipping company with no experience in food marketing, to acquire the firm, once it had pledged not to sell to non-Québécois interests for at least ten years.

The Caisse, which had started out in 1965 at the suggestion of Jacques Parizeau, then an adviser to the Liberal government, deftly administered Quebec's portion of the Canada Pension Plan. Its assets, estimated at $34,000,000,000 in 1990, were sufficient to make it Canada's largest single bundle of capital as well as a stock-market player to contend with.

The Parti québécois's policy pamphlet stated that all Quebec civil servants working for the federal government would automatically be hired by the Quebec government to run its embassies and manage its postal service, training and other programs now under federal jurisdiction. But officials of the Public Service Alliance of Canada—35,000 of whose membership of 170,000 were Quebecers—were understandably skeptical. PSAC leaders doubted that the already notoriously bloated Quebec civil service could absorb so many new employees.

As a first step, the Parti québécois declared that a newly independent Quebec would go to the International Court in The Hague to claim the immense territory of Labrador. Labrador, which had been under Quebec's jurisdiction until 1774, only to be shuffled off into Newfoundland's care again in 1809. Then, in 1825, each claimant was awarded a chunk of the pie, the territory west of Blanc Sablon north of 52 degrees going to Quebec and known for a time as either Côte-du-Nord or Quebec-Labrador. Its borders still in dispute in 1907, the problem was sent to the British Privy Council, which, in 1927, awarded Newfoundland the vast area drained by rivers flowing into the Atlantic.

Problems, problems.

"If Canada is divisible," Pierre Elliott Trudeau once said, "Quebec should be divisible, too."[5]

In the cogently argued *Partition: The Price of Quebec's Independence*, coauthors William F. Shaw and Lionel Albert maintain that an independent Quebec should be limited to the territory of New France, the land settled by the French before the conquest of 1759. Therefore, it follows that the entire area of Quebec north, which was awarded to Quebec as a province and not as an independent country, should revert to Canada:

> Once the emotions aroused by the proposed break had subsided, the negotiators would have to take three major headings into consideration.
>
> The first is the part of the territory known as Rupert's Land that is now the upper two-thirds of the province of Quebec, which was not even a part of Canada at the time of Confederation in 1867, but was transferred by the British government to Canada in 1870 in order to strengthen the union of the British colonies in North America. The Rupert's Land territory would be retained by Canada *without discussion* [italics mine]. It is historically British and, by an act of the British Parliament, Canadian. It does not have any valid French historical character. Moreover, the overwhelming majority of its native inhabitants have persistently made it known that they would not be included in a separating French state.[6]

Under their other two major headings, the coauthors argue that in order to retain its territorial integrity Canadians must insist on a

> land corridor south of the St. Lawrence River containing the principal road, rail, and telecommunications routes between

Ontario and the Maritimes. No negotiating team could accept a compromise . . . [that would] split the country into two separate parts.[7]

Rather, *indépendantistes* would be bound to counter, like Alaska and the lower forty-eight, which have managed very nicely.

The third heading covers the right of self-determination of a large number of Quebecers who would opt to remain Canadian. Among the territories thus affected would be the Western half of the Montreal archipelago, the Ottawa Valley including its tributary valleys, the Timiskaming region, and the lower part of the North Shore of the Gulf of St. Lawrence.
    The reality of the potential of partition is essential to any discussion of the separations of a territory for an independent French state.[8]

The coauthors first met in December 1976 at a meeting that led to the founding of an organization called the Preparatory Committee for an Eleventh Province:

Public meetings were held in Montreal and surrounding regions. The response was remarkable. There was no question that many Quebecers, both English and French, were determined that if Quebec were to separate, central and western Montreal, the inner Eastern Townships, and the Ottawa Valley would certainly not leave with it. The goal was not to promote the break-up of Quebec, but to establish that one of the rationales for partition would be that if Quebec can opt out of Canada, then obviously sections of Quebec that preferred to remain part of Canada could opt out of Quebec. It was based on the example of West Virginia, which opted out of the state of Virginia because it did not wish to secede from the United States when Virginia joined the Confederacy. Most important to us was the destruction of the presumption that the prize of a positive referendum would be the total territory of Quebec.[9]

Should a clear majority of Quebecers opt for independence in a referendum, the fighting response, advocated by Shaw and Albert, while undeniably clever, would certainly lead to more acrimony, possibly even violence, and this is not what Canadians,

English or French, need in the future. All the same, I must admit that the coauthors of *Partition* do get off some good shots. Writing about the Eastern Townships, for instance, they note that its two major population centers, Sherbrooke and Drummondville, were both founded by English-speaking settlers:

> The townships south of the St. Lawrence were in land that was never French and had no French names at all. In a curious passage, the ultra-nationalist magazine *La revue indépendantiste* admits that after thorough research that covered "oral" traditions, Monseigneur Desranleau, Bishop of Sherbrooke, was unable to uncover evidence that there had ever been a French name for the Eastern Townships. That disappointment does not prevent *La revue* advancing some sort of French prior claim to the area because it has been "visited," and even "explored" by Frenchmen.[10]

The eleventh province, as envisioned by the coauthors, would have a population of over a million, more than, respectively, the provinces of Newfoundland, Prince Edward Island, New Brunswick, Manitoba, or Saskatchewan.

In another scenario, this one the invention of an aide to Robert Libman, Quebec West would become a province *within* an independent Quebec, with its own language and schooling regulations and the right to secede if it wanted to. This screwy scheme, published in the *indépendantiste L'aut'journal*, was followed by an interview with Bernadette Devlin, who warned Quebecers that the partition of Ireland had been "the disaster of the century."[11]

Before absorbing Labrador, Quebec would be obliged to get Canada to agree to submit the case to the International Court in The Hague and then it would have to consult the natives of the territory, the majority of whom would most likely opt to remain in Canada. In fact, in 1991, Ovide Mercredi, the newly elected leader of the Assembly of First Nations, would declare, "The aboriginal people have no interest in separating from Canada. If Quebec separates . . . the aboriginal people, in my view, will stay with Canada. [They] should not be forced to be part of a new state that they have not consented to."[12]

Never mind. Blithely taking the acquisition of Labrador for granted, the PQ manifesto declares that the new, expanded Quebec would be the eighteenth-largest country in the world geographically and, given its six and a half million citizens, eightieth in population. Its gross domestic product of $144.2 billion, would be roughly equivalent to that of Austria, endowing it with the world's sixteenth-largest economy, providing of course that it maintained its enormous trade, amounting to 55 percent of its total exports, with a just possibly fulminating English Canada, and that it retained an unrevised free-trade deal with the United States, another open question.

Gordon Ritchie, who was the Canadian deputy chief negotiator in the free-trade deal with the United States, has warned that if American hard bargainers were empowered to reopen the pact, ostensibly to accommodate an independent Quebec, they would certainly question provincial intervention in the economy by the Caisse, the Quebec Federation of Labour's Solidarity Fund, and Hydro-Québec. Hydro-Québec, we would learn in a scandal that didn't break until 1991, had already signed secret contracts with thirteen foreign aluminum smelters, offering them electrical power at less than cost in order to attract them into the province.

Bill Merkin, who figured prominently on the American side in the free-trade negotiations with Canada, told the Southam News Agency that if a sovereign Quebec were accepted by Canada, then the U.S. would have no qualms about dealing with it, but, he added, "If there were a messy situation in Canada with a lot of hard feelings and not a very constructive relationship between Quebec and the rest of Canada, I think that would make it very difficult for the United States to enter into any kind of relationship with Quebec. The U.S. is going to be concerned about maintaining good relations with Canada."[13]

Quebec, according to the PQ manifesto, would hold on to the dollar, retaining a monetary union with Canada for the mutual benefit of both countries. This, of course, doesn't take the likely ill will of English Canada into account and fails to explain how

Quebec could be truly sovereign if its bank rate were set in another country. In fact, it would immediately make the brand-new state of Quebec a distinct society indeed, establishing it as the only industrialized nation in the world to have another state control its monetary policy. Like Liberia and Panama, both of whom use the U.S. dollar, the new country would have no say in determining the value of its currency or setting interest rates. Come to think of it, as Quebec now does have some influence on the shape of the Bank of Canada's policies it would, by choosing independence in name, become even more dependent in fact than ever before. In any event, Quebec's independence would be protected by a small conventional army, and it would immediately apply for a seat in the United Nations.

Javier Perez de Cuellar, then secretary general of the United Nations, speaking in Quebec City where he had come to pick up an honorary degree, had already said that he hoped Canada would remain intact, but, if that were not the case, he would like to see Quebec seated in the UN right next to Qatar.

The PQ's case was given further credibility when *The New York Times* pronounced Quebec's economy strong enough to allow it to separate and become a nation "three times the area of France."[14] A preposterous analogy, given that France is verdant from shore to shore, but most of Quebec's territory, say 98 percent, cannot be cultivated and is unlikely to be ever more than sparsely settled. In support of its view, the *Times* quoted John Kenneth Galbraith, himself Ontario-born and educated, saying, "The economic viability of Quebec is no longer in doubt." On the other hand, Galbraith added, "But this is not the issue. The political and cultural loss to Canadians would be irretrievable."

Fourteen

NINETEEN-NINETY LUMBERED Quebecers with two anniversaries to celebrate, neither of them happy. Ten years earlier, on May 20, we had voted in the referendum on sovereignty-association. Twenty years earlier we had endured the October Crisis, created by the Front de libération du Québec's kidnapping, in Montreal, of British trade commissioner James Cross and then Quebec labor minister Pierre Laporte.

The 107-word referendum question put to us in 1980 was notoriously mealy-mouthed, and justifiably ridiculed by Pierre Trudeau. "You've got to admit," he said, "that for courage of conviction, for nobility of ideal, for spirit of decision, we've seen better."[1] The now-you-see-sovereignty-association-now-you-don't question had been devised by Claude Morin, then the PQ minister of intergovernmental affairs. Morin was the party's acknowledged master *étapiste*, which is to say, if he had set out to rob your home of a thousand dollars, he would have been content to pinch a penny at a time. Soft as the question was, however, it was still traumatic for many Quebecers. Ten years later Pierre Bibeau, who was the Liberal Party's chief organizer during the referendum, recalled, "It was very divisive in the end. It divided Quebec profoundly, to the point where many of the wounds haven't healed. There were quarrels in families, there were hard feelings between colleagues at work and between neighbors at home. . . . Personally," he told the *Gazette*'s Hubert Bauch, "even if it was a very special feeling, it's not something I'd want to repeat. The wounds from the last time still haven't healed completely."[2]

The campaign, hard fought by impassioned advocates of both Yes and No, was, on occasion, silly, sneaky smart, or downright ugly. An increasingly hoarse René Lévesque delivering his stem-winder here, there, and everywhere, actually asking Yes supporters to come forward so that he could reward them with a believer's certificate. Even before the campaign had started, the PQ paid for highway billboards ostensibly to promote a seat-belt campaign, its slogan: *"On s'attache au Québec."* Then the federal government mailed Quebecers what purported to be an anti-drink pamphlet, its message, *"Non merci,"* the same as their referendum slogan.

In the heat of the campaign, Trudeau made a pledge that, so far as he was concerned, he honored when he delivered a Charter of Rights to the country at large. But in the opinion of many Quebecers, not all of them nationalists, it was a promise he reneged on the morning after, as it were. What Trudeau said was, "We are staking our heads, we Quebec MPs, because we are telling Quebecers to vote No, and we are saying to you in other provinces that we will not accept having a No interpreted as an indication that everything is fine, and everything can stay as it was before. We want change. We are staking our seats to have change."[3]

In the end, Quebecers voted 59.56 percent No and 40.44 percent Yes, sparing us the most unpleasant resolution, which would have rendered a Francophone majority vote for sovereignty-association, but an overall No response which could have been blamed on the province's Anglophones and Allophones. In the end, Claude Ryan, leader of the No campaign, proved a sore winner, but both Trudeau and Lévesque showed grace under pressure.

Ryan, once he had been advised of the referendum results, grimly called for the government's resignation. Trudeau, on the other hand, was at his best. He could not forget, he said, "all those Yes supporters who had fought with such strong convictions. . . . Their disappointment prevents me from entering unreservedly into the spirit of celebration." And he then went on to say, "To my fellow Quebecers who have been wounded by defeat, I wish to say simply that we have all lost a little in this referendum. If you take account of the broken friendships, the strained family relationships, the hurt pride, there is no one among us who has not suffered some wound which we must try to heal in the days and weeks to come."[4]

And in Montreal's Paul Sauvé Arena, René Lévesque led his supporters, some of them weeping, many of them waving Quebec flags, in the singing of their national-anthem-in-waiting, Gilles Vigneault's "Gens du pays." Then, his voice cracking, he said, "If I understand you correctly, you are saying, *A la prochaine.*"[5]

It was, and I speak as an unrepentant No voter, an incredibly moving moment in Quebec history, a time when many Canadians felt for Lévesque, who was admired throughout the country, considered to be a politician unlike the rest.

I FIRST MET RENÉ LÉVESQUE in November 1970, only two weeks after the FLQ had murdered Pierre Laporte, informing police that the body of the late labor minister could be found in the trunk of a car abandoned in the South Shore suburb of St. Hubert.

To recap, briefly, the events of the 1970 October Crisis:

On October 5, four armed men kidnapped James Cross from his Montreal home. One of them was heard to say, "We are the FLQ." Five days later, four members of another FLQ cell kidnapped Pierre Laporte from his suburban home. On October 12, the army moved into Ottawa to protect Cabinet ministers and government buildings. Three days later a badly shaken Premier Bourassa asked the federal government to impose the War Measures Act. At 4:00 a.m. the next day the federal Cabinet proclaimed the act. It not only outlawed the FLQ, but gave the police just about absolute powers of search, arrest, and detention without warrant. Something like 1,200 cops made a predawn roundup of anyone remotely connected with the FLQ and, come noon, more than 450 Quebecers were in the slammer. Then, on October 17, the FLQ declared that Laporte had been executed. Two days later, the House of Commons voted 190-16 to approve the use of the War Measures Act. On November 6, the police finally arrested one of the Laporte kidnappers,

Bernard Lortie, in an apartment on Queen Mary Road in Montreal. Just short of three days passed before the police located the apartment where the other FLQ cell had Cross hidden. On December 3, the kidnappers agreed to release Cross in return for a safe conduct to Cuba for themselves and their families. A day later, once the Cuban consul in Montreal had learned that the kidnappers had arrived safely in Havana, Cross was released. Then, on December 27, the other kidnappers of Pierre Laporte, the brothers Jacques and Paul Rose, were nabbed at a house in St. Luc, south of Montreal. Twenty years later, on the anniversary of the kidnapping and murder, a junior college teacher named Heinz Weinman wrote in *Liberté*, the Québécois intellectual quarterly, that 1970 was Quebec's year zero. "[It was] the birth of the Quebec nation."[6]

ROOTED IN LONDON IN 1970, I was preparing Guy Fawkes fireworks in the backyard for our children when *Life* magazine phoned from New York. Could I leave for Montreal immediately?

A few days later I met René Lévesque for drinks in an East End Montreal restaurant. Determined to dissociate the Parti québécois from the FLQ, he dismissed the latter group as "a bunch of bums." At the time, I had no idea that seven years earlier, when the FLQ was much given to planting bombs in mailboxes that could explode in the faces of children, Lévesque had said to André Laurendeau, "You've got to hand it to them, they're courageous, those guys."[7]

On first meeting, I took the chain-smoking, obviously high-strung Lévesque to be an authentic people's tribune. As I wrote in *Life*, he struck me as a man effortlessly in touch with the bookkeeper with sour breath, the wasting clerk with dandruff, the abandoned mother of five, the truck driver on welfare, in fact with all the discontented lives. Only later did I learn that the man had many sides to him.

When he first founded his independence party in 1967, he had objected to it being called the Parti québécois because the name erred on the side of pomposity, implying that all other political parties were either non- or anti-Québécois, but in the end he acquiesced to it.

When PQ zealots first proposed uprooting all of Montreal's STOP/ARRÊT signs, he warned it would make them a laughing stock, but he agreed to that, too.

Then, some years after the fact, it was revealed that Lévesque had feared Bill 101 imposed too many restrictions on the province's English-speaking citizens, but he did not insist on any amendments.

Stroking Quebec's jittery Anglophones, Lévesque would say that they were also Québécois, but when he introduced a new head of Hydro-Québec, Robert Boyd, he assured the faithful that, in spite of his Anglo-sounding name, Boyd was a real Québécois.

The next time I met Lévesque, in 1978, was at Harvard. We were both participants in an extended lecture series ("The Future of North America: Canada, the United States, and Quebec Nationalism") co-sponsored by Harvard's Center for International Affairs and the Institute for Research on Public Policy, based in Montreal. My lecture was delivered to a small group in a classroom, but, appropriately enough, Lévesque, the final speaker in a series that included Robert Bourassa and several federal politicians of note, was to appear in Memorial Hall. This was to be followed by a dinner for fifty or sixty people to which I had also been invited. Afterward we would retire to another room for coffee, where Lévesque would answer questions informally.

Lévesque and I clashed at the cocktail party preceding his lecture. It began when I addressed him as "Mr. Premier," only to be immediately cut short.

"You bum," he said, "you know my name, use it."

His anger stemmed from an article about Quebec that I had recently published in the *Atlantic Monthly*—an article in which I had been guilty of an embarrassing gaffe. Elaborating on Jewish community fears I had written, "and nobody was reassured when joyous PQ supporters sang a French version of

'Tomorrow Belongs to Me,' the chilling Hitler Youth song from *Cabaret*, at their victory rally."[8] Not only had I got it badly wrong, but it served me right, because I had cribbed the "fact" from somebody else's piece in *Commentary* without checking it out. The truth is, the song in question was different from the one in *Cabaret*.

A belligerent Lévesque now told me, "When the writer of our song catches up with you, he's going to punch you in the nose."

Provoked into being equally childish, I replied, "I'm not so difficult to find. My name's in the phone book."

Then we got into other things.

"It is possible to dislike Menachem Begin," Lévesque said, "without being an anti-Semite."

I agreed, hastily pointing out that, although I was not anti-French Canadian, I took Camille Laurin to be an abomination.

Lévesque giggled. "If you only knew how much I dislike him," he said.

"Well, he's in your Cabinet, René, not mine."

Shrugging, Lévesque slid away to join another group, and I found myself face-to-face with one of his bodyguards, an obese young man with a pulpy pale face. "You must know my car dealer in Quebec City," he said, "his name's Isenberg."

"We don't necessarily all know each other," I said.

"First name Issy," he went on, baffled.

There was not an empty seat to be found in Memorial Hall, which was nice, very nice. All the same, I was astonished to hear Neil Nevitte, the fellow for the Center for International Affairs who introduced Lévesque, declare unequivocally that no other Canadian could have attracted such a large crowd. This was ridiculous, of course, because Pierre Trudeau, not to mention Bobby Orr, could have done as well, if not better.

Lévesque, usually an effective speaker, got off to an uncertain start, as if he expected the audience to barrack him. In the event, the students were either uncommonly polite or not punishingly bright, none of them reacting when the premier began with a preposterous analogy. Reminding his audience of the

Boston Tea Party and their own struggle for independence, he went on to say that their example had inspired many people on their path to national emancipation. "I am confident, therefore," he said, "that here in Boston, here at Harvard, there will be, if not necessarily agreement, a basic understanding of our aspirations."[9]

At Harvard, of course, there also should have been a basic understanding that Quebecers in 1978, unlike the Bostonians of 1773, far from suffering from taxation without representation, had one of their own serving as prime minister, backed by seventy-four MPs from the province.

The central fact of language, Lévesque pointed out, "makes Quebec the home base, the homeland, of a compact, very deeply rooted, and rapidly evolving cultural group."[10] But he failed to add that, in the words of a staunch PQ supporter, Quebec economist Georges Mathews, "the federal government has done infinitely more for the cultural advancement of French Canada than has the provincial government."[11]

With legitimate pride, the premier reminded his audience that of all European settlers on this continent, excluding Mexico, "We were the first discoverers, the first pioneers, the first settlers, and now our roots go back a bit further than those of Boston, three hundred and seventy years. We have worked the same land. We were born on it in the Valley of the St. Lawrence; all our forefathers are buried there. The tradition is tied also to a language which made us different."[12]

Allowing that Quebec had once been a reactionary, priest-ridden, folkloric society, he went on to talk of how the Quiet Revolution, begun in 1960, had changed so many things. But he failed to explain that this revolution could never have taken place without the massive support of Quebec's Anglophones because in the 1960 election, a close run, the majority of Francophones still supported the Union nationale.

He filled the students in on the astonishing rise of the Parti Québécois. "[It] grew," he said, "from a few hundred members in 1967 to twenty-three percent of the voters in the first election three years later, in 1970. We polled thirty-one percent in

1973 and we emerged as the official opposition. In 1976 we became the government with a forty-one percent plurality."[13]

Lévesque also made it clear that, campaigning in a province with a history of political corruption, the Parti québécois had done what it could to impose honesty on the electoral process. "The [PQ]," he said, "is the first political party in the Western world, as far as I know, to rise from nothing to become the government while refusing, year after year, any money from any group—either corporate on the right or union on the left—because groups do not vote. We made it a basic principle to keep them at arm's length. No slush funds. With thousands of canvassers all over the place, door-to-door, we solicited citizens' money, which is not supposed to be, of course, a serious factor in politics. It was serious enough to build a party into the government of a society of six million people. And our government has passed Bill No. 2, the legislation of which I am proudest, requiring all parties to open their books."[14]

Lévesque also could have claimed, without fear of contradiction, that his basically honest government had also brought in a refreshingly rational auto insurance plan and a progressive green law to protect the countryside from the avarice of developers.

"Nationalism often has a bad connotation," he said, and then went on to reassure the students that Quebec nationalism, with laws then already in place to suppress the English language and deny parents freedom of choice in education, "is not anti-anyone; it is pro-us."[15]

No sooner were we all seated for dinner at our various tables than a twinkly little Harvard professor of French rose to toast Lévesque. To my astonishment, he echoed General Charles de Gaulle's cry from the balcony of Montreal's City Hall in 1967: "Vive le Québec libre!"

Later I asked the professor how he would have responded in 1864 if Jefferson Davis, following a lecture in Toronto, had been toasted by a rebel yell.

"I was just trying to be nice," he said.

After we had all adjourned to another room for coffee, Lévesque, his mood noticeably improved, fielded questions with panache. Mind you, most of the questions were innocuous and the premier, obviously an expert at playing a room, was more often ingratiating than honest in his responses.

Finally, I did get a chance to speak to a Harvard economist with an international reputation, an adviser to American presidents. "How would people here feel if Quebec separated?" I asked.

"It would be an inconvenience."

"That's all?"

"Yes."

René Lévesque resigned from the leadership of the PQ in 1985, and two years later he was dead of a heart attack. Unfortunately, I never had an opportunity to talk to him again. In this country, where we are served by so many resoundingly mediocre politicians, he was a happy exception to a depressing rule. Charismatic, vulnerable, a leader without whom the separatists would have remained trapped within the fringe RIN (Rassemblement pour l'indépendance nationale), he nevertheless did not merit his reputation for honesty.

My enduring feeling about René Lévesque is that if he had chosen to hang me, even as he tightened the rope round my neck, he would have complained about how humiliating it was for him to spring the trapdoor. And then, once I was swinging in the wind, he would blame my ghost for having obliged him to murder, thereby imposing a guilt trip on a sweet, self-effacing, downtrodden Francophone.

IN JUNE 1990, JACQUES PARIZEAU announced that he saw no purpose in observing the twentieth anniversary of what English Canadians call the October Crisis and French Canadians, *Les événements d'octobre.* "I don't see what we'd have to commemorate in this," he said. "Neither the acts of terrorism nor the abuse of power by our governments toward ordinary citizens. Neither in one case nor the other."[16]

But former FLQ apparatchiks had already declared that they would commemorate October 16—the day Trudeau invoked the

War Measures Act—by marching past the former prime minister's house in Montreal.

Come late September, both an FLQ special shown on TVA, the privately owned French-language television network, and a front-page story run in Quebec City's *Le Soleil* sniffed conspiracy in the twenty-year-old events. There were two suggestions. One, that Pierre Laporte had not been murdered, but, instead, strangled by accident with the chain of his own religious medal during an escape attempt. Two, that Laporte had still been alive when he had been dumped into the trunk of a car abandoned in a field in St. Hubert and if the police hadn't been so tardy in getting there he would still be with us today. Problems. The communiqué from the FLQ's Chénier cell, informing the police where Laporte could be found, stated clearly that he was "executed." And Francis Simard, who served eleven years in prison for the murder of Laporte, stated unequivocally that the former labor minister had died "at the hands of the FLQ."[17]

Yes, but what if Simard, Jacques and Paul Rose, and Bernard Lortie, all ostensibly members of the Chénier cell, were in fact RCMP moles? "Though no one has ever presented any solid evidence to support it," wrote Hubert Bauch in the *Gazette*, "this year's anniversary has provided an occasion to refloat the theory that the whole 55-day kidnap crisis was a put-up job by the federal government; that Quebec Labour Minister Pierre Laporte . . . was actually killed by the police, or even a secret agent dispatched directly by Pierre Trudeau."[18]

In a book that leans heavily on an exchange of letters between John Grube and Jacques Ferron—the former an Ontario academic and the latter a highly regarded Quebec novelist and playwright—it is claimed that the October Crisis was staged by the federal government to discredit Quebec's *indépendantistes*, just as, say, John Wilkes Booth was set up to shoot Lincoln in order to deny actors middle-class respectability in America.

"There are a lot of suspicious elements," Grube told Hubert Bauch. "Put them all together and you have a government scam."[19]

This, Bauch notes, credits three police forces (the RCMP, the

Sûreté du Québec, and the Montreal Urban Police) with rather much, considering that at the time they outdid the Keystone Kops in their ineptitude. During the raids on the homes of suspects after the War Measures Act had been imposed, one cop seized a book on Cubism, convinced he held a Cuban revolutionary tract in his hot hands.

In any event, in 1990 the FLQ kidnappers and murderers were back in Quebec, their taste for Cuba having turned out to be no more than a passing fancy.

Francis Simard, who served his term in prison, was writing film scripts.

Paul Rose was teaching at the Université du Québec in Rimouski, which is to say he was doing penance of a sort. Immediately after the Supreme Court had ruled Bill 178 illegal, he was greeted as a hero at a rally of Francophone students at a junior college in a Montreal suburb. Rose told them that the Supreme Court was "very extremist."[20]

Jacques Rose had gone into the home-renovation business.

Jacques Lanctôt, a member of the Libération cell that had kidnapped James Cross, was now owner of a publishing house, VLB Editeur. "We were romantics," he said. "We saw ourselves going off to war, though we didn't really know what we were doing. We wanted to make a revolution, but we didn't want to kill anyone. I've come to understand that working in the cultural field is a way of making a political contribution."[21]

Jacques Cossette-Trudel, in exile from 1971 to 1979, has been a communications counselor in a social service agency since 1980. His essay about the October Crisis, "L'Histoire séquestrée," appeared in the October 1990 issue of Liberté. "The FLQ of 1970," he wrote, "insisted on distinguishing itself from its predecessors by convulsive rejection of any intellectual effort (and argument would sometimes be dismissed out of hand: 'That doesn't count, you read it in a book!'), by the passage to immediate acts."[22] One of the Cross kidnappers, he obviously didn't remember the British trade commissioner fondly. "As for the British diplomat sequestered by the Libération cell, his greatest misfortune was doubtless to miss the bridge game planned for the evening of October 5, and to eat Quebec food for 59 days. Eat Shepherd's pie in Montréal Nord? *My Lord!*"[23]

Cossette-Trudel was proud of the fact that his FLQ cell was the only one to integrate "women into direct action,"[24] but his wife, a Libération cell member, divorced him in 1983 and complained in her book that the FLQ honchos were male chauvinist pigs. "The guys appropriated all the glory," she complained.[25]

Fifteen

WOODY'S PUB USED TO BE frequented late in the afternoon by a number of lawyers, journalists, and politicians, among them Richard Holden, now a member of the National Assembly, and the ebullient Nick Auf der Maur, gadfly city councillor, *Gazette* columnist and boulevardier. In the summer of 1990, more often than not, Auf der Maur, expounding with gusto on our tribal troubles, was attended at the bar by reporters out of New York, Washington, or London, notebooks at the ready. Like so many English-speaking but fluently bilingual Montrealers, he was increasingly concerned about our situation, but also relished it. Attention was being paid at long last.

I should point out that Canadians traveling in Europe, or even the neighboring United States, have long been reconciled to finding no word of home in the newspapers, save for last night's baseball or hockey scores. In the summer of 1990, however, there was a sea change. Once benign, law-abiding Canada was born again as front-page stuff, one of the world's most unnecessary and goofy trouble spots; Montreal, my Montreal, was the very eye of the storm.

Montrealers, reading about their plight in Canadian newspapers or magazines—say, the Toronto *Globe and Mail, Maclean's, Le Devoir, La Presse, L'actualité,* or *Saturday Night* magazine—tend to dismiss doomsday scenarios as the mischief of indigenous hacks: made-in-Canada, therefore minor-league, of no consequence. But a report run in *The Wall Street Journal, The New York Times,* or the London *Daily Telegraph* or *Economist* predicting the breakup of our nation inevitably reverberates in our own press the next day and commands serious attention here, even an overreaction.

Back in 1988, for instance, a top-of-page-four headline in the

Montreal *Gazette* read:

QUEBEC TRIP 'LINGUISTIC NIGHTMARE' TOURIST WRITES[1]

The article that followed told of a British woman who had visited Quebec City the previous autumn and had described her trip, in a letter to the editor of *Condé Nast Traveler*, as a "linguistic nightmare," adding that she and her companions "felt oppressed because of our ability to speak only English.

"On occasion we felt we were the targets of rude remarks. The lack of English signs added to our frustration."[2]

Her letter, which struck me as more than somewhat arrogant, was in fact a response to a *Condé Nast Traveler* article that had appeared the previous October. Clive Irving's article was, for the most part, appreciative of Quebec City's grandeur, but then he came a cropper:

> It takes a while to realize that there is a persistent strain of lunatic chauvinism.
>
> The first clue is the number of restaurants promoting *casse-croûte*, which, literally translated, means "broken pastry." A regional specialty? The second clue comes as I notice that in place of STOP signs, standard even in France, there are ARRÊT signs. Finally I pass an Auberge Ramada.
>
> What has happened is linguistic genocide. The Quebecers have tried to eliminate the sight of English. Many speak it, but they are not allowed to gaze upon it. *Casse-croûte* is, quite simply, a snack. In France you can see LE SNACK-BAR as frequently as you see STOP. I want to enjoy Le Weekend, but this makes me ornery.[3]

In July 1989, the *New York Times* printed a couple of articles about resurgent Quebec nationalism. In the second article, the *Times* suggested that Premier Bourassa, invoking our constitution's notwithstanding clause to override a Supreme Court ruling and tighten an already restrictive language law, had taken advantage of a "legal loophole."[4]

I thought this was fair comment, but it enraged many a Québécois politician and editorial writer. The same article made reference to, but did not quote in detail, a statement that

Witold Rybczynski had originally made in *Liberté*. What the McGill professor and the author of *Home, The Most Beautiful House in the World* and *Waiting for the Weekend* actually said was, "The once cosmopolitan city of Montreal is in danger of becoming a linguistic Beirut. Sensibilities have become dulled to the point where the presence of an apostrophe or an *accent aigu* is a political statement, and spray paint has replaced civilized discourse. Comparisons with historical examples of intolerance are exaggerated, but it is true that public policy seems to be made as much by vandals as by elected politicians. It is a sorry spectacle, and one which the rest of us view with incomprehension."[5]

The Quebec delegation in New York lodged an immediate protest with the *Times*. Premier Bourassa declared that the *Times* coverage was "so contrary to the real situation it will not have any serious consequences."[6] Jacques Parizeau reminded reporters that when the PQ had first come to power in 1976 the U.S. media had suggested that Quebec would become the "Cuba of the North,"[7] and he went on to say, "If some of the U.S. newspapers are now trying again to describe us in such a way that would be called politically damaging to us, it's probably that we are stronger than we think."

The truth is that Canadians, English and French, are bound together by more than a propensity for bad taste. Both our founding races are also hypersensitive.

Michael Kinsley once wrote in *The New Republic:*

> Now any slighting reference to Canada is bound to produce a flurry of anguished letters, most of them attached to manuscripts. On the other hand, so is any favorable reference to Canada, so it would be futile to add at this point that I think it's a lovely country and we're darn lucky to have it next door, especially considering the alternatives. Yet Canada is, for all its acknowledged merits, a nation of assistant professors, each armed with articles designed to "dispel misunderstanding." These literary missiles are aimed at the American media, ready to be fired at the slightest provocation. Those who are themselves transfixed by subjects like Canada and the Law of the Sea Conference (now there's a title) tend to see misunderstanding where there is actually judicious indifference.[8]

I have had my own troubles with touchy Canadians. In 1982, I wrote a short piece for the sports pages of the *New York Times*, actually about the baseball All-Star Game coming to Montreal, in which I admittedly led off by poking fun at the PQ for lumbering us with *"hambourgeois"* for "hamburger," among other foolish things. But nothing I wrote was as damaging as René Lévesque's reaction to his party's demand to uproot the province's STOP/ARRÊT signs and have them replaced with signs that read ARRÊT only. "If our government did such a thing," he said, "we would become a laughing stock."⁹

A couple of months later Jacques-Yvan Morin, then deputy prime minister of Quebec and minister of intergovernmental affairs, spoke at the Harvard Faculty Club, in Cambridge, in a colloquium on Quebec–United States Relations:

> In all honesty, however, it should be said we have no one to blame but ourselves if we are not better known in the United States. If the news that trickles down here about Quebec is more often than not distorted, either deliberately or through ignorance, right at the source, the reason, all too frequently, is that the person transmitting the message from Quebec may have a particular axe to grind. I know of no better example than an article which appeared recently in the sports section of *The New York Times*. That article, written by Mr. Mordecai Richler, contained a measure of venom against Quebec with which it would be difficult to compete.
>
> Now I must assume that *The New York Times* did not consciously seek out a writer whose objective was to denounce Quebec. It just seemed like a good idea to have a Montreal novelist write a piece on the occasion of the first All-Stars' game ever played outside the United States. I must also assume that the story would not have been printed by a newspaper of that calibre had the sports desk been conscious of its onesidedness. But it was published and that merely underlines the fact that Quebec still has a long way to go to ensure that Americans— even presumably objective people like those who are at *The New York Times*—get to know us better.¹⁰

Of course all Morin accomplished, the silly bugger, was to have a large chunk of his audience, who had never heard of me or read the piece in the *Times*, return to their offices and ask their secretaries to ring the *Times* sports desk and ask them to dig up that article by what's-his-name, I have it written down somewhere.

And while I'm at it, those members of the audience who were knowledgeable about Quebec must have guffawed when the shameless Morin bragged about "Baie James, with everything it implies in terms of progress and know how," and how it reflected "merely part of the image of contemporary Quebec." They would have guffawed because as every Quebecer knows, the massive James Bay hydroelectric facility was the accomplishment of Robert Bourassa and was bitterly condemned by the PQ as an outdated venture, while they stood for the future, which was obviously nuclear power. The PQ only came round to claiming James Bay after public opinion polls informed them that Quebecers were proud of it.

To be fair to Morin, I have endured equally asinine criticism from English Canadians, once more in reaction to something I wrote for *The New York Times*, in this case an article about Wayne Gretzky in which I noted, in passing, that Edmonton did not qualify as one of the world's architectural wonders. With hindsight, this was hardly an original observation. Anyway what I wrote was:

> The capital of Alberta is a city you come from, not a place to visit, unless you happen to have relatives there or an interest in an oil well nearby. On first glance, and even on third, it seems not so much a city as a jumble of a used-building lot, where the spare office towers and box-shaped apartment buildings and cinder-block motels discarded in the construction of real cities have been abandoned to waste away in the cruel prairie winter.
>
> If Canada were not a country, however fragmented, but, instead, a house, Vancouver would be the solarium-cum-playroom, an afterthought of affluence; Toronto, the counting room, where money makes for the most glee; Montreal, the salon; and Edmonton, Edmonton, the boiler room. There is hardly a tree to be seen downtown, nothing to delight the eye on Jasper Avenue. On thirty-below-zero nights, grim religious zealots loom on street corners, speaking in tongues, and intrepid streetwalkers in

mini-skirts rap on the windows of cars that have stopped for traffic lights. There isn't a first-class restaurant anywhere in town. But, for all that, the city of 700,000 has a fascinating history.[11]

Fulminating city officials phoned the New York Times and demanded an immediate retraction. They were informed that this would be impossible, but they could respond with a full-page advertisement if they liked. Yes, right, book the space right now. Then they were told the price and they had second thoughts.

Next, the editor of Edmonton's trashy tabloid, the Sun, printed my home phone number and encouraged readers to give me a tinkle. As a consequence, I was wakened again and again by Edmontonians who would either breathe heavily and then hang up or, taxing their natural wit to the utmost extreme, would holler, "Fuck you, you Jew bastard!" and slam down the receiver.

This had only gone on for a week or so when a reporter from the Sun phoned. "My editor would like to know if you have had many phone calls in reaction to our article on you."

"Could you put your editor on the phone, please?"

"Just one moment, please." A pause. "He's in a meeting."

"May I have his home phone number, then. I'll call him later."

"Just one moment, please." A pause. "It is not our policy to give out the editor's home phone number."

Considering the amount of abusive mail I received, I could only conclude that I had brought financial ruin on a proud city. Obviously, hundreds of thousands of tourists who had been looking forward to spending their winter vacations in Edmonton had read my piece in the Times, promptly canceled their reservations, and now had to settle for London or Paris or Rome instead.

IF CANADIANS RESPOND badly to criticism printed abroad, the truth is they are more often insulted by indifference.

Nineteen-ninety, no exception to the rule, saw my compatriots diminished by the publication of two books: *Spy Wars* and *In the Eye of the Eagle*.

Spy Wars, by J. L. Granatstein and David Stafford, is a study of snooping in Canada from Gouzenko to glasnost. It deals with Quebec only in passing, searching for evidence of possible hanky-panky by the French from the time General de Gaulle performed his political *pirouette en dehors* on the balcony of Montreal's Hôtel de Ville. Looking down on the wretched of the earth gathered below, descendants of true Frenchmen, the general was so moved by the pitiable plight of such an emaciated horde that he cried, *"Vive le Québec libre!"* Presumably the old soldier did not know, or had forgotten, that in his time of need most of the bourgeoisie gathered below, if they were old enough, had probably belonged to the Bloc populaire and been fervent supporters of Marshal Pétain. In any event, it did not seem to bother de Gaulle that he was encouraging sedition in a country, wrote the coauthors of *Spy Wars*, that had left close to 100,000 soldiers "buried in war cemeteries on French soil, killed in Canada's effort in two world wars to keep France free."[12] But aside from the fact that a succession of French officials, conspicuous among them one Philippe Rossillon of the Haut-Commissariat de la langue française, had stirred the waters of our troubled pond, encouraging separatists, there is no hard evidence of any real dirty work on their part. So the authors of *Spy Wars*, obviously a responsible pair, are careful to qualify their speculations. Writing about Rossillon, for instance, they say, "he had some shadowy contacts with terrorist groups in Quebec and *apparently* [italics mine] provided financial aid to . . . the Rassemblement pour l'indépendance nationale."[13] Even Trudeau, justifiably outraged by French mischief-making, could say no more of Rossillon than that he was *"more or less* [italics mine] a secret agent."[14] Trudeau, however, did certainly get off a good one in *Spy Wars*. "France," Trudeau told one of us bitterly, "was always ready to advance the cause of French minorities everywhere in the world—except in France and its colonies."[15] Say, the *pays Basque* or Corsica.

If *Spy Wars* yielded no hard evidence of a French plot to sub-
vert the Canadian government, it was certainly to be hoped
that *In the Eye of the Eagle*, by Jean-François Lisée, would blow
the whistle on Washington's perfidy, establishing beyond doubt
that the Americans were sufficiently interested in us to meddle
in our politics to their advantage. After all, the book's cover
featured a ferocious eagle clutching a wimpy Canadian flag in
its claws, and it promised "Secret Files [that revealed]
Washington's Plans for Canada and Quebec." Furthermore, in
the seventies, the separatists were damn sure the CIA was out
to undermine them. *If not, why not?* Everybody knew that they
had already toppled Allende. Two months after the military
coup in Chile, Claude Castonguay, a former Cabinet minister in
the Bourassa government, said, "The United States has shown
many times that it does not like instability. What makes anyone think [it] would look passively on Quebec separation?"[16]

Clearly, American intelligence would have been remiss had it
not maintained a watching brief on Quebec, but Guy Joron, the
former PQ energy minister, was absolutely right when he reproached his more paranoid colleagues, saying, "Let's not over-
estimate our own importance. Quebec's plans don't rock
Western civilization. They don't crack the columns of Wall
Street's temples, and they probably don't change even the last
decimal point on General Motors' sales projections."[17]

The secret Washington file unearthed by the resourceful
Lisée, formerly *La Presse*'s Washington correspondent, turns out
to be both prescient and fair-minded. Commissioned by Henry
Kissinger, dated August 1977, it was prepared by Tom Enders,
then U.S. ambassador in Ottawa, and supported the idea of a
special status for Quebec within confederation, which is precisely the idea we are struggling with today.

"The Quebec Situation: Outlook and Implications" begins
by reminding Americans that Quebec nationalism did not begin with the founding of the PQ. "The five million francophone Québécois, 80% of the Quebec population, have an
ethnic identity and solidarity of their own. They have also had
long-standing grievances, real and perceived, against both

English Canada—symbolized by Ottawa, and anglophones in Quebec—symbolized by West Montreal. These grievances include such matters as a feeling of inferiority, second-class citizenship—both in Canada as a whole and, more importantly, in their own province of Quebec."[18] Then it goes on to point out, "Quebec is no longer the backward area with uneducated farmers ruled by the church and corrupt politicians of a few decades ago—when the only chance for the best and the brightest was federal service or national politics. Over the past decades there has been a tremendous surge in industrialization, urbanization, education and opportunities for advancement in the province."[19]

Pondering the PQ's language law, the report speculates that it will create tensions, especially in Montreal, and prompt many Anglophones to quit the province. Then the report reflects on the five possible outcomes of the impasse:

1. Considering *Maintenance of the Status Quo*, it predicts correctly that "if the PQ should be defeated, the next provincial government will have to keep on demanding concessions from Ottawa, though perhaps not such sweeping ones."[20]

2. The alternative of *Devolution of Powers to All Provinces* from the federal government it adjudges "the only realistic way in the long term to keep Quebec in Canada."[21]

3. Another possibility, *Devolution of Powers to Quebec Only*, it pronounces highly questionable, as the other provinces might not agree to it.

4. There is no question, according to the report, that the negotiation of *Political Sovereignty with Economic Association* "would be extremely difficult since [it] would involve such matters as a common market for trade and possibly energy, a monetary union, and control over foreign trade."[22]

5. If a frustrated Quebec should opt for a *Unilateral Declaration of Independence*, based on the outcome of a referendum, the report points out that the size of the majority would be the most important factor. It also notes that "both Trudeau and Clark [then leader of the federal Tories] have said they would not use force to keep Quebec in Canada if a clear majority of the Québécois chose independence."

Considering this last option, the report ventures, "While Quebec would certainly be a more viable state than most UN members, it could well, to begin with, be less viable as an independent country than as a province. Canada, if it could survive at all, would be less viable as a country without Quebec."[23] It then goes on to point out that an independent Quebec, "having established once and for all the supremacy of its French character in language and culture, might well become less xenophobic."[24] It is less sanguine about the future of the larger English Canadian rump:

> The first flush of Quebec independence could bring about greater cohesion, at least temporarily, for the rest of Canada, and could result in an increase in anti-U.S. feelings as a means to preserve a separate Canadian identity deprived of the French peculiarity. Strong regional divergencies, the natural North-South pull, and the exposed situation for the maritime provinces would probably inexorably in time lead to one or more of the provinces or regions breaking away from Ontario/Ottawa domination. Once started, it is questionable whether the process could be stopped. Some of the provinces or regions would try it alone, some would seek some form of association with the U.S. The effect would be that the U.S. would be faced with either new responsibilities and/or opportunities, or a number of small and weak, although probably friendly, countries to the North.[25]

The report concludes:

　　a. The U.S. considers the Quebec situation to be one for the Canadians themselves to resolve;
　　b. The U.S. considers Canadians completely capable of resolving the question; and
　　c. The U.S. prefers confederation.[26]

If *In the Eye of the Eagle* FAILED to deliver on its promise of revealing America's secret (and no doubt nefarious) plan for Canada and Quebec, it is nevertheless informative, entertaining, and rich in revelations about the Parti québécois. On the evidence, it would seem that the party that was determined on independence from Canada was simultaneously pathetically dependent on American goodwill, its leaders, Lévesque, Claude Morin, and Parizeau, outdoing each other in groveling to Ambassador Enders and Terry McNamara, the American consul general in Quebec City. "At the top of the list of American 'sources,'" wrote Lisée, "was René Lévesque."

> In private meetings with the ambassador and the consul general, he laid out his latest strategic information as if it were yesterday's news. Prognoses for the referendum, comments on his political adversaries, his plan to nationalize the asbestos industry—nothing was taboo. It should be said, however, that the geopolitical value of this information was tempered by the fact that the premier changed his mind almost every month. All the same, his American interlocutors had, on average, thirty days' head start on the public—and on most of the ministers in his cabinet.[27]

Claude Morin was also out to ingratiate himself. Before Lévesque had bothered to apprise his own electorate, Morin reported to McNamara that sovereignty-association would mean, among other things, a monetary and customs union with Canada, as well as a common central bank. Finance Minister Jacques Parizeau, equally hot to trot with the Americans, gave their consul general advance notice of just about all his intended moves in the expropriation of the US-owned General Dynamics Corporation.

Mind you, according to Lisée, some federalist politicians were equally obsequious, reporting to Washington cap in hand, as it were. Among them federal Cabinet minister Bryce Mackasey:

> American diplomatic dispatches concealed scoops which, had they been leaked, would have made front page copy in Canada and seriously embarrassed many high-ranking officials. What inspired Canadians to offer their secrets to the first American to pass their way? Quebec separatist leaders wanted absolution. Getting acquainted with Washington's representative was a start. Being invited to dine with him was akin to promotion

from the status of local player to participant in the continental games. It is more difficult to explain the Canadian federalists' attitude, caught up as they were in the struggle for national identity. They had just endowed the country with a flag and they were involved in a permanent campaign to prove that Ottawa, not Washington, was the center of the Canadian universe. Were they trying to let the US know that things were under control in Quebec? Were they sending messages to calm Washington's frayed nerves?[28]

Sometimes it appears to me that Canada, even an intact Canada, is not so much a country as a continental suburb, where Little Leaguers govern ineffectually, desperate for American approval. Brian Mulroney is a case in point. Going into the 1988 election he assured Canadians that, unlike his opponent John Turner, he knew George Bush *personally*. He had actually been a guest at Kennebunkport. Following his election, interviewed for a *Time* cover story, he also proved that you couldn't take Baie Comeau out of the boy. "I'm very good friends with George and Barb," he told the *Time* writer.

Lévesque, coming from a distinctive society, when in doubt borrowed from another one. "We have nothing to fear but fear itself," he wrote in *Option-Québec*, and his sovereignty-association manifesto issued in 1979, in time for the referendum, was titled *Quebec-Canada: A New Deal*.

Sixteen

INSULTS, EVEN INDIFFERENCE, from abroad were small beer when set against the real shocks that would reverberate through Quebec in the summer of 1990. On June 22 the Meech Lake Accord collapsed. The accord was a constitutional compromise that, so far as Premier Bourassa was concerned, would have yielded Quebec its absolute minimum demands, enabling it to sign the Canada Act of 1982. Then, on July 11, a force of one hundred provincial police, armed with assault rifles, concussion grenades, and tear gas, attacked a Mohawk blockade in Oka, some forty miles west of Montreal, retreating after one of their number was shot and killed.

Meech first.

Benumbed by three years of repetitive, cliff-hanging constitutional negotiations, endless op-ed pieces pro and con in our newspapers, urgent television specials tarted up with doomsday music, speeches warning us of the national apocalypse to come, and contradictory polls by Gallup, CROP, Southam, *Globe*-CBC, Decima, SOCRAM, and the rest that seemed to test the pulse at least once a month, punch-drunk Canadians wakened to big black banner headlines on Saturday, June 23. The one in the *Gazette* ran:

MEECH IS DEAD[1]

In a brief statement to the National Assembly, Premier Bourassa expressed his "profound disappointment" that the Meech Lake Accord had not been ratified and concluded by reminding English Canada that "Quebec is today and forever a distinct society capable of ensuring its own development and destiny."[2]

"Meech is dead," a jolly Jacques Parizeau proclaimed in the

National Assembly. "Long live a sovereign Quebec, and quickly."[3]

There was a pleasing symmetry in that what had begun as a wasting tribal quarrel between Canada's two founding races finally came unstuck through the efforts of a descendant of Canada's original peoples—Elijah Harper, a hitherto unknown aboriginal member of Manitoba's legislative assembly—even as other Indians beat on drums outside the building.

That Meech foundered and finally expired was inevitable, seeing that it suffered from the Polish syndrome.

In the mid-fifteenth century, Poland acquired its first Diet, the Sejm, all its appointed members noblemen. No statute could become law unless the Sejm agreed to it unanimously. Put another way, it only took one bumpkin to block any piece of legislation. Obviously inspired by this model, the Canada Act of 1982 required provincial unanimity before a constitutional amendment like Meech could become law. This meant that Mulroney's constitutional fix could be undone by tiny Prince Edward Island or Newfoundland, most of whose citizens traditionally wintered on welfare. This meant that if the Meech Lake Accord were to become law, and not turn into a pumpkin, it had to be passed by all ten of Canada's provincial legislatures before midnight, June 22. The Manitoba legislature, another victim of the Polish malaise, just happened to need unanimous consent in order to extend its June 22 debate on the accord so that members could vote on it. At 12:26 p.m., June 22, Elijah Harper, the former Ojibway-Cree chief who was the member for Rupertsland, was asked if he would acquiesce to unanimous consent. And this Ojibway-Cree named after a Hebrew prophet—Elijah, the Tishbite, the champion who had protected his people against the scourge of Ahab, importer of the heathen cult of Baal into the land along with his squeeze Jezebel—replied, "No, Mr. Speaker."[4] Moments later the legislature adjourned indefinitely, and that was that.

Canada's natives had objected to the accord because it failed to acknowledge that they, like the Québécois, also comprised "a distinct society," a fundamental characteristic of Canada.

Harper, holding his sacred eagle feather, addressed several hundred supporters outside the legislature. "Now," he said, "the Canadian people know our concerns about the national disgrace of this country's treatment of its aboriginal people."[5]

At Woody's, we were obviously dismayed by the refusal of the Rest of Canada (ROC) to officially hail Quebec as a distinct society, a slight to our insecure Francophone brothers and sisters. In a spirit of compromise, one of our number suggested that it might possibly be acceptable to Quebec, as well as our First Nations, if ROC agreed to be designated indistinct instead—confirming what the rest of the world thought of us in any case. Unfortunately, the proposal never caught fire, as it were.

THE NEXT MORNING's *Gazette*, surely unaware that it was echoing the slogan of the Jewish Defense League, featured the following front-page banner headline:

Bourassa to Canada:
NEVER AGAIN[6]

In the heat of the morning after, Premier Bourassa—uncharacteristically painting himself into a corner—stated that he would never again negotiate constitutional reform with the other provinces. "Do not ask me to go back to the bargaining table," he said. "Dignity will prevent me from doing that." Then turning on Trudeau, his old nemesis, he said, "Do not forget that the source of the problem is the fact that in 1981 the premier of Quebec was put aside by the federal government."[7]

Certainly on November 5, 1981, an isolated and infuriated René Lévesque, who was then premier of Quebec, did refuse to sign the agreement on "patriating" the BNA Act. And thereafter, so far as Quebec nationalists were concerned, their province, humiliated at the conference, had been excluded from the Canadian family, the victim of an Anglophone conspiracy yet again. But as Andrew Cohen pointed out in *A Deal Undone:*

The Making and Breaking of the Meech Lake Accord, "The fact is that the 'injustice' was undertaken by a Liberal government with overwhelming representation in Quebec. The prime minister was a Quebecer who had been elected with large majorities from his native province since 1968. A third of his cabinet was from Quebec, including senior ministers in finance, health and justice. Moreover, the Liberals had elected seventy-four of seventy-five MPs from Quebec, seventy-one of whom supported the package. A good many provincial Liberals supported it too. If this was humiliation, it was at the hands of les Québécois."[8]

Three years later the flamethrowing federalist dragon repaired to his cave, Trudeau retired, and on September 4, 1984, the Conservatives, led, in the absence of St. George, by Brian Mulroney won the federal election. Bourassa was back in office in Quebec before 1985 was out, and on May 9, 1986, Gil Rémillard, Quebec's minister of intergovernmental affairs, presented the province's five conditions for rejoining the family, as it were, at yet another conference on the future of Quebec and Canada. The first condition, ostensibly innocuous, even oddly touching, that Quebec be officially proclaimed as a "distinct society," would turn out to be the most contentious. "We must be assured," said Rémillard, "that the Canadian constitution will explicitly recognize the unique character of Quebec society and guarantee us the means necessary to ensure its full development within the framework of Canadian federalism."[9]

Quebec also wanted a veto over any future constitutional amendments and a limitation put on federal spending powers, allowing the province to "opt out" of federal programs with financial compensation. It demanded sole control over immigration into its territory, and it wanted its right to fill three of the nine Supreme Court appointments enshrined in the constitution.

The following spring Canada's ten provincial premiers met with Prime Minister Mulroney at Meech Lake, in Gatineau Park, only a twenty-minute drive from downtown Ottawa, and agreed to an amending formula.

Each Canadian province would now have a role in choosing its senators, which is to say it could reward its own superannuated bagmen and other political nonentities, rather than those favored by Ottawa. Quebec would be recognized as a distinct society within Canada, its legislature entitled "to preserve and promote the distinct society of Quebec," even while acknowledging that Anglophones, like acne, were a fundamental characteristic of that society. This was interpreted as window dressing, a sop to the insecure, by most of the premiers, but Premier Bourassa told the National Assembly that "as a result, in the exercise of our legislative jurisdictions, we will be able to . . . gain new ground [in our] cultural, and our political, legal and economic institutions."[10]

Quebec, with roughly a quarter of the country's population, attracted only 15 to 17 percent of Canada's immigrants. Now it would be entitled to newcomers equal to its population plus 5 percent, which was simply swell but also baffling, if only because there was no need for immigrants to linger in the province for longer than a week. In fact, it would soon emerge that rich immigrants from Hong Kong and Korea, who had been welcomed to Quebec with special visas as they were pledged to set up businesses here, were using the province as a jumping-off spot, actually bound for Toronto or Vancouver, where they could educate their children in the language of their choice.

The accord guaranteed Quebec the right to three Supreme Court justices. It would allow provinces to opt out of federal programs with financial compensation. Furthermore, not only Quebec, but now every province, would be able to veto certain kinds of future constitutional amendments, including any that might call for senate reform or the creation of additional provinces. For the rest, a general amending formula would call only for the agreement of seven of the ten provinces, provided the seven (or more) contained at least 50 percent of the population.

Pierre Elliott Trudeau was not pleased. "With the assurance of a creative equilibrium between the provinces and the central government," he wrote, "the federation was set to last a thousand years. Alas, only one eventuality hadn't been foreseen: that one day the government of Canada would fall into the hands of a weakling. It has now happened. And the Rt. Hon. Brian Mulroney, PC, MP, with the complicity of ten provincial premiers, has already entered into history as the author of a constitutional document which—if it is accepted by the people and their legislators—will render the Canadian state totally impotent. That would destine it, given the dynamics of power, to be governed eventually by eunuchs."[11]

The former prime minister was equally scornful of Québécois nationalists. "The provincialist politicians," he wrote, "whether they sit in Ottawa, or in Quebec, are also perpetual losers: they don't have the stature or the vision to dominate the Canadian state, so they need a Quebec ghetto as their haunt. . . . That bunch of snivellers should simply have been sent packing and been told to stop having tantrums like spoiled adolescents. But our current political leaders lack courage. By rushing to the rescue of the unhappy losers, they hope to gain votes in Quebec; in reality, they are only flaunting their political stupidity and their ignorance of the demographic data regarding nationalism.

"It would be difficult to imagine a more total bungle."[12]

In any event, the accord didn't have to become law for three years, and there was the rub. In that time the premiers of three new governments elected to office in the provinces of Manitoba, New Brunswick, and Newfoundland took against it. So, for that matter, did a majority of Canadians in every province but Quebec, for which Premier Bourassa himself bore considerable blame. Until he had invoked the notwithstanding clause and imposed Bill 178 on the province, most Canadians, weary of endless bickering, were disposed to allow Quebec's status as a distinct, very distinct, or even unique society to be cobbled into the constitution, but not any more. Many feared that Quebec's license to "promote [its] distinctive identity" would enable it to introduce even more restrictive language laws, stifling individual rights. It is also fair to say that others, who were anti-French in the first place, were delighted to be handed Bill 178 as a cudgel with which to beat the Québécois.

BETWEEN 1988 AND 1990, Canadians, traditionally history's couch potatoes, were obliged to weigh two hard choices, either of which could enhance or limit their futures. In the case of the free-trade deal with the United States, settled more or less in 1988, everybody could vote on what was the primary issue in a federal election, but in the case of Meech, the electorate was not given an opportunity to pronounce. The original deal was devised by eleven men working late into the night in a lakeside cottage, and then the accord was put to every provincial legislature, except for Newfoundland, only to have a lone Indian naysayer put the kibosh to it.

In the opinion of separatist firebrand Pierre Bourgault, Elijah Harper was a dupe of the Anglophones. In *Now or Never! Manifesto for an Independent Quebec*, Bourgault wrote:

> Everybody thought the Savages had been put in their place long ago. But they'd forgotten the last of the Mohicans who was still hanging around, and who'd gotten himself elected in Manitoba.
>
> He stood up straight in the Legislative Assembly and, with a slash of his tomahawk, chopped the Accord into little bits. Damned Indian!
>
> And that was that. It was all the Indians' fault.
>
> The hypocrites among the Conservatives, Liberals, and NDP rent their garments and went into convulsions of feigned pain. They had done everything in their power to block the agreement and torpedo it using every possible tactic. Now it was all the system's fault: it had allowed one man to grind the process to a halt.
>
> Finally, we had our scapegoat. Use him for all he's worth, then let's get back to important things.[13]

Insofar as English Canadian intellectuals were concerned, there was a symbiotic relationship between the free-trade deal and the Meech Lake Accord.

In the months leading up to the 1980 Quebec referendum on sovereignty-association, English Canadian intellectuals in the ROC made it clear that in their opinion Quebec was entitled to self-determination. The usual Toronto suspects signed a petition to that effect in *Canadian Forum*. For the benefit of non-Canadian readers, I should point out that *Canadian Forum* is a left-wing monthly review modeled on the old *New Statesman*, but it has never, even when it was being edited by the late Northrop Frye, approached it in quality or prestige. At best the *Forum* is as well meant, but also as appetizing, as health food. At worst, it publishes fiction and poetry that have obviously already been rejected by magazines that can afford to pay their contributors. Astonishingly, the *Forum* petition was not signed by a single Quebecer, English- or French-speaking. Or possibly it was not so astonishing, considering that the *Forum* is published in Toronto, Ontario. Look at it this way: when a group of Ontario investors launched a commercial television channel *whose signal could only be received within the province*, they dubbed it Global TV. Anyway, at the time I could not help thinking that if Quebecers had had the audacity to put together a petition calling for a better deal for the Inuit without bothering to get a single Inuit to endorse the document, the *Forum* would have been the first to condemn such paternalism.

In any event, English Canadian nationalists who were vociferous supporters of Québécois *indépendantistes* in 1980 have since changed their minds or been struck mute. The problem was the free-trade deal, supported by a majority of Quebecers, English and French, but not by most of the voters in the rest of Canada. In *Letters to a Québécois Friend*, Philip Resnick, a former Montrealer who is now an associate professor of political science at the University of British Columbia in Vancouver, bitterly reproached his former Québécois nationalist chums for their stance on free trade:

> And yet, *cher ami* (and you are a friend, or even closer, what Baudelaire might have termed *un semblable, un frère*), something has changed in my sentiments towards you and, I fear, those of many English-speaking Canadians, something which will leave an indelible mark on this country for a generation or more. A feeling of profound hurt has come over many of us, especially those who, in the recent past, were most sympathetic to Quebec and its national aspirations. The feeling, quite simply, is one of betrayal.[14]

Reviewing Resnick's book in the Montreal *Gazette*, Gérard Pelletier, one of Trudeau's closest friends and the former secretary of state in his government, made a valid point. Quebecers, he wrote, did not vote massively for the Tories in 1988 in support of free trade, but simply continued the province's history of supporting the winner, in return for which, he might have added, adapting a phrase of Bourassa's, they expected to collect their booty. A case in point was the federal government's decision, in 1986, to award the contract for the maintenance of the CF-18 jet fighter to Bombardier (Canadair) in Montreal rather than to Bristol Aerospace of Winnipeg. This, in spite of the fact that documents later obtained by the Toronto *Globe and Mail*, using the Access to Information Act, revealed that the Bombardier proposal would cost taxpayers 13 percent more in the first four years of the contract and 18 percent more each year after that and furthermore that the government's advisers had preferred the Bristol bid "based on a significantly higher technical assessment."[15] Put plainly, the *Globe* editorial writer was right to say that the contract had been awarded to Bombardier only because "the Mulroney Conservatives wanted to curry favor in Quebec."[16] Unfortunately, this blatant bribe also incurred Manitoba's wrath, as Pierre Fournier noted in *A Meech Lake Post-Mortem*:

> In Manitoba, the 1986 federal government decision to award a CF-18 contract to Bombardier (Canadair), despite the recommendation of an Ottawa task force in favor of Winnipeg's Bristol Aerospace, also helped to sustain bitterness towards Quebec and the federal government. Although the impact on Meech is hard to measure, it was probably considerable.[17]

In *Letters to a Québécois Friend*, a seething Daniel Latouche, a professor at the Université du Québec à Montréal and an adviser to René Lévesque during the referendum, responds to Resnick. Assessing Quebec and Canada, Latouche adjudges them strange bedfellows and then, confusing his Jewish comics, possibly because they all look alike to him, goes on to write, "I am reminded of Woody Allen's famous quote: 'I don't want to become a member of a club that would accept me as a member,'" a paraphrase not calculated to delight the ghost of Groucho.

If nothing else, the Meech fiasco has inspired a number of angry books, English and French, none as badly written as Pierre Bourgault's *Now or Never!* (*Maintenant ou jamais!*), which is dedicated "For Jacques Parizeau, in tribute," a stigma the PQ leader will no doubt overcome, given time and a more literate diet.

Bourgault, who was once leader of the RIN, may very well be, as claimed by the *Gazette*'s Benoît Aubin, the "best, fiercest, most explosive political orator Quebec has produced in this half of the century," but he is also, on the evidence of his latest book, a perfectly appalling writer. This is not to say that I doubt his sincerity, but sincerity on some levels of intelligence, as Kenneth Tynan once observed in another context, is downright embarrassing. Bourgault's book, which *La Presse* hailed as "luminous, powerful, electrifying," is not only devoid of original ideas, but it is rendered unreadable by a plague of snappy, one-sentence tabloid-style paragraphs and polluted by recurring exclamation points. I prefer to think he dictated it while shaving, but Bourgault claims he wrote his tract in "a white heat." He informs us that, after years of neglect, beginning in 1988, all at once he found himself in demand by the young as a speaker:

> Suddenly, the invitations came pouring in. And they weren't coming only from schools with immigrant majorities. They came from all over Montreal, and from outside the city, where all the faces were white and all the words spoken in French.[18]

Bourgault, it should also be noted, is a writer who is not troubled by self-awareness, as witness the following passage about Quebec's aboriginals, which, to be fair, follows a plea by the author for more understanding of their plight. All the same, it reads like a parody of the impatient case many make against French Canadian nationalists:

> On their side, too, they have abandoned all sense of reality, especially when they start calling upon ancestral rights that take

them back to a bygone era, denying contemporary history in the process.

They have a habit of forgetting that a lot of things have happened in the last 300 years, and that now, in North America, there are 250 million non-aboriginal people.[19]

This, from a radical spokesman for a people whose motto, stamped into every vehicle licence plate in the province, is *Je me souviens* and whose flag, the fleur-de-lis, was the banner of the Bourbons, and doesn't even take the French Revolution into account. The mind boggles.

A shared characteristic of all the post-Meech books I've read by Québécois nationalists is a tendency to lapse into incoherent rage at the very mention of Trudeau's name.

Of course, there is a case to be made against Trudeau. By inclination, while in office, he pursued a privileged life, festooned with glitter. The people he cultivated were uncommonly bright or beautiful or accomplished, whether they were writers or academics or architects or filmmakers. He mingled with the stars, not the studio chars. Mean lives, the condition, after all, of much of the electorate, were not in his idiom. This is not to say that he didn't care, but that, on his part, it had to be an effort of will. His arrogance is legendary. Yes, yes, but Pierre Fournier, a professor of political science at the Université du Québec à Montréal, is so carried away by his animus against Trudeau that he runs off the rails in *A Meech Lake Post-Mortem:*

> Even if the former prime minister emerged victorious from the Meech round—after having contributed in large measure to its failure—this farce at least helped demystify the man and his ideas. An ally of the most reactionary and most anti-francophone elements in Canadian society, Trudeau would finally be unmasked to the Québécois, who were now ready to purge themselves of the influence of the man who, more than anyone else, had stood in the way of the normal evolution of Quebec.[20]

Fournier, an academic untroubled by doubts, could not have anticipated that a Quebec public opinion poll, measuring the pulse in the spring of 1991, would discover that 51 percent of

Quebecers would vote for Trudeau were he to run for prime minister again, a level of support far exceeding anything on the table for his rivals.

Then, in *Quiet Resolution: Quebec's Challenge to Canada*, economist Georges Mathews, a formidable advocate of independence, brought me up short when he wrote:

> How did Pierre Trudeau's vision, *which did not have support of a majority in Quebec* [italics mine], draw the country into such a mess?[21]

Whether Trudeau drew the country into a mess is highly debatable. However, if he served as prime minister for a total of seventeen years it was only because he had the support of a majority in Quebec.

Paranoia also disfigures a good deal of the writing by *indépendantistes*. In *A Meech Lake Post-Mortem*, Fournier writes:

> The principal reasons for English Canada's rejection of the accord, including the rights of linguistic minorities, Bill 178, the role of native peoples and ethnic groups, and Senate reform, were merely pretexts aimed at concealing feelings and attitudes that were profoundly anti-francophone and anti-Quebec. The accord's opponents, although their ideas were rarely convincing, only managed to preach to the converted precisely because they were so adept at exploiting deeply held prejudices regarding Quebec.[22]

There is no denying that the nutters who support the Alliance for the Preservation of English in Canada, as well as many westerners who have found a home in the new Reform Party, have been anti-Francophone for years. To suggest that a majority of English-speaking Canadians subscribe to an anti-Francophone cabal, however, is an outrageous distortion. Speaking for myself, I do not need to live in Quebec. I could function just as well, or even better, back in England, where I was rooted for twenty years, or in the United States. I live in Quebec because it's home and I happen to like it here.

INJUSTICE COLLECTING IS ANOTHER shared characteristic of Francophone nationalists. Beginning with Pierre Vallières's *White Niggers of America (Nègres blancs d'Amérique)*, which sued for French Canadians filling the office of blacks in the American South—a ridiculous conceit—there has been a tendency for the separatists to overstate their case wildly. Fournier, in *A Meech Lake Post-Mortem*, writes:

> When circumstances change and fears evaporate, people change course with unfeigned enthusiasm. Just ask the East Europeans.[23]

And Georges Mathews writes in *Quiet Resolution:*

> It is all the more amusing to see English-Canadian columnists going round in circles, trying to hide their inability to grapple with the nexus of the Canadian problem. They do not hesitate one minute to condemn Soviet intransigence towards Lithuania, but who is suggesting that Canada should be offering a new deal, a *really* new deal, to Quebec.[24]

To compare the situation of Quebec within Canada to that of the Baltic states coerced into the Soviet Union in 1940, implying that the act of Confederation was interchangeable with the Stalin-Hitler Pact, not only demeans the suffering of those who were murdered by the KGB or wasted in the Gulag, but makes the *indépendantistes* look like simpletons.

Finally Fournier and the rest, also offend by trying to have things both ways. Meech, Fournier argues, would in no way have served Quebec's interests. It would have led to "major setbacks" for the province. But, on the other hand, the rest of Canada rejected Quebec by turning it down. For once I am bound to agree with Claude Morin, the former PQ minister. Pronouncing on Meech, he said, "We [in the PQ] are in a win-win situation." And then he went on to say, "I don't know if the distinct society clause has any concrete effect. No one knows exactly what [it] means. But it will certainly be used to the utmost extent by the PQ whenever it is re-elected."

"If I were a Cabinet minister and [Newfoundland] had certified the Meech Lake Accord, I would start tomorrow by asking for the patriation to Quebec of federal powers over communications, manpower policy, social policy, anything that deals with the family. I would also try to extend Quebec's international role and things of that kind."

Elaborating on the ambiguity of the "distinct society" clause, he said, "Either the notion of a distinct society works and has a concrete effect, or it doesn't because it has no concrete application.

"If it doesn't, then the people of Quebec who believe that it means something will be quite disappointed and this will be used by the PQ to show to what extent the whole thing was based on hypocrisy."[25]

Seventeen

Lucien Bouchard sprang from a working-class family in Chicoutimi, a small town on Quebec's North Shore. He and Mulroney became chums when they were students together at Laval University Law School. Later, when Mulroney was appointed to the three-man commission that was to look into hooliganism in Quebec labor unions, he brought in Bouchard as the commission's associate counsel.

In 1983, when Mulroney was pursuing the Tory Party leadership, he denounced his rival, Joe Clark, for "coseying up to separatists" and promised that he would never give René Lévesque "a wooden nickel"[1] if he did not make a commitment to Canada. All the same, at his nomination meeting in Sept-Iles, on August 6, 1984, Mulroney read a speech that had been written for him by Bouchard, a nationalist activist. "In Quebec," Mulroney said, "and it's very obvious, there are wounds to be healed, worries to be calmed, enthusiasm to be rekindled, and bonds of trust to be established." And this he promised to do, making it possible for the Quebec National Assembly to sign the constitution "with honor and enthusiasm."[2]

Bouchard, who also helped draft Mulroney's 1984 victory statement, was rewarded that same year by being named Canada's ambassador to France.

Bouchard, who had supported the New Democratic Party when he was a student, and then became a Liberal, joined the Parti québécois in 1971 and two years later worked to elect PQ candidate Marc-André Bédard in his constituency of Chicoutimi. In 1980, he served as that town's chairman of the Yes side in Quebec's referendum on sovereignty-association. So his appointment to represent Canada in Paris—a hive of separatist sympathizers—was not greeted with hallelujahs in

English Canada. Instead, it was seen as a harbinger of the shameless cronyism to come.

Discussing English Canada's reaction to his appointment, Bouchard told the *Globe and Mail* in 1990, "That hurt. It left wounds . . . when I saw the reaction I was tempted to resign then and there, and blast English Canada."[3]

I can understand exactly how Bouchard felt. After all, if the Pope had named me a cardinal in Quebec, in return for services rendered, and devout Francophone Catholics had the bad taste to object, adjudging me an unconvincing spokesman for their beliefs, I would also feel hurt. It would leave wounds.

In any event, the Bouchard story did not end there.

Mulroney, who had already lifted this small-town lawyer out of obscurity not once, but twice, extended his healing hand yet again. Bypassing the forty-seven members of his own Quebec caucus, whom he clearly considered inadequate, the prime minister summoned his old buddy back from Paris and, on March 30, 1988, announced his appointment to the Cabinet as secretary of state. All this, mind you, before Bouchard had even been elected an MP.

John Turner, then leader of the Liberal opposition, was not pleased. "Mr. Bouchard," he told reporters, "had no known connection with the Conservative Party except that he is a close buddy of the prime minister. I should say to the Conservative backbenchers: I feel sorry for you who haven't gone to school with Brian Mulroney—you haven't much of a chance of promotion."[4]

As for Bouchard, responding to questions after his swearing-in, he said, "I don't like the word 'separatist.' You know it is a loaded word. It's not the reality. You know many people voted 'Yes' [in the referendum] for negotiation. . . . I feel since Quebecers have decided in a democratic way that their future was within the federation . . . it is the duty of Francophone Quebecers to make it work." Then, icing the cake, he added, "I am very proud to be a Canadian. I showed the flag in Paris for Canada, for Quebec and all the provinces. I proved it is possible to be a committed Canadian and Quebecer at the same time."[5]

If the appointment of the then forty-nine-year-old Bouchard

to the Cabinet seemed precipitous, it is worth remembering that at the time Mulroney, not waving but drowning in his own government's sleaze, was in desperate need of a Mr. Clean from Quebec. Of the eight Cabinet ministers who had had to resign or who were hanging in under a cloud since the Tories had bounced into office, five had been Francophone Quebecers. This only helped to feed a dearly held English Canadian prejudice that Quebec pols were more prone to corruption than their own, which was not the case. In fact, within three years Canadians would be able to boast that it was not the Grey Cup football game that unified the nation, but dishonest politicians from sea to fabled sea. Or, looked at another way, it wasn't a pigskin that bound us together so much as the hogs themselves, snouts in the trough. In 1991 the premier of Nova Scotia, several of his Cabinet ministers already badly tainted, would find himself under investigation by the RCMP, and the premier of British Columbia would be charged with accepting $20,000 in cash from a real estate agent, and would be obliged to resign. While I'm at it, I must also protest the canard that Tories are necessarily more inclined than their Liberal counterparts to solicit bribes, dispense patronage, accept freebies, demand a little vigorish for contracts rendered, or—based on inside information—turn a quick personal profit in a stock market deal or real estate flip. Their problem is that after all those years on the opposition benches they were hungrier and less adroit at the game than the Liberals. They also tended to be less sophisticated. Look at it this way: no Liberal pol, the morning after being charged in a land scam, would pull up outside the courthouse in a brand new Mercedes-Benz, alighting in a new ankle-length fur coat to protest his innocence before the assembled television cameras. Instead, continuing to tool about Ottawa in his four-year-old Toyota, he would have committed the number of his Swiss bank account to memory.

AFTER HE HAD BEEN SWORN IN, Bouchard was asked by reporters if he had been chosen the Mr. Clean who was to purify the Tory image in Quebec.

"I believe it is very important," he said, "for us to transpose in Ottawa and in the whole of the country a real image of what Quebecers are." Then he went on to say that Quebecers were essentially an honest, hardworking people who "raise their children so that they excel academically."[6]

Only a week into his campaign to be elected the MP for Lac St-Jean, Bouchard no longer qualified as anybody's Mr. Clean, standing by mute as his jittery sponsor, Brian Mulroney, manured the constituency, shoveling millions at it. "What a metamorphosis in just seven weeks," wrote political columnist William Johnson in the *Gazette*:

> The Progressive Conservatives' star candidate began the campaign as a recycled Péquiste. He ends it as a throwback to the Union nationale in its glory days.
>
> *"Les élections ne se font pas avec des prières"*—elections are not won with prayers—Le Chef used to say, echoing Wilfrid Laurier's electoral wizard, Israel Tarte.
>
> Tarte and Maurice Duplessis would both be moved if they left their choirs in heaven to see the campaign of Bouchard, who is also the secretary of state of Canada.
>
> They bought the electors with a few hundred feet of paved road, a school or a refrigerator.
>
> Bouchard can promise a paved road from Chibougamau all the way to James Bay. And throw in a space agency for Montreal, and a $500-million development fund for Quebec's excentric "regions," of which Lac St-Jean just happens to be one.
>
> Why bother mentioning a mere $1.5 million grant for a job creation centre in Alma, rushed through in the dying days of a flagging campaign?
>
> The price of buying voters has leaped since 1896 or 1952, Tarte and Duplessis would agree, dazzled to see so much pork expended on a mere byelection.[7]

The Lac St-Jean constituency purchased, Bouchard, in receipt of his parliamentary seat and installed as secretary of state, now made it clear that, unlike his prime minister, he thoroughly approved of the language restrictions inherent in Quebec's Bill 101 and anticipated that the Meech Lake Accord would license Quebec to impose even more limitations on the uses of languages other than French. This he described as an "asymmetrical" language policy, explaining that under Meech the treatment of minority-language groups throughout Canada would differ. "Giving the same weight," he said, "to French [minorities] as to English [is] unacceptable because it doesn't take into account that French is the only one of the two official languages that is threatened in Quebec."[8]

Then, in the early spring of 1989, Meech now in trouble in both Manitoba and New Brunswick, Bouchard told reporters that if the accord didn't pass he would have to reevaluate his position in federal politics. He might quit. Even if Meech were passed, he said, "In the future, it could be that more [powers for Quebec] would be needed."

Next that legendary fly fisherman Jacques Parizeau cast a long one into the turbulent waters of the Tories' Quebec caucus. The PQ would welcome any one of them, he said, doing a number on Mulroney's 1984 speech, "with honor and enthusiasm." Trailing his own party in popularity, the PQ leader dismissed questions about Bouchard as a potential rival in the future, calling them hypothetical. "Bouchard did some things," he said, "that were quite remarkable from my point of view." But, taking the job of Canadian ambassador to Paris, he added, "impressed me less."[9]

Following his swearing-in as secretary of state in 1988, Bouchard had denied to reporters that he would be the Tories' savior in Quebec. "I will not be savior," he said. "I don't like the word. I will be part of a team. I will always be part of a team."

Two years later Bouchard, then minister of the environment, was staying with a friend in Paris when he was faxed a copy of the Tories' Charest Committee Report, an eleventh-hour package of recommendations hastily stitched together in an attempt to save the foundering Meech Accord. In response, Bouchard revealed to Canadians for the first time that he was blessed with an instinct for political theater which far exceeded the capabilities of his rivals. Instead of replying to repeated calls to him from the Clerk of the Privy Council, he went to the Canadian Embassy and faxed a message to a Parti québécois group that was meeting in Alma in his own constituency on the tenth anniversary of the referendum on sovereignty-association. His fax noted that the referendum anniversary was a good time "to recall loudly the frankness, the pride and the generosity of the YES which we then defended, along with René Lévesque and his team."

The next day Bouchard flew back to Ottawa and then met with Brian Mulroney and resigned from both the Cabinet and the Progressive Conservative Party at a time calculated to do the most damage to the delicate Meech negotiations and the cause of Canadian federalism. Interviewed by the *Globe and Mail*'s Graham Fraser a year later, Bouchard denied that his departure had been planned. But Stanley Hartt, then the prime minister's chief of staff, did not agree. "You may see 'his resignation' as an act of high principle," he told Fraser, "[but] I see it as a staged stunt."[10]

In his May 21, 1990, letter of resignation, Bouchard said that he would retain his seat as the member for Lac St-Jean. The letter, addressed to the prime minister, began:

> When, in answer to your call, I entered active politics a little over two years ago, every head of government in the country had agreed to follow you on the road to national reconciliation. They all understood that this road went, first and foremost, through an act of redress from the whole country toward Quebec, ostracized by the *coup de force* of Pierre Elliott Trudeau.[11]

He went on to complain, justifiably, that the new premiers of three provinces (Manitoba, New Brunswick, and Newfoundland) had reneged on a Meech deal that had been approved by their predecessors:

> I trusted that the signatures freshly appended to the Meech Lake Accord would be respected.
>   Like all Quebecers, I then witnessed with increasing sadness and dismay the adverse reactions that came to light across English Canada. Instead of the planned demonstration of generosity and

respect for Quebec this country's fault line was emphasized and an outpouring of prejudice and emotions arose that would put anyone to shame. Rather than being asked for forgiveness as it should have been, Quebec was hauled on the carpet.

Francophones throughout the country were subjected to new demonstrations of intolerance. While Quebec's flag was being trampled, supporters of the Yes side in the referendum were accused of racism and treason. I was surprised to see, among other things, that those who profess to value freedom of expression cannot tolerate that a federal minister, 10 years after the event, recalls the generosity, nobleness and pride of René Lévesque and the Yes supporters. The mere mention of the right to self-determination gives them a rash.[12]

Then he set out his personal agenda, as it then stood:

I will sit as an independent in the House of Commons. I will use my newly found freedom of speech in the best interest of Quebec and Canada.

I deeply believe that we need to rethink this country. We must stop trying to fit Quebec into a mold of a province like the others. Beyond the legal arguments, there is one argument that is unanswerable: Quebecers do not accept this mold. Their very reality shatters it. Quebecers, especially, must redefine the degree, structures and conditions of their participation in Canada as a whole.

For me participation, whether it is called association, confederative or other, will require another negotiation: a real one this time, dealing with the fundamental issues. . . . Only a Quebec state democratically invested with a clear mandate, based on the recovery of all its powers, will have the political authority needed to negotiate the Canadian association of tomorrow.[13]

Revealed was a twister, perhaps, but also a pol who could write a better letter than most of the others in Canada. His resignation was followed by that of a Tory backbencher nobody had ever heard of before: Gilbert Chartrand, who had been elected in 1984 to represent the Montreal suburb of Verdun–St. Paul.

At the press conference called on May 22, immediately following his resignation, Bouchard told reporters that English

Canada would have to choose between confronting the world as "a small country," sans Quebec, or including Quebec in a sovereignty-association arrangement.

Obviously aware that many suspected him of opportunism, a betrayer of his long-standing friend and patron, he protested that he was a man of integrity, the victim of a biased Anglophone press. He complained about one English newspaper story in particular, a column that speculated on how many Québécois Cabinet ministers would resign over Meech. "The story," he said, "quoted a senior Tory official saying that Quebec ministers have principles, but that given the choice between principles and the company car, the car wins." And he went on to say that he had recalled that story as he had deliberated over his future the previous week in Paris. "I thought, Will the car win? Will a damn black Ford win over my principles?"[14]

The last week in June had to be a bummer for the Tories. On the twenty-sixth, another three Tory backbenchers, as well as one Liberal, resigned over the rejection of Meech.[15] Then, on the twenty-ninth, two Tory backbenchers from Quebec were charged with fraud and breach of trust for demanding payola from contractors and pocketing Commons funds.[16] The same day there was some reassuring news for the prime minister. Bouchard, whose Tory followers now numbered six, told reporters, "We don't want to destabilize the government: we think it important that Mr. Mulroney continues to be prime minister." He also announced that he and his followers had agreed not to form an official political party.

The following week the Liberals took one on the chin. Gilles Rocheleau, the member for Hull, quit the party, saying he couldn't work for its new leader, Jean Chrétien, whom he denounced as "a traitor, a hypocrite, and a liar," a man who was "a Judas"[17] to Quebec, the chief villain responsible for the collapse of Meech. Rocheleau, who had backed another candidate for the Liberal Party leadership, had an interesting history. The previous autumn, he had described Jean Alfred, a black PQ candidate in the provincial election, as "crazy as hell" and "a darkie just out of the psychiatric hospital."[18] On another occasion, he had stated that two of his fellow Liberal MPs from Quebec, both of them Jewish, were out of touch with the province's texture and roots. In any event, Bouchard and his band now numbered eight. Taking into account the quality of invective and the intellectual muscle that Bouchard's followers had demonstrated so far, it was inevitable that one of the wags I drank with at Woody's dubbed them "Lucien and the Seven Dwarfs."

Before July was out, the sovereigntists announced that they had picked a name of their own. From now on they wished to be acknowledged as the Bloc québécois in Parliament, but, according to their recent recruit, former Liberal MP Jean Lapierre, they would not vote as a block and neither, he reiterated, would they become a party. Party discipline, he suggested, demands too many compromises. "Not being tied to a political party is the best position," he said. "Other MPs will be so jealous [of our freedom] they will want to join us."[19]

A month later the nonparty ran a candidate in the east end of Montreal and, with the help of the local PQ organization, won the first federal by-election since the collapse of Meech with a handsome majority. "It seems to be a clear-cut message to English Canada,"[20] Bouchard said. A Gallup Poll released the following week showed that the BQ could count on the support of 21 percent of Quebecers, which put it in third place behind the Liberals, supported by 35 percent of decided voters, and the Tories, who could still claim to be backed by 29 percent of Quebecers.[21]

Even with its new member, the BQ was still several bales short of a load in parliamentary terms. Under Commons rules, it needed twelve members before it could qualify for official recognition, a status that provided for research monies, as well as salary hikes for the party leader, house leader, and party whip.

Eighteen

L ESS THAN TWO MONTHS AFTER he had reminded English Canada that Quebec was capable of ensuring its own development and destiny, an embarrassed Premier Bourassa had to call in the Canadian Army to help him put down an increasingly acrimonious Mohawk uprising at Oka and Châteauguay. "On a legal level," he said, "it is the Government of Quebec that has called on the Canadian Army and thus, finally, it is the Government of Quebec that will give instructions for the use of the army."[1]

Parizeau would have none of it. Bourassa, he charged, had turned to "big brother" in his moment of need.

The next morning the equally predictable *Gazette*, steadfast voice of Anglophone Quebecers, weighed in with a lead editorial, introduced with the following headlines:

IT IS QUEBEC'S ARMY, TOO
No Apology Needed for Calling Canadian Forces[2]

No apology, possibly, but a sense of irony, certainly, for the Mohawks' complaints reflected those of Quebec itself as seen through a distorting mirror. A minority within *la belle province*, they, too, wished to be recognized as a distinct society with the right to self-government. In fact, they were only the most militant of Canada's 500,000 aboriginals, Indian and Inuit, who looked to the courts to restore their ancestral rights to 85 percent of Quebec's territory, and they wanted nothing to do with independence. "If they want to pull out with fifteen percent of the land, we'll let them go," said Max Gros-Louis, chief of the Huron Nation in Quebec. "Most of that fifteen percent is polluted anyway."

Billy Diamond, a Cree chief, told the Toronto *Star*, "What Quebec should be talking about when it talks about separating is only the Montreal and Quebec City area and that's it."[3] The trouble had flared up in Oka when the town's mayor had moved to expand a nine-hole golf course into an old Mohawk burial ground adjoining their settlement of Kanesatake. On March 11, the Mohawks set up a barricade to stop work on the golf course, and three months later, on July 11, one hundred officers of Quebec's provincial police force—founded in 1870 and renamed Sûreté du Québec in 1968—attacked, retreating when one of their number was shot and killed in an exchange of gunfire.

The Sûreté, made up of 4,460 officers, is exceeded in size in Canada only by the Ontario Provincial Police and the RCMP. It is handicapped by the least stringent personnel policy of the three, accepting recruits with no more than a high school education, while the OPP and the RCMP, as well as most other Quebec forces, insist on at least two years of junior college or the equivalent. The Sûreté's unenviable but well-deserved reputation for brutality is rooted in its activities during the late forties and early fifties, when it served as Premier Duplessis's personal goon squad, cracking the heads of strikers and Jehovah's Witnesses and breaking up the meetings of any group of political opponents the premier condemned as "Communist." Then, in 1964, fearful of FLQ violence during the Queen's visit to Quebec City, the Sûreté outdid itself in what became known as *"le samedi de la matraque"* ("Truncheon Saturday"). Sailing into crowds on the parade route with their billy clubs, bopping demonstrators and spectators with equal abandon, they injured almost a hundred people and arrested thirty-four. Since then, preceding the 1990 confrontation with the Mohawks, they have been accused of favoring gratuitous violence in maintaining the law in other native settlements: Les Escoumins, Malieotenam, and Restigouche.

In any event, following the Sûreté's attack on Kanesatake, there was a show of sympathy by other natives. The Mohawk Warrior Society at the Kahnawake Reserve near Châteauguay set up barricades on all roads leading to the Mercier Bridge, one of four bridges connecting South Shore communities with the island of Montreal. Inevitably, things began to heat up. The Mohawks, on their side, threatened to blow up the bridge and fulminating residents of Châteauguay, who now had to make endless detours to get to their jobs in Montreal, burned Indians in effigy. This led *Le Devoir*, seemingly unaware of its own long and disgraceful history of anti-Semitism, to discover that there was latent racism in Quebec, as elsewhere. Alain Dubuc, chief editorial writer of *La Presse*, was gratified by a poll that indicated 69 percent of Montrealers felt the Mohawks had legitimate grievances. How Quebec resolved this crisis with one of its own minorities, he felt, would weigh heavily in post-Meech thinking. Then, in mid-July, the Quebec Human Rights Commission sent a team into Oka which established that the besieged 1,600 natives behind the barricades were being denied food and medical services. On July 24, the commission declared the Sûreté's action in Oka illegal, a violation of the Quebec Charter of Rights and Freedoms.

Humbug. Codswallop. So far as freedom-fighter Jacques Parizeau was concerned. The PQ leader told reporters that the Sûreté should have stormed the armed Mohawk blockade on the Mercier Bridge immediately after it went up. "There are times," he said, "when one has to act."[4]

On August 14, much to the relief of Mohawks who feared the vengeance of the Sûreté, that force was displaced by a Canadian Army regiment, 2,500 strong, moving into place opposite the barricades. Night after night, through the rest of the summer, no Canadian television newscast was complete without an ugly clip of soldiers and masked Mohawk warriors, both fully armed, standing nose-to-nose in the woods, cursing each other. American civil rights lawyers slipped into the Mohawk camp, and one night Jesse Jackson, trailing a spoor of television cameramen and reporters, made an appearance, only to be politely denied entry to Kahnawake by the army. Late in August, Prime Minister Mulroney dismissed the Mohawk demand to negotiate with Ottawa, nation-to-nation, as bizarre. In response, Georges

Erasmus, president of the Assembly of First Nations, said, "if Mulroney really believes we are bizarre in seeking more control over ourselves, then I suggest that he also tell the people of Quebec . . . that they are all wet and that their claims are bizarre.

"I wonder if Canada is to use force on them when they start to exercise some of the sovereignty they wish."[5]

Happily, the army, rendered redundant by a more effective peacemaker peculiar to our country, never did mount an assault on either Oka or Châteauguay. The first cold snap had hardly hit when the Mohawk warriors, pledged to fight to the death, agreed to a truce, and on September 6 the barricades came down everywhere and the Mercier Bridge was opened to traffic again.

Unfortunately, the truce had been preceded by an ugly incident in the last week of August. As cars evacuating native women, children, and elderly people from the Kahnawake Reserve crossed the Mercier Bridge, a mob of more than 500 people gathered at the north end pelted them with stones and lumber. This revolting scene, caught by the television cameras, clearly showed the police standing by idle. Later, the Sûreté would claim they had failed to intervene because they had been outnumbered. An outraged Alain Dubuc wrote in *La Presse:* "The passivity of the SQ agents when the white savages stoned the Mohawk refugees showed that we cannot let these complacent, if not compliant, policemen take charge of the investigations against the Warriors without risking unacceptable outbreaks."[6]

Then Quebec, already deeply embarrassed by the television images of the standoff at Châteauguay which had been seen abroad, was dealt a slap on the wrist. The United Nations human rights committee criticized Quebec for its treatment of the Mohawks and admonished the government for invoking the notwithstanding clause to override a decision of the country's Supreme Court. Next Quebec judge Jean-Charles Coutu, the coordinating judge of the itinerant court in northern Quebec, accused the provincial government of stalling on its promise to give natives more control of the justice system in their communities. "There doesn't seem to be the political will," he said, "to implement the required changes."[7]

The Oka dispute was ostensibly settled when the mayor relented on his fatuous golf club scheme and the federal government declared that it would buy the burial ground and turn it over to the natives. However, this being Quebec, nothing could be resolved before paranoia came into play and conspiracy theories were factored in.

In the first instance, the *Gazette*'s saucy editorial-page cartoonist Terry Mosher lit the fuse. His cartoon of September 7 portrayed a dog wearing shades and a Sûreté cap, its badge a doughnut symbol bearing the inscription *"chien chaud."* A couple of days later an unsigned statement released by the Sûreté accused "a Montreal Anglophone daily newspaper"—only the *Gazette* fits that description—of slandering the agency in an attempt to "settle accounts . . . since the discussions and failure of the Meech Lake accord."[8] This was baffling, if only because the *Gazette*, with the exception of William Johnson, had been an ardent supporter of Meech, and the French press, by and large, had been equally critical of the Sûreté.

If there was any defense to be made of the Sûreté, it was that after one of their own had been shot and killed in their initial assault on the Oka barricades, the warriors at Kanesatake had gone out of their way to mock them. They had, for the benefit of the television cameras, painted on a barricade cement block in Day-Glo orange: "They came, they saw, they ran." It must also be said that many of the warriors, far from being knights in shining armor, were a foulmouthed lot involved in immensely profitable cigarette smuggling and running gambling halls on the reserves, much to the displeasure of the traditional elders. And self-conscious Quebecers did have cause to complain that their police force, singled out for so much disapprobation by the press in the rest of Canada, was actually no more brutal than the Manitoba police force, which would be condemned in a judicial inquiry a year later, its treatment of natives proclaimed "an international disgrace."[9] Or worse than the

RCMP, which in 1991 would also be denounced as racist for its dubious role in the investigation of a young Cree woman's murder in a northern Manitoba lumbering town. The sour truth is that the Sûreté didn't beat natives to a pulp more often than the California State Police cracked open the heads of blacks or Hispanics or—much as I hate to admit it—Israeli soldiers broke the bones of Palestinian children.

Then there were the conspiracy theories.

Naturally, some Québécois nationalists sniffed Oka and identified the stench as Anglophone, an obvious cabal to discredit the Québécois, bent on independence, in the eyes of the world. After all, who had done in Meech in the first place, if not another aboriginal, Elijah Harper, and—as Don MacPherson observed in the *Gazette*—didn't the Mohawks speak English rather than French, and hadn't they fought the French and traded with *les maudites Anglais* in colonial times? And—the clincher, this—during the crisis, hadn't the Mohawks insisted on negotiating with Ottawa rather than Quebec? Nationalist conspiracy theories, wrote MacPherson, were based on two widespread assumptions:

> One is that the English and their institutions aren't really a part of Quebec, and their loyalty to it is suspect. A couple of weeks ago, *Le Devoir* columnist Daniel Latouche saw something sinister in the fact that most of the principal characters in the Mohawk drama, on both the Quebec government and Mohawk sides, were English-speaking.
>
> The other assumption is that the English [in the rest of Canada] are as obsessed with Quebec as Quebec itself is, and are constantly out to get it.[10]

Finally, as far as the Oka Mohawks were concerned, the Sûreté was out to get them in revenge for Elijah Harper doing in the Meech Accord.

Nineteen

GIVEN ITS CONTINUING LOW birthrate and flight of Anglophones, Quebec is in dire need of immigrants in order to increase, never mind maintain, its population. Should the province opt for independence, this problem would be exacerbated by the inevitable mass exodus of even more Anglophones and Allophones. Jacques Parizeau had something to say about this in October 1990. Continuing in the time-honored Canadian political tradition of saying one thing in French and another in English, the leader of the party that had introduced repressive language laws in the province and had done everything possible to make English-speaking Quebecers feel unwelcome, whistled a different tune when he slipped into his soft-shoe routine in an appearance before the American Association of Sunday and Feature Editors at Le Grand Hôtel in Montreal. Suddenly possessed by amazing grace, he said, "English-speaking Quebecers have been in a sense the real builders of large parts of Canada and Quebec as we know them today. These people are in a very real sense as much real Quebecers as the so-called *Québécois de souche*, the home-grown Quebecers." As such, he went on to say, "we cannot for one moment say to these people who have been here for a very long time . . . 'Well, we're going to trample on your rights.' English-speaking Quebecers have rights with respect to schools, social services and that's that.

"Their rights are not adequately protected in the present with respect to health and social institutions . . . and I think they will have to be."[1]

There is no saying how this sophistry went down with the American conventioneers, but two weeks later Charles Bronfman, co-chairman and one of the controlling shareholders of Seagram

Co. Ltd., told the *Financial Post* that Seagram would have a big problem remaining in Quebec if it separated. "I'm a Canadian," he said. "Stay? No. I put my country before my province. Seagram makes VO and Crown Royal Canadian whiskies in Quebec. Canadian whisky cannot be produced and bottled in another country other than Canada."[2]

Commenting on the interview, Parizeau said, "Most of those who wanted to leave have already left." And he reminded the *Financial Post* that Bronfman had also threatened to leave after the PQ came to power in 1976. "The first thing he said after the election was that 'they're bastards.' We all know Charlie and he's been saying that for years."[3]

Be that as it may, "Charlie" had already announced that he wished to sell the Expos, the baseball franchise he had brought to Montreal in 1969. A friend of Bronfman's, familiar with the proposed sale, told the *Gazette*'s Michael Farber that Bronfman "had been saddened by the seeming rise of anti-Semitic incidents, including the desecration of Jewish cemeteries around Montreal, and the political direction of Quebec in recent years."[4] But Bronfman's sister, Phyllis Lambert, proclaimed that she felt comfortable with the idea of an independent Quebec, which provoked an indignant column in the *Gazette* by Don MacPherson:

> Don't you suddenly feel just warm all over about the prospects of Quebec sovereignty, now that a political dilettante such as Seagram's heiress Phyllis Lambert has told us she's not worried?
> What, Lambert worry? Of course, she's not worried. She's 63 years old and one of four heirs to a fortune estimated at $36 billion. Even in Quebec dollars that would be a lot of money. So what's she got to worry about? Becoming merely the richest woman in Quebec, instead of in all of Canada?[5]

Over the years, Quebec has attracted less than its share of immigrants to Canada, relative to its percentage of the country's population, because most prospective immigrants see it as a quaint French-speaking isle, its possibilities modest, adrift in an English-speaking sea, where opportunities abound. They

also fret over the province's long history of xenophobia, endowed with resonance by the repeated street cry of *"Le Québec
aux Québécois!"* So the chances of a newcomer from Italy, Greece,
or Portugal, never mind Scotland or Wales, don't strike potential immigrants as being so hot. Look at it this way: while
Francophone Quebecers have protested for years that they have
been discriminated against in Canada at large, the truth is that
two of our most distinguished prime ministers (Laurier and
Trudeau) have come from Quebec. On the other hand, there has
never been a non-Francophone premier of Quebec and, given the
province's rampant tribalism, there never will be one, unless
there is a drastic change in the ethnic makeup of the population.

Ideally, the powers-that-be in Quebec would like to attract
thousands of people from France to the province, and there's
nothing wrong with that, except why would any sane French
person quit Provence or Brittany or Lorraine or Burgundy for
Baie-Comeau, Rivière-du-Loup, or Chicoutimi? Not only is
France more prosperous than Quebec, it also abounds in beautiful buildings, lovely villages, and affordable wines, and is
blessed with an enviably benign climate. Quebec's most cher-
ished folk singer, Gilles Vigneault, can continue to sing his signature ballad over and over again—

> Mon pays ce n'est pas un pays,
> C'est l'hiver. . . .
>
> (My country, it's not a country,
> It's winter. . . .)

—but as far as most foreigners and even some Quebecers, including this one, are concerned, it only confirms that we endure
a vile climate in this raw northern outpost: say, six weeks of
summer, given a vintage year, and then six months of frost,
blizzards, slush, black ice, frozen pipes, and hazardous roads
and sidewalks that lead to multiple car crashes and broken
limbs. The typical newcomer to Montreal, already driving a
rented taxi for twelve hours a day, also has to cope with huge
heating bills and the cost of a complete set of winter clothes for

his family. If he is black, Asian, or Muslim, he will also have prejudice to contend with.

In the nature of things, there *is* a pool of French-speaking immigrants available to Quebec, but they would have to come from Senegal, Morocco, Tunisia, Algeria, Vietnam, and Haiti— a prospect that is already seen as menacing by those, *pace* Ms. Lise Payette, maker of the documentary "Disparaître," who sense a threat to their racial purity. This, mind you, before the first mosque has even gone up in Trois-Rivières or Rimouski.

Quebec's Department of Cultural Communities and Immigration has reported that, according to the last census, in 1986, more than 40 percent of the foreigners admitted to Quebec were Asian and the country that sent the most immigrants was Haiti. The census also revealed that, in 1986, 18 percent of Quebec's population was made up of nonwhite newcomers or "visible" minorities, as they now say, but the same group accounted for only 3.6 percent of the province's bloated civil service.[6]

In November 1990, Michel Pallascio, chairman of the Montreal Catholic School Commission, issued a statement calling for the province to recruit more immigrants with what he called Judeo-Christian values. "If it's permitted and desirable to encourage the arrival of Francophones, it should be equally considered that people who share with us the Judeo-Christian values are candidates who integrate more easily into our society.

"People leaving their countries expect to adopt a new language, but are much more reticent to abandon their spiritual values or their religious convictions."[7]

In response, Quebec's minister of immigration, Monique Gagnon-Tremblay, said her government would never adopt a policy that favored immigrants with "Judeo-Christian values" over others. It was, she said, contrary to both the Quebec and Canadian charters of rights, and "totally unacceptable."[8]

A month later Bernard Landry, the PQ's vice president, pinched a statute from the Israeli constitution and announced that a sovereign Quebec would have its own *loi de retour*. René Lévesque, he said, had always regretted calling Francophones who lived outside of Quebec "dead ducks." Once sovereignty was attained, they would be welcomed home as would the estimated 140,000 Anglophones who had left between 1976 and 1981.[9]

Then, on December 4, 1990, Minister Gagnon-Tremblay tabled a new policy proposal on immigration. It said Francophones should make up 40 percent of the immigrants to Quebec, but, the minister said, "We don't want Francophones at any price. We want to increase Francophone immigration but that doesn't mean we won't choose other immigrants and it doesn't mean we won't continue to give points for knowledge of English."[10]

At the time, although Quebecers made up 26 percent of the country's population, they attracted only 17.7 percent of immigrants to Canada. So Quebec was pleased to learn, before the year was out, that Ottawa would yield a good deal of the responsibility for immigration to Quebec. The two governments agreed, as if it were within their jurisdiction, that from now on Quebec would get 25 percent of the immigrants coming to Canada. A senior federal official, however, did have the temerity to point out, "How do you guarantee that Quebec will receive a certain proportion of immigrants, when you've got free movement of persons in Canada?"[11]

In any event, the $332 million deal gave Quebec exclusive control over the selection of independent immigrants, that is to say, those who did not fall into the refugee category and who hadn't come to Canada under the family reunification program.

Twenty

Accustomed to unexpected moves by that artful dodger who was our premier, I experienced difficulties all the same in comprehending a page four headline in the *Gazette* of October 27, 1990:

SOVEREIGNTY DOESN'T MEAN SEPARATION: BOURASSA[1]

It seemed that Bourassa, interviewed on radio station CKAC, had said that even though 60 percent of Quebecers now supported sovereignty-association, "I don't believe the majority of Quebecers wants Quebec passports. And if we don't want Quebec passports and we're instead looking for mobility for our people and our goods, then we need a Canadian economic living space administered by a body with certain powers."[2]

As if that weren't sufficiently mind-boggling, he went on to say that those who were intent on sovereignty-association also wanted to remain a part of Canada: "There are maybe sixty percent who support sovereignty-association, but three-quarters of them want to continue sending politicians to Ottawa."[3]

Confounding Quebecologists even more a month earlier, he had suggested alternative remedies for the Canadian malaise: "neo-federalism" or a "political superstructure" or a "supra-national parliament."[4]

Lise Bissonnette, publisher of *Le Devoir*, promptly slapped him on the wrists. "Mr. Bourassa is not a Jean Monnet," she wrote, "proposing to the warlike nations of Europe to unite. He is rather involved in the process of deconstructing Canada as we know it."[5]

Following the Meech debacle, Premier Bourassa had announced with a straight face that he would appoint a nonpartisan commission to deliberate on Quebec's future either within or beside Canada. As he and Parizeau could not agree on the name of a chairman, they settled for each leader nominating one of the two committee co-chairmen. Bourassa picked Michel Bélanger, chairman of the National Bank of Canada and considered to be a federalist; Parizeau's choice was Jean Campeau, a former chairman of the Caisse de dépôt et placement, who was said to favor independence. The Bélanger-Campeau Commission, with thirty-five commissioners not counting the co-chairmen, was to convene for seven weeks, beginning on November 1, scheduled to listen to at least 500 briefs in Montreal, Quebec City, and nine smaller centers and then to report back to the National Assembly on March 28, 1991.

Commissioners ranged from impassioned *indépendantistes* through defensive federalists to some who were committed to neither side. And there was, if you took the recent Mohawk troubles into account, a startling omission—no place was reserved for an aboriginal representative. This seemingly calculated insult was quickly explained by Liberal House leader Michel Pagé. "How," he asked, "can a community participate on the future of Quebec in political and constitutional terms when the community refuses to be considered a member of Quebec society?"[6]

The nationalists, emboldened by polls that indicated they now enjoyed the support of 65 percent of Quebecers, managed to twist the hearings into a platform for their cause, squelching federalists who appeared before them with ridicule or with long and convoluted questions that ate into the time allotted for their presentation. Then, on December 17, only a week after he had been returned to Parliament the winner of a by-election in New Brunswick, Jean Chrétien appeared before the commission. Depending on which page of the *Gazette* you read, the new Liberal leader either did well or disgraced himself. The page one headline ran CHRETIEN SAILS THROUGH GRILLING but the head on Don MacPherson's editorial page column read, LIONS CHEW UP JEAN CHRETIEN and William Johnson's editorial page column led off with a statement of the obvious, not usually the case with him: CHRETIEN SHOWS HE'S NO PIERRE TRUDEAU.[7] Whatever, there was no doubt that Chrétien made some important points in his appearance. "It would be irresponsible to believe," he said, "that an agreement [between an independent Quebec and Canada] could be concluded easily and quickly. It would take years to achieve and resolve. . . ." He hit out at Gérald Larose, the commissioner who was also president of Quebec's Confederation of National [sic] Trade Unions. "I hope," he said, "your main preoccupation will be to tell workers what price they will pay for independence. . . . In fact, only two thousand bourgeois will profit from it."[8]

Larose responded, "Workers are in favor of sovereignty; it is the bourgeois who are against it."[9]

Chrétien maintained that an independent Quebec, lumbered with its share of the national debt, which he calculated to total $81.8 billion, would be among the most indebted nations in the industrial world. The rest of Canada, he said, would not take the breaking up of their country lightly. Quebec's borders would be disputed, including the territory covering the James Bay hydroelectric development, and the province would be billed for federal assets on its soil.

The hearings of the Bélanger-Campeau Commission did make a couple of useful points. First of all, although the action was broadcast many nights on Radio-Québec's television channel, hardly anybody was watching. According to A. C. Nielsen, the audience for the hearings ran from a low of 25,000 to a high of 87,000, drawn from a population of 6.7 million.[10] Second, it did establish the chilling depths of *indépendantiste* anger. In his appearance before the commission, the popular Québécois novelist Yves Beauchemin, author of *Le Matou* and *Juliette Pomerleau*, pointed out that the so-called rights of Quebec's English-speaking minority were in fact privileges that had been won on the Plains of Abraham. "Bilingualism exercises a devastating effect on our collective unconscious," he said. "It undermines our confidence in ourselves; it shrivels our soul."[11]

Léon Dion, the Laval University law professor who had advised Premier Bourassa to impose Bill 178 in the first place, warned the commission, "English Canada will not make concessions . . . unless it has a knife at its throat."[12]

Professor Dion recommended that Quebec allow English Canada one last chance to offer the province an acceptable constitutional deal, but if that failed it must be prepared to opt for independence.

In spite of the fact that in just one month the previous spring, even before the Meech Lake Accord had collapsed, nervous European and Japanese investors had unloaded a billion dollars' worth of Government of Canada bonds, nationalist economists assured the commission that separation would not foment a financial crisis. The cost of sovereignty, they said, would be negligible. One economist, a former banker, ventured that Quebec's share of the national deficit of $400 billion would come to only 18.5 percent, even though, based on the traditional measure, Quebec's cut of the country's population, it would come to something like 25 percent. Servicing this debt, he said, would lead to Quebec's tolerating an annual deficit of $9 billion, no worse than that of Denmark or Austria.

The commission also heard from an important dissenter, Jacques Henripin, who had founded and still ran the department of demography at the Université de Montréal, but his contrary brief was all but totally ignored by the French press. Henripin was a darling of the nationalists in the sixties, when his prediction that Francophones could become a minority in Quebec by the year 2000 had helped spawn Bills 22, 101, and 178. But now, having examined the entrails yet again, he pronounced his earlier findings wildly flawed. In a seven-page brief submitted to what he called the Bélanger-Campeau "circus," he stated that if Quebec's paramount dilemma was still its low birthrate, it also had to cope with emigration, mostly Anglophone, and the assimilation of Allophone immigrants. Between 1966 and 1986, he said, an annual average of 9,000 Francophones and 20,000 Anglophones left Quebec for other Canadian provinces. The Anglophones, he said, take with them their furniture, their qualities, their capital "and—something that is never mentioned—a form of collective wisdom that

usefully complements that of the French Canadian majority."
He was against the banning of other languages on signs inside
or outside. "Let us also note," he said "that it has never been
demonstrated, to my knowledge at least, that one-quarter of
English or Italian on a sign carries risks for the survival of
French." In fact, he said, "if today French is threatened," it
wasn't the fault of *les Anglais,* "it's more by the poor quality of
the spoken and written language."[13]

Then, as the year drew to a close, Jacques Parizeau, who had
already been to New York to sweet-talk Wall Street, assuring
them that separatism was inevitable, packed his bags and flew
to Toronto to deliver the same message to a joint meeting of
the Empire Club of Canada and the Canadian Club. Addressing
an audience of 600 he said, "Quebec has no political or historical accounts to settle with Canada. Not now, at any rate, not
any more. The future is exciting enough not to get bogged
down in past irritants and conflicts."[14] After three weeks of haggling, he said, he had no doubt that the problem of the national
debt would be settled, Quebec assuming responsibility for
something like a quarter of it. "Quebecers by and large," he
added, "would find it more comforting to keep the Canadian
dollar as their currency. In spite of the criticism often levied at
the monetary policy pursued by the Bank of Canada, [they]
would prefer to maintain a common monetary policy if they
could have some say on the way it is run."[15]

The PQ leader was received politely but without enthusiasm.

THE ST. LAWRENCE RIVER, once bright with salmon, has
become a sewer. One of the busiest bridges connecting the island of Montreal with the South Shore, the Champlain has been
allowed to slide into such a state of disrepair that it has been
adjudged dangerous. Our hospitals are notoriously understaffed
and our universities underfunded. But just before Christmas it
was the language of signs that was the major preoccupation of
our politicians once again. On December 20 the chairman of
the Montreal Urban Community Transit Corporation (MUCTC)

declared himself amazed to have been informed that bilingual signs had been posted both on Montreal buses and in its métro system, and he assured the MUC that he would have the offending ads removed as soon as possible.

The ads in question, posted by the federal government, sought recruits who might be interested in the army reserves as a "part-time adventure—*l'aventure à temps partiel,*" and their placement earned the cash-poor MUCTC $800,000 annually. Absenting himself from Woody's for a while that evening, Councillor Nick Auf der Maur pointed out that the transit systems in Hull, Sherbrooke, and even Quebec City all ran the ads with impunity. The next morning Ludmilla de Fougerolles ordained, "These are not MUCTC ads. They belong to the federal government and are ruled by the Official Language Act. Legally, the federal government can post ads in both languages in Quebec."[16]

Jacques Parizeau wasn't pleased. "Principles have cost us so much in the past," he said, "that eight hundred thousand dollars is peanuts."[17]

A spokesperson for the Office de la langue française declared the signs legal because the federal government was not subject to Quebec's language laws. "However," he added, "if we had a Quebec army these ads would be illegal."[18]

AT YEAR'S END, a *Maclean's* poll revealed that the majority of Canadians would just sit back and let Quebec separate if that's what it wanted. According to the Decima Research Company poll, 51 percent of Canadians thought Canada should "just let them go" if Quebec wished to separate. Implicit but unspoken in that sentiment was the "good riddance" felt by so many who had had enough of Quebec's demands or who had never liked French Canadians in the first place.[19]

The same poll showed that 68 percent of Quebecers believed that their province would be independent before the decade was out.[20]

And so, as Tiny Tim, observed, "God bless Us, Every One!"

Twenty-one

EARLY IN THE NEW YEAR Woody's shut down without notice and its congregation, myself included, was lumbered with the inconvenience of finding other winter quarters. Required was a watering hole that was well lit, cashed personal checks, did not blast its patrons with rock music, and employed a barmaid who never acknowledged to phone callers that you had even been in that afternoon, never mind that you stood there right now, unless you agreed to it with a nod. These days such an agreeable retreat is as hard to come by as a Chinese laundry, a real barbershop, or a doctor who makes house calls. So we were understandably upset when Woody defected to Costa Rica, where he owned a hotel. Slipping on galoshes, scarves, overcoats, and earmuffs, we wandered out into the blowing snow and, bent into the January wind, avoiding icy patches on the sidewalk, were fortunate enough to find refuge in Grumpy's basement bar only four doors down Bishop Street.

Nineteen-ninety-one promised to be a downer for perplexed federalists. The first of what would no doubt be 101 public opinion polls, this one a CROP reading of the fever chart published in the January issue of *L'actualité*, reported that 62 percent of French-speaking Quebecers now favored sovereignty. One of the questions put to the collectivity ran: "Do you think it possible to reach an agreement with the rest of Canada, or will Quebec have to decide its political future unilaterally?" Fifty-four percent responded that a unilateral decision was called for, while 39 percent felt that it was still possible to cut a deal.[1] Worse news. The latest issue put out by Archie Comic Publications Inc., which sold an estimated three and a half million copies a year, brought adorable Archie's shapely girlfriend north, *but not to Montreal*. The cover of "Veronica in Canada" showed the young lady wearing a sweater with a maple leaf knit into it, thinking aloud, "I thought I was the *coolest* thing in North America . . . until I visited *Canada*."² Four cities, each one framed by a maple leaf, were shown in the background: Toronto, Quebec City, Vancouver, and Halifax. Michael Silberkleit, president of Archie Comic Publications, professed to be surprised that Montreal hadn't been on Veronica's itinerary, especially, he said, "as Archie is the best-selling French comic strip in Quebec."³ Then the country at large, already threatened with the loss of its heartland, suffered a symbolic blow. The Hudson's Bay Company, that honorable company of adventurers that first received its charter in 1670, the onetime proprietors of the vast Prince Rupert's Land, announced its decision to stop selling furs. Understandably, the president of the Fur Council of Canada denounced the decision as a betrayal of our country's heritage. "The Bay's roots were in the fur business and the country was formed on the fur trade," he said.⁴ Meanwhile, back in Quebec, it turned out that 1990 had been a good year for fruitful bonking. The cash-for-babies program was paying dividends. 95,423 babies had been born in 1990 as compared with only 89,883 in 1989.⁵ If this pleased Bourassa, then Parizeau was cock-a-hoop over the second public opinion poll to be published in 1991. The Gallup Poll brandished by the PQ leader showed that 75 percent of English-speaking Canadians were willing to risk Quebec separating from Canada rather than submit to its demands for more powers. "The impact of this poll is like a bomb," said Parizeau. "After a poll such as this one, there isn't a politician in Canada who would dare try to sell the kind of major constitutional reform that the Liberals are expected to propose."⁶

It was in this climate, on January 16, that I finally caught up with the hearings of the Bélanger-Campeau Commission in Montreal. They were taking place, appropriately enough, on a faded scene of yesterday's WASP grandeur, the former ballroom of the once modish Windsor Hotel, which had closed in 1981 and been converted into an office building. There, on a day that Israeli children were practising their gas mask drills, and

America and its allies were preparing to launch a massive air attack in the Persian Gulf, their armies anticipating a chemical counterattack, twenty-six obviously bored commissioners prepared, almost as an afterthought, to listen to briefs presented by minority groups—Hungarians, Ukrainians, Syrians, all of them fearful that an independent Quebec would put minority rights at risk. "We come from war-torn countries," said one of them, "so we can best appreciate the peace and tranquillity we find in Canada."[7] Then a retired train conductor of Polish origin, a World War II veteran, told how he had traveled the country from sea to sea, had come to love it, and did not wish to see it dismembered. Commissioner Gérald Larose, a union leader committed to outright independence, asked the old man if he was not familiar with the plight of other small nations, say Latvia, Estonia, and Lithuania, and was he unaware that the Québécois were also a people.

The Bélanger-Campeau Commission was only one section of what was actually a three-ring circus, and not the one that earned the most audience laughs either. That unenviable office was filled by the Citizens' Forum on Canada's Future, cobbled together by the prime minister the previous November under the chairmanship of Keith Spicer, a former newspaper editor, who was to be helped in his labors by eleven other commissioners. These twelve seekers after Canada's soul were to travel the country coast to coast, listening to Mr. and Mrs. Front Porch and their children, gathering—as it turned out—more bromides than verities. Come winter, in Quebec City, they were at each other's throats. Things came to a boil when Commissioner Robert Normand, publisher of Quebec City's *Le Soleil* and a former senior adviser to René Lévesque's government, blamed the others for putting the problems of Canada's aboriginals before those of Quebec. "Don't worry about the barn," he said, "when the house is on fire."[8] Then, according to an account published by Mark Kennedy and Roy MacGregor in the Ottawa *Citizen*, Normand referred to the native peoples as *"les cristis sauvages,"*[9] that is to say, those goddamned Indians. When the meeting in the Château Frontenac was over, Normand proved himself a snitch as well as no friend of our native peoples. The commissioners, he told reporters, were charging $600 a day for their services, some of them billing the public for as much as twenty-five days a month.

Meanwhile, Premier Bourassa had a committee all his own, headed by lawyer Jean Allaire, to ponder Quebec's future. Its sixty-two-page report, *A Québec Free to Choose*, released on January 29, was to be voted on at the Liberal Party's convention in March.

The Allaire Report allowed Canada eighteen months to agree to its conditions or, alternatively, suffer a referendum on sovereignty in Quebec. It demanded that Ottawa yield jurisdiction to Quebec over no less than twenty-two fields, including social affairs, agriculture, education, culture, energy, environment, industry and commerce, health, natural resources, and, of course, language. It would agree to share authority in ten areas, among them native affairs, financial institutions, taxation and revenue, and foreign policy. It would grant Ottawa exclusive authority over defense and territorial security, customs and tariffs, currency and common debt, and equalization. Equalization, I should explain, is a federally imposed policy that obliges the wealthy provinces (British Columbia, Alberta, Ontario) to pay equalization monies to the poorer ones, including Quebec.

Quebecers would still elect members of Parliament, but would adopt their own constitution and charter of rights. The report also called for an end to the Supreme Court's authority in Quebec and the abolition of the Senate.

Here I should explain, for the benefit of non-Canadian readers, the nature of our senate. In our unending struggle to make it absolutely clear that we are neither Americans nor British, but something nicer, we often compromise, settling for the worst of both worlds. Our much-ridiculed senate lacks the clout of the American one and is without the cachet of the British House of Lords. A non-elected body, established by the BNA Act, its original purpose was twofold: it was to represent the country's regions and to review legislation passed by the

House of Commons, putting at least a temporary brake on bills it adjudged ill-considered. But senators are appointed by Ottawa, not the provinces, and the senate's majority is usually of the same stripe as the House of Commons or can be adjusted accordingly. Traditionally, appointment to the senate is a patronage plum, enabling the prime minister of the day to reward cronies. Such appointments are much in demand by superannuated bagmen and other political hacks, and with good reason. In New York or London, where the hotel desk clerk or *maître d'* is invariably unaware of the difference between an American and a Canadian senator, it will help to get a room upgraded as well as to secure a decent table in a restaurant. Then there are the money and the perks to be considered.

Senators are paid $64,100 a year, a pot sweetened by a $10,000 tax-free allowance, first-class Air Canada passes for themselves and their spouses, their children and grandchildren, and other insurance and health care goodies too numerous to catalog here. Put plainly, it is the ultimate welfare scam. Tiffany all the way. However, it is worth noting that, on the evidence of *The Senator's Handbook/Guide du Sénateur*—the new boys' and girls' guide to tuck shop favors and freebies—a distinction is made between draftees sprung from our two founding races, who are obviously adjudged unequal in sensual appetite. The *Handbook's* bilingual "Finger Tips" list of services that can be arranged by a phone call differs on one count. The French-language pages offer the solace of a masseur, but there is no such listing in the English-language pages.

In order to qualify for the senate, a candidate must be thirty years old and own debt-free property in his province with a net value of four thousand dollars. Until 1965 he or she was appointed for life, but since then a senator must retire at age seventy-five, his compensation a pension usually calculated at 75 percent of his average salary during his last six years of service. Numbering 104 in normal times, 24 of them from Quebec, the senators are expected to sit three afternoons a week while Parliament is in session, but the attendance record of many of them is, to say the least, notoriously spotty.

The lead editorial in the January 31 edition of English Canada's national newspaper, the Toronto *Globe and Mail*, ventured that Premier Bourassa had set in motion "a profound process of change," and concluded, "If Brian Mulroney is not to preside over the disintegration of the Canadian state, he must be the catalyst in redefining it. That is what history demands."[10] But on the bottom of the same page, Jeffrey Simpson, the most influential of our political columnists, noted that "Mr. Mulroney is already viewed as a constitutional snake-oil salesman because of Meech Lake."[11]

Simpson, clearly a worried man, wrote two more columns on the subject within a week, one titled "All the formulas and proposals in the world won't keep Quebec in Canada"[12] and another "After Quebec leaves, Canadians will be embroiled in new, crucial debates." In this column, he wrote:

> But some time later, after the disengagement deals have been signed and the pain has subsided, Canadians will forget about Quebec, a small, proud, inward-looking place where people speak another language. Instead, Canadians will confront the problems of their new, unwieldy, unbalanced, awkward, artificial country.
>
> Within that country will be a nagging French-speaking minority with its constitutional guarantees and special funding. These rights and funds will be either quickly scrapped or gradually eroded, since Canada will have no need of two official languages after Quebec goes.
>
> The breakup of Canada will mean the end of the English-French arrangement that prevailed for so many decades and gave rise to these rights and programs. The French-speaking minorities will become what they always insisted they were not: multicultural Canadians with social clubs and folk dances but no rights.[13]

Without Quebec, Simpson concluded, the larger debate about relations with the United States will subsume all others. Next Conrad Black—*rara avis*, a newspaper publisher who is also literate—was heard from. Black, who now lives in London, wrote that "if the lure of the U.S. proved irresistible [to English

Canada shorn of Quebec], this would not be a tragic fate either."[14] He suspected—or hoped—"that most Canadians would prefer an American Canada to a socialist one and would rather deal with George Bush than Robert Bourassa [or Brian Mulroney]," which was to present his countrymen with a Hobson's choice unworthy of him. In an article that he wrote for the *Financial Post*, Black made his own preference clear:

> [It] remains, as it has been all my conscient life, for a bicultural federal state guaranteed by an adequately endowed federal jurisdiction and based on the principle of reciprocal respect for sufficiently numerous minorities, and not on coercion.[15]

This, Black felt, had been rendered impossible since the Quebec government had brought in Bill 178, breaking the social contract. Bourassa, in his opinion (and mine, too, for that matter), was "never a federalist, he is without convictions, a charming chameleon adapting with agility to economic requirements and the arithmetic of the polls." The province, he wrote, had one true ambition: independence with continuing equalization payments. As for the Allaire Report,

> This constitutional document is so egregiously hostile to anything that even the most naïve Canadian federalist could abide, that there can be no danger of that. Those who rhapsodize hopefully that it can be a basis of negotiation do not inhabit the same planet as the rest of us. There can be no negotiation over the suggestion that Quebec set up its own Supreme Court, co-manage the Canadian mint and Canadian foreign policy, have a pre-eminent or exclusive jurisdiction over at least three-quarters of public policy, yet continue to accept equalization grants from English Canada."[16]

Put another way, in a Canadian world reborn according to Allaire, Quebec would settle for hemi-semi-demi-independence, providing the rest of Canada was willing to pay it rent, if only to keep it in the country, sort of. Meanwhile, Quebec executives were voting with their feet. Only a week after the Allaire Report appeared, head-hunting firms in Ottawa were inundated by inquiries from executives who wanted out of the province. "It started as a trickle," said David Perry, of Perry-Martel International Inc., to the *Gazette*, "but it's beginning to look like a downpour."[17]

Interestingly enough, according to Perry, at least half of the inquiries came from Francophones who didn't have the energy to cope with yet another referendum on sovereignty. "People aren't afraid," he said. "They are just fed up. They don't want to go through this any more."[18]

Certainly those of us who now gathered at Grumpy's had thrown more than one farewell party for a good companion departing permanently for Toronto, Vancouver, or, in one case, even Hamilton. Imagine that. And we continued to endure American reporters who had come to town to churn out an in-depth piece on whither Quebec. Riding a sufficient quantity of Grumpy's Scotch, they inevitably took to teasing us about being citizens of a non-country in any event, the difference between English-speaking Canadians and Americans marginal at best. Happily, we were able to counter such condescension with evidence gathered from *Maclean's*, quoting the magazine's annual Decima Research poll that finally established some crucial differences between the two countries:

42. Do you own a handgun?
    No 93
    Yes 6
    DK/NA..1
    (Don't know/No answer)

43. (For those who answered No) If there were no gun laws in Canada, would you get a gun?
    No..86
    Yes 14

44. Generally speaking, are you afraid to walk the streets of your community at night alone?
    No..74
    Yes..26

45. Have you ever been mugged or physically assaulted?

No...90

Yes ....10 [19]

Early in February we were blessed with even more evidence with which to pummel patronizing American reporters. I had used to believe, I had once even written, that the U.S. was where the action was and Canada only where it reverberated. I was wrong. I now discovered, reading a report by Ken MacQueen of Southam News, that, mirroring Quebec's *visage linguistique* policy, there was now an English-only movement in the United States. The movement was a response to the fact, unsettling to some, that in 1991 there were 19 million Hispanics in the U.S., and, according to the American Census Bureau, their numbers were multiplying at five times the national rate and could soar to 47 million within thirty years. As a consequence, seventeen states, including California, had passed laws making the English language official. There is even a city, Monterey Park, California, that has set out to limit foreign languages on business signs and attempted to stop publication of a Hispanic Yellow Pages and to limit licensing of Spanish-language broadcasts.

MacQueen interviewed Stanley Diamond, the California chairman of a one-language advocacy group called U.S. English, in his office on Market Street in San Francisco. "We always point to Canada as the horrible example of what can happen with two official languages. The passions are deep. They are divisive. They are irreversible."[20]

Diamond, married to a Hispanic himself, was instrumental in getting Proposition 63 on the California ballot in 1986, its purpose, *pace* Camille Laurin, "to preserve, protect and strengthen" English. Seventy-three percent of Californian voters supported Proposition 63, but the campaign, begun in 1982, to have English enshrined as America's official language in a constitutional amendment has not yet succeeded. However, U.S. English now claims 400,000 members, and it is worth noting, in passing, that its mentor is an eighty-five-year-old expatriate Japanese Canadian, former U.S. senator S. I.

Hayakawa of California, who was born in Vancouver, raised in Winnipeg, and educated at McGill University.

EVEN AS THE REST OF CANADA was still choking on Allaire, Lucien Bouchard was heard from again. That former political grazer, who had belonged at one time or another to each of Canada's three major political parties (the New Democratic Party, the Liberals, the Progressive Conservatives) and found them wanting, now chose—contrary to a pledge he had made seven months earlier—to create one in his own emotional image. Bolstered by polls indicating he could win sixty of Quebec's seventy-five seats in a federal election, he decided, on February 11, to apply for official party status in the House of Commons for the Bloc québécois. "We are the party of sovereignty, not a party of politicians," Bouchard said.[21]

Actually, if a political party, like a work of pornography, could gain safe passage only if it could claim redeeming social value, then the BQ would have met with an immediate ban. Seeking parliamentary recognition, Bouchard allowed that the BQ would not try to develop a "wall to wall"[22] political platform. This, of course, was no more than a recognition by Bouchard that he led a very motley crew indeed, his gang of eight made up of six X-brand Tory backbenchers, two renegade Liberals, and Gilles Duceppe, a former member of the Communist Workers' Party. The nine of them, surely, could agree on no more than to be as contrary as possible in the House of Commons, bringing down plagues on Ottawa, disbanding only after the government had let their people go. Meanwhile, Bouchard was proving himself a skilled orator, stoking tribal angers. A force in the boonies and the east end of Montreal, he might yet prove to be too angry for the more cultivated nationalists.

FEDERAL AND QUEBEC MINISTERS signed their immigration pact, actually agreed to the previous December, in the first week of February. The accord granted Quebec exclusive responsibility for the selection of independent immigrants and awarded it $332 million over four years in compensation for the services it would take over from Ottawa. There were murmurs from the other provinces when it was discovered that Quebec, which lured only 20 percent of immigrants to Canada, now collected 32 percent of the federal funds available for immigrant settlement and language training. André Juneau, the executive director of immigration policy for the federal Immigration Department, reflected on the situation and then declared Quebec's disproportionate share of funds was in part motivated by "political considerations."[23]

One Quebecer who was worried by the new policy was Sylvain Simard, head of the Mouvement national des Québécois and a former vice president of the PQ. Some Francophones, he said, felt threatened by the number of people "from cultural communities" who had settled in the Montreal area. A solution to the problem, he thought, taking either South Africa or Russia as his model, would be to force new immigrants to move into outlying regions. "With those who are already here we have to do our best," he said, "but for the future we will have to adopt a policy of regionalization."[24]

Simard's odious notion was immediately opposed by Denis Langeois of the Montreal Ligue des droits et libertés.[25] The provincial Charter of Rights, he said, would prohibit a sovereign Quebec from passing a law that forced immigrants to settle in far-flung areas.

Article 10 of the charter reads:

> Every person has a right to full and equal recognition and exercise of his human rights and freedoms, without distinction, exclusion or preference based on race, color, sex, civil status, religion, political convictions, language, ethnic or natural origin or social condition.[26]

However, Article 10 also guaranteed full and equal recognition of rights, including language, and that certainly had not prevented the enactment of Bill 178. So, notwithstanding what was guaranteed by the Quebec charter, it would seem that a sovereign Quebec could oblige immigrants to settle in Alma or Abitibi or Sept-Iles. Meanwhile, it was clear that they were not welcomed by the Ste-Croix School Commission, which ran nineteen schools in the Montreal suburbs of St. Laurent, Town of Mount Royal and Outremont. As things stood, 41 percent of the commission's 8,000 students were Allophones. Judith Lortie Hinse, head of the school commission, said Montreal was in for "a cultural shock" unless the immigrants were scattered in other parts of the province. "You can't integrate immigrants to immigrants," she told a committee of the National Assembly studying the province's new immigration policy. "You have to integrate them to the population of Quebec. We won't be Quebecers any more. It will be all sorts of cultures."[27]

The Quebec Federation of Catholic School Commissions presented a brief objecting to the government's immigration policy. "Look what happened in Brossard [a Montreal suburb] where we welcomed a wave of rich and powerful Hong Kong immigrants. Far from integrating easily into Francophone society, these immigrants create a strong pressure to obtain services they need in English, rather than in the language of the mainly Francophone society receiving them in Brossard."[28]

In yet another brief, this one presented by the Montreal Island School Council, it was claimed that if immigrants continue to settle in Montreal, within ten years barely half of the students attending French-speaking schools would be Francophone. The brief concluded that "these tendencies inescapably lead to an island of Montreal that is in the majority Anglophone and Allophone and the rest of Quebec that is in the majority Francophone."[29]

A day later Immigration Minister Monique Gagnon-Tremblay came out for tolerance of a sort. Obviously insensitive to the insult to immigrants implicit in her statement, she said, "Montreal is no worse than all the other big cities, like Vancouver and like Toronto." Admitting that something like 86 percent of immigrants to Quebec chose to settle in Montreal, she went on to say, "We have to be quite flexible about the first generation. As for the second and third generations, they have to speak French and this is the message we have to send outside the country."[30]

Then the PQ MNA for Pointe-aux-Trembles, in the east end of Montreal, stood up for the immigrants and reproached the city's Catholic school board. "The fact that they regularly stand by racist statements doesn't help," said Michel Bourdon.[31]

Next a draft of a document prepared by a task force that had been put together by the federal multiculturalism minister, Gerry Weiner, was leaked to the *Gazette*. The document, labeled "final report," said, "In Quebec, racism is alive and well living under the guise of Quebec nationalism but is not confined solely to Francophones."[32] It went on to urge minorities to speak out clearly against dangers that threatened their quality of life. "As Quebec moves toward becoming more French it pushes aside and ignores other cultures," the report said. "Quebec has long argued that Canada has turned its back on this province. Now we see Quebec doing the same to a significant proportion of its people."[33]

The task-force chairman said that the racism charge, which had been dropped from the document, had appeared only in an in-house first draft and did not represent the views of a majority of task-force members. Gerry Weiner said, "I reject categorically that linkage [between Quebec nationalism and racism]. It is false. It is malicious. I'm a Québécois. I've been comfortable there all my life. And whoever's trying to draw any kind of analogy has no understanding of the Quebec society that we've all come to know and accept and love."[34]

Weiner's statement posed a problem. Either he was incredibly thick-skinned or a man absymally ignorant of the historical roots of Quebec nationalism. In either case, he did establish that he was capable of delivering the politically correct comment when required.

Within weeks, the provincial Immigration Department, backsliding, declared that it did want more immigrants to settle outside of Montreal and suggested that matters would be helped if Quebecers in the boonies were more welcoming to newcomers. Quebec, it announced, had attracted 40,000 immigrants in 1990, a 17 percent increase from 1989, and Francophones—many of them from troubled Lebanon—had accounted for 37 percent of the total. But Monique Gagnon-Tremblay cautioned that Lebanese immigration would ease once the country became more stable. "The pool of Francophones interested in, and interesting for, Quebec are not numerous," she said.[35]

Other statistics released by the department revealed that, in the seventies, 35 percent of immigrants left Quebec for other provinces. Then Jacques Henripin, speaking at a junior college, declared that immigration won't stop Quebec's population from declining early in the twenty-first century. "Shortly after the turn of the century," he said, "Quebec's population will start to level off, decline slightly and then very rapidly." He had no trouble identifying the problem. Since 1945, two-thirds of the three million immigrants to Quebec had moved out. "This is not a very high retention rate," he said. "It may be very pleasant to live in Quebec, but apparently it is much more agreeable elsewhere."[36]

Twenty-two

ON MARCH 26, the Bélanger-Campeau Commission, its public hearings complete, its secret deliberations ended, recommended that the National Assembly pass a bill calling for a referendum on sovereignty by October 26, 1992. If a majority of Quebecers supported independence then the province would become a sovereign state within a year.

The proposed bill, seemingly straightforward, also came, as is the tradition here, with a built-in escape hatch. Should the ROC put together a binding offer on renewed federalism that appealed to Quebec, then they could vote on that proposal, rather than on sovereignty in a referendum.

The omens, such as they were at the time, defied analysis. Though Quebecers were obviously in a truculent mood, scornful of Ottawa, applications from them for federal civil service jobs had doubled from 1989 to 1990, escalating from 17,692 to 32,733. And if the polls were to be credited and it was true that more than 60 percent of Quebecers favored sovereignty-association, it is important to grasp that many of them also thought they could have that and continue to send MPs to Ottawa as well. Nothing had changed, it appeared, since the Québécois comedian Yvon Duchamps had observed, *"Ce que les Québécois veulent, c'est un Québec indépendant dans un Canada fort et uni."* ("What Quebecers want is an independent Quebec within a strong and united Canada.")

In late March the Quebec Liberal Party held its annual convention to deliberate, among other things, over the Allaire Report.

Given the strictures of the Allaire Report, Canada had a potential problem I had not seen discussed in either the English or the French press. For twenty-two of the past twenty-three years the prime minister of our country has been a Quebecer born and bred. Prime Minister Mulroney was a Quebecer, and so was the new leader of the federal Liberal Party, Jean Chrétien. Should Quebec become sovereign in 1993, neither leader could be trusted to negotiate for the ROC. In fact, neither man, suddenly born-again foreigners, could fill the office of Canadian prime minister.

"In that case," said a Grumpy's regular, "it must be allowed that sovereignty has its positive side."

On the question of who might then be called upon to fill the diminished office of PM of the ROC, it was agreed with a groan that Joe Clark was the most likely choice. Or, put another way, sovereignty's positive side could be short-lived indeed.

"If Joe Clark were not a politician but a baseball player," ventured somebody at the bar, "he could be counted on to hit into a double play each time he came to the plate—even if two men were already out."

THE ALLAIRE REPORT, which proclaimed itself Quebec's "final and decisive test" for the ROC, was adopted by the Liberal party convention with only one amendment. Disgruntled federalists within the party managed to have the clause calling for the abolition of the Senate softened to read that the institution terminated "in its current form"[1] which allowed for the possibility of an elected senate in the future. In his closing speech to the convention, Premier Bourassa stated that the preferred choice for the Liberal Party was federalism within Canada, but the country had already been cautioned against the elixir prescribed by Allaire. Gordon Robertson, the retired Ottawa mandarin who had advised four prime ministers on constitutional matters, said that it would leave Canadians with "a country so weak, so incompetent in dealing with the problems ahead of us that it would be far worse to have that weak a country than to have two countries that were effective."[2]

The projected borders of these two countries were also

becoming increasingly controversial.

Responding to a mischievous suggestion from the Equality Party that federalist enclaves should be carved out of an independent Quebec, possibly with a cookie cutter, Claude Ryan said, "I don't like this concept very much [and] it is extremely difficult to function in practice. When you establish sovereignty over a territory it has to apply everywhere."[3] Ryan did, however, concede there were historical precedents in both Europe and Asia, but he did not wish to speculate on their ever becoming Quebec's lot. "My objective," he said, "is to work so that Canada continues functioning as a country, so don't ask me to go into negative or pejorative suppositions, which are not part of my frame of mind."[4]

Then there was renewed squabbling over what would pass for the local wampum should Quebec separate.

In *La Souveraineté: Pourquoi? Comment?*, a cocksure PQ had argued that if the rest of Canada wouldn't welcome Quebec using its dollar then, *tant mieux*, the new republic would mint its own. Since then Parizeau had obviously seen polls indicating that nothing softened his potential referendum support more, especially in rural Quebec, than the sobering news that Quebec might soon be printing its own bucks. So now Parizeau adjusted his stance, declaring that Canada couldn't stop Quebec from making the Canadian buck its legal tender. Not so, said Bourassa. "I don't think there is any precedent of a country that will use the dollar against the will of another country."[5]

Lucien Bouchard, as usual, had ideas of his own. If Quebec fails to get more, say, in the deliberations of the Bank of Canada, he said, then it might switch to the U.S. dollar, which suggested that the American Treasury Department, unlike the Canadian, would appreciate Quebec's advice on setting the interest rate.

Québécois economists who favored sovereignty, writing off its costs as negligible, were fond of brandishing a leaked 1990 report from the New York office of Merrill Lynch, an investment firm which just happened to be one of the biggest underwriters of Quebec bonds in the U.S. market. In the world according to Merrill Lynch, the independence of Quebec was inevitable and, furthermore, "Given the economic strength of the province, one can argue that a sovereign credit rating would not be that much different from its rating as a province."[6] But a year later other reports were being leaked, including one from the First Boston Corporation, an underwriter of Hydro-Québec bonds, that concluded the continued dithering over Canada's future made for "an element of risk for foreign investors." Even as things stood, Canada had to offer an interest rate that was 1 or 1.5 percent higher than the American rate in order to peddle their bonds.

Depending on where you paid your political dues, an independent Quebec's share of the national debt would come to either $80 or $100 billion, but the notion that the province could thumb its nose at Canada if its estimate of liability was unacceptable was dismissed as a huge canard by Jeffrey Simpson in the *Globe and Mail:*

> An independent Quebec could not walk away from its share of Canada's national debt; if it did, its reputation in world financial markets would fall to zero. Reneging on past debts is no way to raise money.
>
> Quebec's provincial debt is the highest in Canada. If Quebec left Canada, and took along its share of the national debt (say 25 percent) Quebec would be a heavily indebted new country.
>
> If Quebec left Canada, it would forgo equalization payments that currently account for roughly 12 percent of provincial revenues. It would also forgo transfer payments that have historically benefited Quebec.[7]

Nationalist economists, toting up the independence bill, failed to take into account what Premier Bourassa, his eye fixed on the bottom line, had once described as "profitable federalism,"[8] which yielded the province, in another phrase of his, a good deal of "booty." Take, for instance, the Quebec dairy farmers' bonanza. Under the present system, Canada restricts the import or export of milk and dairy products, but guarantees Quebec's dairy farmers the right to supply 48 percent of the country's industrial milk at a guaranteed price. But should

Quebec secede, other provinces would happily take up the burden and Quebec's share of the milk market could be governed by the General Agreement on Tariffs and Trade, which means it would have to compete with other foreign producers for a 2.8 percent share of the Canadian market. In an independent Quebec, it should also be noted, the province's 52 percent share of Canada's 60,000 clothing manufacturing jobs could also be at risk.[9] And, in the opinion of many economists, the U.S. would not automatically accept an independent Quebec as part of the U.S.-Canada free-trade deal. Instead, it might welcome a chance to question the activities of the Caisse de dépôt et placement and Hydro-Québec, charging that they provide unfair subsidies.

Meanwhile, there is no doubt that Montreal is paying a steep price for the continuing uncertainty. A confidential report to the Quebec government, leaked by *La Presse*[10] in March, stated unequivocally that Quebec's Francization policy had done considerable damage to the city's economy. More than 200,000 Anglophones had quit the city over the past fifteen years. Also in March, but fourteen years after the fact as it were, we learned that René Lévesque had had his doubts about Bill 101, the French Language Charter. Speaking at a seminar devoted to the late premier's career, Camille Laurin, father of the bill, told students at the Université du Québec à Montréal, "[Lévesque] was concerned that we were going too far. He was torn, he was ambivalent on several questions." But, so far as Laurin was concerned, Bill 101 had been needed. "It had become necessary to make a law for us, not a law directed against the others," he said, "a law that would put the resources and the support of the state at the service of the individual rights of a majority that had been poor and dominated for too long." Lévesque, he went on to say, was against the clause that prevented English-speaking children born elsewhere in Canada from attending English-language schools in Quebec. The premier had also considered the sign laws "excessive, not really justified, and would have us attacked for intolerance."[11]

In March we also discovered that Montreal now had the

highest unemployment rate of any major city in North America. Even so, Francophone Quebecers seemed to have been shocked by the results of a CROP Poll published in April. It claimed that one out of three Anglophone Quebecers planned to leave the province within the next five years, but should the province actually separate, 44 percent of the respondents said they would emigrate.[12]

Then, early in June, *La Presse* ran a front-page story saying that a large proportion of Anglophone doctors born and bred in the province, educated at the taxpayers' expense, planned to practice elsewhere. Dr. Augustin Roy, president of the Quebec Doctors' Association, told *La Presse* that out of the 103 Quebecers who had graduated from McGill's medical school in 1991, 33 were leaving the province.[13]

A *La Presse* editorial, pleading for understanding of the Anglophone plight, asked, "When will the purgatory of the Anglophones be over?"[14] A columnist warned that should English-speaking Montrealers quit the city en masse, we would be left with "nothing more than a big Quebec City." Then a young writer in the nationalist weekly *Voir* asked, "How long are we going to drag out this old cliché about the arrogant Anglophone? When are we going to stop demoralizing them with laws like Bill 178? When are we going to stop acting like a besieged, threatened people? How many credit unions . . . do we need to feel secure?"

Possibly it was in response to these outbursts that Premier Bourassa, unrivaled at sniffing any wind of change in public opinion, appointed the distinguished McGill philosopher Charles Taylor to the Conseil de la langue française. Taylor, a twelfth-generation Quebecer, known to be understanding of Francophone anxieties, surprised everybody with his initial statement to reporters: "I think the notion of a predominance of French without the actual outlawing of any other language is what we want.

"The actual banning of another language is a measure of hysteria, frankly. There is absolutely no case that it really promotes French.

"The *affichage commercial* [commercial sign] clause of Bill 101 and 178 is totally indefensible. It's utterly ridiculous. It's a product of mass neurosis. I am disgusted at the way it has not been discussed rationally."[15]

Next, Lucien Bouchard surprised everybody with another quick change in the political phone booth. Sovereignty could not be achieved, he told *Le Devoir*, without the support of Quebec's Anglophones. "I'm uncomfortable with Bill 178," he said. "I'm not big on preventing English from being used. . . . Inside, outside, it's a clumsy compromise. We have to reestablish a balance."[16]

The Parti québécois called for Taylor's resignation, but he refused to quit. Instead, he was even more refreshingly outspoken the second time around with reporters. Quebec, he said, has paid a big price for Bill 178: "It's made us look bad in the world. It has created a tremendous gulf between the communities in Quebec, which is not good for society."

A couple of weeks after Taylor's appointment to the Conseil, a poll undertaken by the Southam newspaper chain led to the following front-page headline in the *Gazette* of Sunday, June 2:

QUEBECERS PREPARED TO PULL PLUG

ON SIGN LAW FOR RIGHT DEAL

The poll claimed that 56 percent of Francophones were willing to tear up the sign law, providing the rest of Canada obliged with an acceptable new constitutional deal. Adding vigorish to the pot, slightly more than 50 percent of Francophones said that, in a trade-off for renewed federalism, they would allow any Quebecer to educate his or her children in English. The same Sunday another poll, this one undertaken for *Le Soleil* and Montreal radio station CKAC, indicated that for the first time since February 1990 a majority of Quebecers were opposed to sovereignty. According to the poll, 51 percent preferred Quebec to remain in Canada, while 48.9 percent were for sovereignty.[17]

Then a tiny fissure seemed to appear in Bill 101, hitherto

sacrosanct in all its clauses. On Thursday, June 13, Quebec's minister of education, Michel Pagé, responded to some chilling statistics which suggested that, in a province where we had been led to believe French culture was threatened with extinction, it was actually the English-speaking community that might be at risk. In 1976 there had been 236,000 students in English-language public and private schools, but by 1988–1989 the number had dwindled to 114,000 and the next year it was expected to sink to under 100,000. Pagé, in an interview with the *Gazette*, said he was willing to consider a change in Bill 101 that would lift the ban on English schooling for the children of immigrants from English-speaking countries. A task force would be set up in his department to study the problem, and if it turned out to be in favor of adjusting Bill 101 for English-speaking immigrants, he would ask the Cabinet to consider the matter. The very next day, however, he made it clear that he had never told the *Gazette* he would support such a change. "It is not in the program of our party," he assured the National Assembly, "and there isn't any sign the government will go in that direction."[18]

Twenty-three

THE SPRING AND SUMMER of 1991 yielded some choice cuts even to the most jaded of whither Quebec watchers. To begin with, there was the sight of a shameless Brian Mulroney trotting out visiting statesmen to deliver "spontaneous" panegyrics in favor of a united Canada. In March it was George Bush. Responding to reporters' questions about Quebec, he said that he had not come to Ottawa to interfere in the internal affairs of Canada and then did exactly that. "We are very, very happy with one unified Canada that has been friendly," he said, "has been allies, staunch allies, and when you have the unknown, you have to ask yourself questions. . . . The U.S. is in support of the integrity and unity of Canada because past experience has been very advantageous, not only for Canada but so too for our allies."[1]

The president of Mexico came through with an endorsement, and soon it was the turn of German Chancellor Helmut Kohl to oblige an Ottawa press conference. "Nobody else in the world can understand what is happening to Canada," he said. Then he elaborated on the meaning of *Heimat*, a sense of home. The chancellor himself, for instance, felt most at home in his native Palatinate region. "This is what I would tell a friend in Canada: it is important to retain one's identity *and* one's sense of *Heimat*, and I believe this is still possible in this time of federalism."[2]

Hardly a day went by without providing a political nugget of one sort or another. Take, for example, the June 15 issue of *L'actualité*, which reported that a Ph.D. thesis submitted by Esther Delisle, *"Antisémitisme et nationalisme d'extrême droite dans la province de Québec, 1929–1939"* ("Anti-Semitism and Nationalism of the Extreme Right in the Province of Quebec, 1929–1939") had created something of a stir at Laval University in Quebec City. Ms. Delisle insisted that anti-Semitism was essential to Abbé Groulx's idea of a French Canadian nation-state. Groulx, she wrote, was fascinated with totalitarianism. "In 1934 he was interested in the camps where German teachers were indoctrinated with a national mysticism to pass on to their young charges. An anti-Communist, he still thought the Soviet Union had done the right thing to create a revolutionary mysticism and regiment its young people."[3] Groulx, she pointed out, used the same language as the Nazis in very precise contexts. He wrote about Jews as "corrupters of the nation,"[4] and favored biological images, comparing them to microbes, a form of putrefaction, and so on.

In her thesis, Ms. Delisle also noted that, in the thirties, *Le Devoir* had assumed some interesting editorial positions. It advocated the deportation of Jews already settled in Quebec or, failing that, at least denying them Canadian nationality, revoking their right to vote, furnishing them with special passports, and establishing ghettos.

L'actualité's article about Ms. Delisle's thesis, by Luc Chartrand, began by observing that a chain of mountains, schools, a junior college, and a major Montreal métro station have all been named after Abbé Groulx. Responding to the piece, admirers of Groulx dismissed his anti-Semitism as a minor flaw in the character of a great man. They were also quick to point out that anti-Semitism was modish at the time, which suggested that it was comparable to the rumble seat or the fox trot. Sorry, no. These two fads usually led to nothing more serious than some heavy petting, but virulent anti-Semitism made the Holocaust possible.

NEXT, GRUMPY'S ITSELF was dealt a blow, when one of its regulars, Buck Rodgers, who also happened to be the most popular manager in the long, increasingly sad history of the Expos, was dumped by the management. The affable Rodgers, who had always enjoyed Montreal, lamented that the thriving city he had come to in 1985 seemed to have sprouted FOR RENT or

FOR SALE signs everywhere. "If nothing is done," he said, "the city could become a ghost town in ten years." Then, commenting on our endless independence quarrel, he added, "You are killing yourselves."[5]

At the time, Montreal's 22 percent poverty rate was the highest in the country, an estimated 615,000 people living under the poverty line and 203,000 officially listed as unemployed. "And [Montreal] was," said a grieving Warren Allmand, the MP for Notre-Dame-de-Grâce, "once the metropolis of Canada."[6]

Then the Equality Party's Gordon Atkinson delivered a Churchillian rebuke to Jacques Parizeau, after the PQ leader, addressing the National Legislature, had painted a glowing picture of an independent Quebec. "I was not elected to preside over the dismantling of the nation of Canada," Atkinson said.[7]

Advice, sensible but unsolicited, was on the way, the Group of 22 riding to the country's rescue with a report—"Some Practical Suggestions for Canada." The group, which had been brought together by Maurice Sauvé, a former federal Liberal minister, included two former provincial premiers, three defrocked federal Cabinet ministers (including Sauvé), a Tory apparatchik known for his wit, a distinguished economist, and a number of the truly rich. Its recommendations, unlike those shackled to Meech, had been subtly engineered so that none of them, in the opinion of the 22, required the unanimous consent of the provinces, but could be riveted in place by the approval of seven provinces with 50 percent of the country's population. The Group of 22 was in favor of aboriginal self-government and seats for natives in the Commons, the Senate, and at first ministers' conferences; it called for a transfer of responsibility for social programs, including health and welfare, to the provinces; and now that we had free trade with the U.S. it ventured that it would be simply dandy if the same courtesy were extended to the movement of goods and workers between the provinces. The group also wanted a reformed senate, renamed the House of Federation, its mandate restricted to fussing over federal relations.[8] Nowhere in the twenty-eight pages of its report did the Group of 22 utter the contentious words "distinct society." A damn good thing, too, because the most recent Gallup Polls revealed that, outside of Quebec, opposition to dubbing Quebec distinct ranged from 61 percent in the Maritimes to 82 percent in the prairie provinces. But in Quebec, 61 percent wanted the province to be recognized as distinct.

As if our cup of troubles weren't already overflowing, the next thing we knew the very symbol of Canadian rectitude was imperiled. The RCMP was being pilloried by the World Wrestling Federation. Performer Jacques Rougeau, cast as a villain, was habitually climbing into rings throughout North America wearing a stiff-brimmed Stetson, a scarlet tunic, and striped pants. His signature hold was to handcuff opponents to the ropes and then jolt them with a bogus 4,000-volt cattle prod. Compounding the offense, Rougeau traditionally finished off his opponent by beating him over the head with the prod, a technique he claimed to have learned during his own officer training. But Rougeau never could have served with the RCMP because, in 1986, he was convicted of punching out a fan in Chicoutimi.[9]

Understandably, the RCMP wanted the World Wrestling Federation to put a stop to Rougeau's antics. "We took one hundred years to build our credibility," said Inspector Yves Juteau, a spokesman at RCMP headquarters in Ottawa. "We don't want it ruined in a short time."[10]

Coming up next was the St. Jean-Baptiste Day parade, the traditional celebration of Quebec's patron saint, and many a non-Francophone Quebecer was apprehensive. After all, on 1990's St. Jean-Baptiste Day, following the collapse of the Meech Lake Accord, some 200,000 belligerent Quebecers had taken to the streets, waving fleur-de-lis flags and chanting, "Quebecers to the streets! Canadians on the sidewalk!"[11]

In the event, the 1991 parade—its Hallmark Cards theme *"Heureux ensemble"* or *"Happy Together"*—a calculated attempt to refute post-Oka charges of racism—turned out to be a benign affair. The parade's theme was endorsed by both Bourassa and Bouchard.

Bourassa said, "[It] should be a celebration of all Quebecers of all parties, as July 4 is the celebration of all Americans and July 14 the celebration of all the French."[12]

In effect, our premier was asking Anglophones, most of whose bilingual children had been driven out of the province, to clap hands and dance, if only to commemorate their empty nests. In a statement cunningly drafted not to offend nationalists, he failed to mention that *all* Canadians, just like all Americans and French, also had a national day: Canada Day, July 1.

A couple of weeks earlier, Bouchard showed us yet another side, his all-you-need-is-love Beatles face. Speaking at a BQ convention, he said, "Quebecers are not only the Tremblays of Alma, the Dutils of the Beauce or the Rivards of Montreal . . . it is also the Soares of St. Lawrence Boulevard, the Rosenblooms of Chomedey, the Nguyens of Brossard and the Murphys of St. Henri who help build Quebec, who love it and who wish to stay here."[13]

Greeks joined in the celebrations on the day of the Fête nationale. So did Haitians, Chinese, Portuguese, and Iranians. Why, there was even a group of wheelchair athletes performing the chant *"Le Québéc aux Québécois!"* in sign language. Street vendors peddled T-shirts embossed with René Lévesque's face or showing a map of a Republic of Quebec. The most inventive, I thought, had the slogan *"Enfin le Québec aux Québécois"* printed over the picture of a frog kicking a beaver in the face. Twenty-five-year-old Randy Debonis claimed to have sold 1,300 of his T-shirts at ten bucks each. "A lot of people found the one with the frog kicking the beaver offensive," he said. "Just wait until Canada Day. We have a beaver kicking the shit out of a frog."[14]

How many people had actually turned out for the parade on the Fête nationale depended on whether you read Montreal or Toronto newspapers or credited statements made by the St. Jean-Baptiste Society. According to the *Gazette*,[15] Montreal police refused to speculate on the size of the crowd, because the year before, when they had estimated the turnout at 160,000, organizers claimed that there had been twice as many people there. But the *Globe and Mail* reporter wrote that Montreal

Urban Community Police estimated the parade crowd at about 100,000, compared to well over 200,000 the year before.[16] However, Jean Dorion, president of the St. Jean Baptiste Society, assured reporters that this was the largest crowd ever. Jacques Parizeau, who was also there, told reporters that the size of the ethnic turnout should lay to rest the myth that Quebec is intolerant or that the nationalist movement suffered from an undercurrent of racism.[17]

Whatever, the good-natured crowd, only a few of them chanting *"Le Québec mon pays, Canada mon cul"* ("Quebec my country, Canada my ass"), deserved a much better show than was delivered. For it turned out that the theme of the day, which organizers had promised would be apolitical, was not only *"Heureux ensemble,"* but also Quebec, a country for giants. This, certainly, was the message on the banner that preceded the first float in the parade—a map of Quebec. It was followed by floats supporting twenty-foot-high giant figures, representing Quebec's history, economy, and sports. These figures of habitants, workers, and hockey players were uniformly crude and ill-made. In procession, they suggested nothing so strongly as the May Day parade in a Stalinist Third World country, circa 1950. Clearly no nationalist myself, but a Quebecer all the same, I was deeply embarrassed. Not so Serge Turgeon, honorary president of the parade. "To take giant steps," he said, "means to advance toward the future. I didn't see anyone this afternoon look at the giants while stooped. But I saw you all, like them, standing tall, proud, life-size."[18]

UNFORTUNATELY, BEFORE THE SUMMER was out the twin themes of the Fête nationale had both come into question. Charges of racism were flying in Quebec again, the accusations made by Montreal's black community, which numbered about 150,000, and by the Crees of northern Quebec; and the near collapse of Quebec's—no, the whole of Canada's—largest engineering firm, the legendary Lavalin Inc., burdened with an enormous bank debt.

On July 3, Marcelus François, an unarmed black man aged twenty-four and the father of two, was shot by a police sergeant during a bungled surveillance operation by an MUC SWAT team. François, a victim of mistaken identity, died of massive head wounds a couple of weeks later, the second unarmed black to be shot and killed by Montreal police within a year. Then Quebec Justice Minister Gil Rémillard announced that he would not bring charges in the incident, and the city's black community, understandably outraged, demanded a public inquiry.

The aboriginal troubles that heated up during the summer actually arose out of a chain of events that preceded the St. Jean-Baptiste parade. June 17, 1991, is as good a date as any to move into the story. That was the day that William Nicholls, a representative of the Grand Council of the Cree of James Bay, accompanied by other native spokesmen and environmentalists, went down to Albany to urge New York State officials not to buy power from Hydro-Québec until a proper environmental study had been done. As things stood, the New York State Power Authority had two contracts with Hydro-Québec, one to begin in 1995, the other in 1999, to pay an estimated $19 billion (US) for 1.8 million kilowatts of power from the James Bay II project. But this project involved the damming of rivers and flooding of forest land equivalent in area to two-thirds of Prince Edward Island.

Nicholls, speaking for the 10,000 Cree of James Bay, told the New York State officials, "I don't see how you can in clear conscience purchase power in advance from the Great Whale River project without taking direct responsibilities for your actions, which would be poisoning my people, destroying our way of life."[19]

Six weeks later Premier Bourassa, talking to a meeting of Liberal Party youth delegates in the small town of St. Augustin, told them that "the hardest blow in history to Canadian unity"[20] had been struck by Elijah Harper, and now the natives were threatening the projected $12 billion Great Whale hydroelectric scheme. Sixty-three thousand jobs were at risk, he said, and the environmental damage was no more than a "marginal drawback" when you considered the pollution, or dangers, implicit in drawing on alternative energy sources: coal, oil, or nuclear. The premier insisted that his government would go ahead, late in 1992, with the construction of the roads and airports necessary for the Great Whale development, and a year later work would begin on the power stations, enabling Quebec to honor its energy export contracts with the northeastern states.[21]

A couple of days later Konrad Sioui, a French-speaking Huron who was head of the Assembly of First Nations in Quebec, denounced Bourassa for linking Meech and the Great Whale. "By playing the Meech card all the time, by regularly attacking Indian people in his statements, Mr. Bourassa is just encouraging discrimination against natives.

"It's sowing the seeds of racism."[22]

The same day Cree grand chief Matthew Coon-Come told delegates from Cree communities in northern Quebec that, such were global concerns over the environment, they had a good chance of stopping the Great Whale project. "People across the world," he said, "are realizing that our struggle is their struggle—that this is not just denial of industrial development by an isolated group in James Bay. It is part of a global decision to choose between two paths: respect for the environment and the need for sustainable development, or continuation of the rape and pillage of the environment."[23]

Repeated visits to Albany and New York City by Cree and Inuit were beginning to yield results. On August 5, Mayor David Dinkins of New York City dealt a major blow to the Great Whale project. He asked the state to delay the purchase of approximately $19 billion worth of Hydro-Québec power until there had been a proper study of the environmental, economic, and social costs of the contract.[24] In response, Hydro-Québec, whistling in the wind, said the news was not the end of the world. A day later, its largest export sale at risk, Hydro-Québec announced that it might consider changing the terms of its deal with New York State, extending the deadline for negotiation. "If we can find new terms that might be mutually advantageous, then why not?"[25] said a spokesman. Then Ovide Mercredi, the leader of the Assembly of First Nations, went to Mistassini, in northern Quebec, to address the Cree. Bourassa's attack on Harper, he said, was unforgivable: "When the premier of this province decides to attack our national hero, he is doing it not only to the personality but to all the aboriginal people, the original inhabitants of this country. We are proud of Elijah Harper and we take great exception to any politician, particularly non-aboriginal, who tries to undermine the character of one of the strongest defenders of our rights and freedoms."[26]

Parizeau, sniffing yet another English and Indian conspiracy, now barged into the fray, claiming the Crees were spreading lies round the world about Great Whale in an attempt to scupper Quebec's voyage to independence. Furthermore, he told reporters, recent boasts by the aboriginals that their territory in northern Quebec would remain part of Canada if Quebec separated was "an operation of disinformation and blackmail" aimed at tarnishing Quebec's image internationally by questioning the legitimacy of its borders. "If it is not stopped," he said, "it could have the effect of complicating the international recognition of Quebec as a sovereign nation." The truth of the matter, the PQ leader added, is what really excited the Cree was not Great Whale, but their "appetite" for financial compensation. In any event, he said, they could not stop the hydroelectric project because they had surrendered their aboriginal claims to northern Quebec when they signed the James Bay Agreement in 1975.[27]

Four days later Parizeau was back on stage. Possibly he had been informed that not only the Cree, but many Quebecers, some of them even PQ members, had strong doubts about the validity of the Great Whale project. So now he called for an "irreproachable" environmental study, blaming Bourassa for trying to push on without one. "The absence of credibility of the preliminary steps," he said, "has left the field open to . . . international reaction that is far from flattering to Quebec."[28]

If Parizeau's statement was meant to mollify the aboriginals, it did nothing of the sort. A week later the eloquent Ovide Mercredi told the country's provincial premiers, "No province can unilaterally decide for First Nations the path we will follow. We will oppose these fantasies of unilateral secession." Aboriginal rights, Mercredi pointed out, have a priority over Quebec's demands in both Canadian history and international law. "Any attempt to take away these rights . . . will be an international violation of our right of self-determination on our homelands."[29]

Only a day later, Premier Bourassa announced that Hydro-Québec and the New York State Power Authority had decided to add a year to the date when the two parties could renege without penalty on their estimated $19 billion deal to buy a thousand megawatts from the province, based on the juice flowing out of Great Whale. This delay, Bourassa said, had come about only because of economic reasons, a slackening of demand.[30] But the following day he was contradicted by Richard Flynn of the New York State Power Authority, who said New York had asked for a delay because of concerns over the environmental impact of dams and river diversions. The new start date, he said, "simply reflects that understanding that there would be a whole and complete environmental review that won't be truncated."[31]

August also saw Lavalin nearly go belly-up with a debt of $860 million, largely due to the company's diversification into fields about which the management knew nothing: petrochemicals, mass transit, aircraft leasing, real estate, health-care services, weather-information programming and hydroponic farming. The problem, wrote most financial critics, was the giant ego of the privately owned company's president, Bernard Lamarre. Lamarre, said a former Lavalin executive, had "the charisma of a religious leader," but, he failed to specify whether he had Jimmy Swaggart or Mother Teresa in mind. However, according to Stephen Jarislowsky, one of Canada's most influential investment counselors, his political touch was "Machiavellian."[32]

Certainly Lamarre, either through altruism or cunning, had found jobs at Lavalin for many an out-of-office but still connected politician. Admirably nonpartisan, Lamarre, at one time or another, employed Tories, Liberals, and Péquistes, among them federal defense minister Marcel Masse, former PQ Cabinet ministers Yves Bérubé, Clément Richard, and Denis de Belleval, and a number of Liberals who had also once served in either the federal or provincial Cabinets.

Senate speaker Guy Charbonneau, a former Tory bagman, played a big part, according to the *Gazette*, "in helping Lavalin win major contracts abroad."[33] And Lamarre, an art collector of note, his private collection reportedly worth $5 million, included among his prized paintings at least one work by Madame Charbonneau, but then Madame Charbonneau is an artist of note. In recognition of her gifts, she was once awarded a medal by an official representing Nicolae Ceausescu, the last Communist ruler of Romania.

At five minutes to midnight, even as banks were moving in to take over Lavalin Inc.'s assets, it was saved by the intervention of its former rival, the SNC Group. SNC's acquisition of Lavalin was made possible by a Bourassa-sponsored sweetheart deal. Quebec granted SNC a loan of $25 million for thirteen years, at 10.75 percent interest, with no payments for five years; and the federal Export Development Corporation kicked in with $5 million under the same terms.[34] Having swallowed if not yet digested Lavalin, SNC with a staff of 6,000, was now rated as one of the world's top five engineering and construction companies. The vice-president of SNC-Lavalin, Yves Bérubé, surprised nobody by saying it would make a strong pitch for the Great Whale and other James Bay hydro projects.

NOAH, SEEKING A LANDFALL, sent his dove out again and again. Prime Minister Mulroney, without benefit of a single dove in the Ottawa aviary, plucked Keith Spicer out of the Canadian Radio-Television and Telecommunications Commission (CRTC), which he was serving as chairman, to fly across the land, in the company of eleven other commissioners, to determine what was bothering the hoi polloi. The Bible doesn't tell us whether the dove, returning with a twig in its beak, was rewarded with corn kernels or whatever, but Spicer did go on the record to Robert Mason Lee, of the Ottawa *Citizen*, with the following story: "On Halloween, the night before his commission was announced, [Spicer] was telephoned by a very important public official. The official offered him the job of ambassador to Tokyo in exchange for chairing the commission."[35] Spicer went on to say that he had felt "sullied"[36] by the offer, which struck him as a crude attempt to ensure that he would make nice when, eight months later, he sat down to churn out his Report to the People and Government of Canada. Whether or not it cost him a cushy job far from the second coldest capital city in the world, Spicer certainly did not stroke Mulroney in his Chairman's Foreword to the Citizens' Forum on Canada's Future. His preamble, a tad overwritten, began:

> Canadians used to believe—and many still hope—that they harbour some special genius for compromise. It's at least as easy to prove that our real knack is for turning opportunities into problems.
> Seen from abroad by both foreigners and Canadians, Canada looks like paradise. Long queues of immigrants—seeking freedom, tolerance, and prosperity—say so. . . . Yet seen from within, Canada looks to Canadians like a pessimist's nightmare of Hell. That's the message we get from almost all our elites—politicians, bureaucrats, media, business and unions, even, sometimes, our artists—who, outside of Quebec, tend to be eloquent, but often voluptuously anxious about Canada; and inside Quebec studiously indifferent.
> Let's be honest: we're all a bit guilty of running down Canada. Dumping on this sprawling, fragile nation without nationality is our homegrown idea of flag-waving. The only exceptions? Recent immigrants who haven't yet got the hang of it.[37]

Then he stuck it to the prime minister, saying the consensual editing of Part II of the report did not adequately echo the anger directed at him.

The top person is of course always a lightning rod. And it is true that Canadians show little regard for opposition leaders, or many provincial ones either.

But people wielding great power must be held responsible for how they wield it. And I think that, from most citizens' viewpoint, our report lets the PM off too lightly. At least for now, there is fury in the land against the prime minister.[38]

The problem was that, having spent $23 million over eight months, shuttling back and forth across Canada, bickering amongst themselves, looking silly more often than not—after that, *and* gabbing with 400,000 adults and 300,000 elementary and secondary school students—the news the commissioners brought back from the Rialto only confirmed what we already knew. In fact, the admittedly obstructive Robert Normand made a valid point about the report that was delivered with such pomp in Ottawa on Canada Day, July 1, when he wrote in a dissenting comment: "[the commission] basically limited itself to gathering only the superficial views of those Canadians who addressed it, in a fashion similar to that of open-line radio shows."[39]

Of course, the Citizens' Forum on Canada's Future was doomed from the onset by a sentimental and badly mistaken initial premise. There simply aren't 400,000 people worth consulting in Canada about the country's future, never mind 300,000 pimply adolescents or children even younger. Surely, this is democracy gone berserk.

Mind you, were I in favor of sovereignty for Quebec, I could argue, after having gone through the 168-page report by the commissioners, that its subtext did suggest a dangerous difference between Quebec and the ROC: each sings its own false notes. Quebecers, on the day of their Fête nationale, would have us believe that they were *"Heureux ensemble,"* while the rest of the country, on Canada Day, would rather that we remained unhappy together.

FOR THE REST, IT WAS a summer like any other, rendered entertaining by continuing tribal idiocies, the activities of volunteer tongue-troopers, and other diversions.

In July, there came a report from Quebec City of a Bill 101 controversy that was rocking the province's most expensive museum, the $40 million Musée de la Civilisation on Dalhousie Street. Like rival schools of Talmudists disputing a passage in the Torah, the Office de la Langue Française and the Commission de protection de la langue française were at odds over whether the signs inside the Quebec City museum should continue to be French-only or include English, as a show of *politesse* to visitors from outside the province. The Office, quoting a section of Bill 101 that stated only French signs were allowed in government buildings, was against tolerating English. But the Commission, quoting another section of Bill 101, maintained that signs with languages in addition to French were allowed because a museum has products to describe.

Since 1988, it was estimated that 400,000 of the museum's two million visitors had come from outside the province. The museum's director, Guy Boivin, said, "We are well aware that American tourists and tourists from other Canadian provinces can't get as much out of the exhibits when our signs are only in French." There were some bilingual tour guides, he said, as well as an English handbook. "But the handbooks are hard to follow," he added.[40]

Actually, the museum's sign debate was sparked, albeit inadvertently, by an Anglophone informer. The museum did have bilingual signs in place for its sneak opening in 1987. So a gracious English-speaking visitor wrote a letter to the editor of *Le Soleil* in appreciation of the museum's courtesy. The letter obviously inflamed Quebec's ever vigilant Lise Bacon, who was minister of cultural affairs at the time.

Boivin said, "We received a letter from Lise Bacon, which stated we must strictly obey the law, and signs must only be in French."[41]

Then we learned that while we possibly had to await real independence before we had our very own Red Guards, Montreal could meanwhile make do with a nineteen-year-old student named Philippe Tremblay and his Action-Québec.

On Tuesday, July 16, the temperature in the low 80s (28 degrees Celsius), the dedicated Tremblay was prowling up and down Sherbrooke Street, in primarily English-speaking Notre-Dame-de-Grâce, looking for store owners who were not heeding Bill 178. With the help of thirty other volunteers, he had already been able to file 350 complaints with the Commission de protection de la langue française. In one case, Tremblay cited a sign outside J.R.'s Bar that read "Orchestre/Live Band."

"Ninety-five percent of my customers" are English, the owner of J.R.'s Bar protested to a *Gazette* reporter.[42]

JACQUES PARIZEAU SEEMED TO SPEND most of his summer serving as the PQ's traveling salesman, hitting the road with a smile and a shoeshine and a suitcase full of self-serving statistics, doing his silvery-tongued best to peddle sovereignty. He appeared to grow increasingly petulant. Trailing his own party in the opinion polls (a more popular people's tribune, Lucien Bouchard, breathing down his neck), Parizeau lapsed into idiocy in August. Addressing a PQ think tank in Beauport, he declared that the apparent dismantling of the Soviet Union showed that Quebec's notion of separating from the rest of Canada wasn't so barmy after all. "With all that is going on in the world," he said, "we should be considered visionaries, nearly prophets.

"It has been years that we have been saying the idea of a little people wanting to have a country isn't an idea of the past. It's not the past, it's the future.

"And all that is happening in the U.S.S.R. just confirms our ambitions; that maybe we weren't so stupid, that we weren't behind but in fact the opposite and what René Lévesque described in the virtues of a little nation, was maybe true."[43]

Parizeau's comparison of Quebec's plight to that of the Baltic states was not only offensive to English Canada, but also to Quebec's French press, which reprimanded him for such bad taste. But the Beauport conference was not over yet. It still had to hear from another invitee to its think tank, political science professor Edouard Cloutier of the Université de Montréal who said that a sovereign Quebec would have to create its own national guard to put down Anglophone and native saboteurs. The greatest danger to the integrity of Quebec's borders, he explained, would come not from English Canada or the U.S., but from discontented Anglophones and natives within the new republic. The Westmount *maquis*. The Mohawk Warriors. Or, put another way, force would have to be deployed by Quebec against those who would dare ask to secede from the secessionist province. "What is most important is maintaining the present boundaries in the few weeks that follow the application of sovereignty," said the professor. "To do this we don't need to think in terms of a big army or a fleet of frigates, but rather a small but effective force that could stop acts of sabotage on the land, cuts in communication, that sort of thing. What I'm talking about is a little like civil protection."[44]

THEN, EARLY IN SEPTEMBER, the trees in the hills surrounding Lake Memphremagog beginning to flare every possible shade of yellow and red, morning ground frost the unhappy rule, it was, I suppose, inevitable that the next threat to national unity should revolve round an ice hockey crisis. What happened is that Eric Lindros, the most promising junior hockey player to come along since the incomparable Wayne Gretzky and a prize coveted by every one of the twenty-one National Hockey League teams, but the legitimate first draft choice of the Québec Nordiques by dint of their having finished last in the 1990–91 season, said that he was not going to play in Quebec City no matter what. The eighteen-year-old Torontonian at first said that he had come to this conclusion because of business reasons, i.e., Quebec City did not constitute a major market and, aside from a salary of a million or two, he also anticipated picking up another couple of mill in endorsements. But soon enough, the Francophobe cat was out of the bag. Lindros told the *Gazette*'s Michael Farber, "It's not one thing about Quebec, it's a lot of things. It's taxes and the size of the place. Language is another. If I'm making a wave now, what happens in a couple of years? What if the separation problem grows? Why get stuck there? Why not try to avoid the whole issue? The way it is is the way it is. I don't want to change anything. Just don't involve me."[45]

Involve him? Short of trampling on the fleur-de-lis, Lindros couldn't have done more to set himself stage center in the national quarrel. He was on the front page of just about every French-language newspaper in Quebec, denounced for his avarice, and also appeared on the cover of *Maclean's*. Still to come was a book-length autobiography of this six-foot-five behemoth who had yet to score a goal in the National Hockey League. Meanwhile, in an interview with *Maclean's*, he did make a good point about the questionable nature of a draft system that can rule where a youngster will play hockey, like it or not. "The people that come out of high school with the best grades go to the best universities," he said. "The people with the lower grades have fewer choices. Why should a player who comes out of junior hockey with top marks go to a city that is not his choice?"[46]

Next Prime Minister Mulroney pronounced, saying it might have been worse, Lindros could have been drafted by Winnipeg. He was right, but I doubt that the sentiment did Mulroney any good in Manitoba. Then things really began to heat up. Lindros, who had made Team Canada, was to play with the team in its game against the Russians in Quebec City on September 9, the city's hockey fans already fulminating. Lindros didn't make things any easier for himself by telling reporters the day before the game that his decision was "not political and it's not racist. I like the French people. I like the culture [but] Quebec City is not for me. It's a great place to visit. It's a great place to go out and have a good time. It's a great place to vacation. But this is a business decision. I want to spend the fifteen or seventeen years of my career in the place I like."[47]

The actual game the following night in Quebec City served to establish two things: the Nordiques fans, who booed Lindros good-naturedly and then cheered him when he made a stylish play, were a classy bunch, while the organizers of the Canada Cup, on the other hand, were a craven lot. Rather than risk the national anthem—traditionally sung half in French, half in English—being booed, they cunningly brought out a pianist to play "O Canada" sans lyrics.

The Lindros case is still unsettled, but the penultimate word on it was written by Win Hackett, a former New Brunswick deputy minister, on the op-ed page of the *Globe and Mail*. "I wish someone would offer me $2 million to live in Quebec City," he wrote, "one of my favorite places. It has some of the best restaurants, best bars and best jazz in Eastern Canada. Two million would do me fine. I could dine regularly at Guido's, the Café de la Paix, or the Continental, then go enjoy good jazz at L'Anse aux Barques or the Clarendon."[48]

Twenty-four

As I WRITE, LATE IN SEPTEMBER 1991, Quebec is pledged to definitely, but not necessarily, hold a referendum on sovereignty by next October. Or, on the other hand, the referendum could deal with the rest of Canada's binding offer for renewed federalism. Or, if such an offer were near, the referendum could be delayed. Or, instead of a referendum, there could be an election in 1993 to settle the question once and for all, but only for another decade.

Certainly Premier Bourassa, having put through the enabling legislation, Bill 150, would still not be so foolish as to sanction a referendum if he thought the vote could go against sovereignty, wrecking Quebec's bargaining position with the ROC. So if the polls continue to show declining support for independence, there will be no referendum. This, in spite of the propensity for tough talk by Quebec's minister of intergovernmental affairs, Gil Rémillard. It is essential, he has said, that Quebec be recognized as a distinct society, and Canada must be radically changed; otherwise, there will be a referendum on sovereignty. Meanwhile, the wily Bourassa, reeling in the enthusiasm of nationalists within his own party, has announced that he will set up two committees; one to ponder binding offers from the rest of Canada and another to study the actual costs and disadvantages of sovereignty. If Quebec wants economic union with the ROC, he has said, then it must suffer political union as well, or it will be bound to endure a "democratic deficit," that is to say, economic policies dictated by a Parliament in Ottawa in which it is not represented.

In the meantime Quebecers continued to be battered by variations on the same old mixed signals.

In a survey of Québécois business leaders undertaken by the

Conseil du patronat, 70 percent responded in favor of a revision of Bill 178.[1] This, in turn, provoked a knee-jerk reaction from the far-from-unpredictable Jean Dorion, president of the Montreal St. Jean Baptiste Society. Quebecers, he said (contradicting one poll after another, over the wasting years), would never tolerate a return to bilingual signs. "Everyone would see it as a backward step for French," he said.[2]

Next to be heard from, wearing his favored no-more-cakes-and-ale expression, was Claude Ryan. "For the moment I maintain the position that I have defined several times," he said, "that Bill 178 and Bill 101 continue to apply as currently formulated. We have no intention of proposing any modifications to Bill 101, which includes Bill 178, either in the next session or in this year."[3]

The most original solution to the language impasse was outlined by Daniel Latouche. He offered Anglophones a Faustian bargain. Support sovereignty and—presto!—your language rights will be restored. Latouche argued that the harsh language laws that could fly in one of the world's provincial backwaters would be downright embarrassing in a real country. "Provinces and states," he wrote, "can have such restrictive language and cultural laws but full-fledged nation-states, those who aspire to play among the big boys (and the big girls) of international relations, cannot afford to be caught with such restrictions on their hands."[4]

Absolutely convinced that Quebecers comprised a distinct society, the endearing Latouche proved that within every Québécois nationalist tiger there was a timorous Canadian pussycat waiting to get out. Language rights would be restored not as a matter of principle, but because the new little country, just like the old big one, wouldn't dare offend the United States:

> After sovereignty, English in Quebec will no longer be the language of a majority. It will become a minority language that also happens to be the official language of two members of the UN Security Council, one of them the United States, the country whose sympathetic ear is absolutely needed by Quebec if it

is ever to make it on the independence road.

One can easily imagine the reaction of a sovereign Quebec to the polite suggestion of a state department official that there is no room in the North American free trade zone for any country which imposes such discriminatory measures against the language and cultural life of one of its trading partners.

Such restrictions might even be considered a non-tariff barrier to trade. Quebec would probably nullify Bill 178 and Bill 101 so fast that few will have time to take notice.[5]

While we waited for the language bills to be lifted, Philippe Tremblay and his loyal Action-Québec troopers, having done their utmost to cleanse Sherbrooke Street W. of linguistic impurities, took their crusade to the Eastern Townships. There, in only two little towns, Beebe and Stanstead, they discovered 103 violations of Bill 178 and advised the Commission de protection de la langue française accordingly. Happily, their intrusion into a region where there was no discord between French and English neighbors aroused a voice of reason. Jean-Guy Dubuc wrote an editorial in *La Tribune* of Sherbrooke that appeared under the following head and subhead:

THE ABSURDITY
OF BILL 178
It Puts Intolerance
on a Pedestal.

Many Francophones, he wrote, had been embarrassed by Bill 178, which deprived people of their right of expression. And he concluded:

> Residents of Stanstead and other towns will have to abuse their heads as well as their hearts to comply with a law of such idiotic censorship. The rules of today's lay people are as absolute as for those of yesterday's church.
>
> But the church has matured. It would be unfortunate if the new religion of nationalism creates a hell that burns more people than the hell of the dogmatists of yore.[6]

Canadians, confronted by a clear political choice, have an exasperating habit of not saying yes, not saying no, but only maybe. So the last time a political issue generated real emotional heat here, in the 1988 debate over the Free Trade Bill, they voted the Tories, advocates of the deal with the U.S., back into office, but split the majority of the popular vote between the two parties that were vehemently opposed to the bill, the Liberals and the New Democrats. Presented with a clear political choice, the Québécois, a far more subtle lot, tend to confound everybody else in the country by voting both yes and no. Traditionally, they send MPs committed to federalism to Ottawa, but put a nationalist government in place in Quebec City and then settle back to enjoy the ensuing scrimmage. In 1980, a vintage political year, they voted 60–40 against sovereignty-association in a referendum and eleven months later hoisted the Parti québécois, a party founded to promote that status, back into office.

Whichever way Quebec votes in another referendum, if we have one, the decline of Montreal will not stop. Anglophone Quebecers, the bilingual young in particular, will continue to leave because they feel so unwelcome here. Between January and May 1991, some 12,000 people quit Quebec for other provinces.[7] Even if you factor in new arrivals, there was still a net loss of more than 4,000, most of them young, and educated in universities. Down the road we will have something like *de facto* separation, an almost totally French-speaking province, as the most ambitious and highly skilled immigrants are bound to pass over Quebec for more tolerant societies, where they are free to educate their children in the language of their choice.

In the short term, the least likely but most unpleasant possibility is that the country will stumble into partition through error or ineptitude. Brian Mulroney, it must be said, is an intensely disliked prime minister, consistently supported by less than 20 percent of the voters in polls taken over the last two years. And the alternatives do not excite anybody. Unhappily, in this hour of Canadian need there is no politican of the stature of Trudeau to speak for the country. Even so, the likelihood is that next year the Québécois will retreat from the precipice once more. Abjuring sovereignty or sovereignty-association, they will probably settle for something called renewed federalism, whereby Ottawa will surrender still more of its powers to Quebec. Then, in the absence of the Wizard of Oz, the prime minister will present the province with a scroll that declares it "a distinct society," making the painfully obvious official, as it were. And, in 1993, if the polls are correct, a grateful Quebec will boot Robert Bourassa out of office, elect the Parti québécois, committed to outright independence, and once more settle back to wait for the fireworks.

MEANWHILE, A CAUTIONARY TALE for Quebec *indépendantistes*, the details of which I have cribbed shamelessly from a splendid piece in the Montreal *Gazette* by Hubert Bauch, which could have been called, had it been written by the Brothers Grimm, "The Little Mayor and the Big Tower." The tower in question rises out of Montreal's Olympic Stadium, or the Big Owe as it has long been known here. This is the billion-dollar folly which, in the words of its present director—Pierre Bibeau, head of the Olympic Installations Board—has made Montreal "the laughing stock of the world."[8]

The story begins in the early sixties when His Worship Mayor Jean Drapeau, our bush-league de Gaulle, bent on civic *gloire*, determined to leave Montreal with monuments to his reign. What he had in mind, in particular, was a majestic tower, without which, he believed, no city could claim to be "world-class." To begin with, the mayor thought it would be a neat idea to dismantle the Tour Eiffel, crate it, and bolt it together again in Montreal, where it would stand for the duration of Expo 67. Then he had a second brainstorm. Instead of borrowing the Tour Eiffel, he would build one of his own, a "Paris-Montreal" tower to commemorate Quebec's French heritage, and it would soar precisely 1,066 feet high to celebrate the 1066 Norman conquest of England. Unfortunately, when the model of what Drapeau dubbed "a poem in concrete"[9] was unveiled in 1964, journalists described it as resembling nothing so much as an oversized celery stalk or a golf driver from the land of the giants.

Then, in 1972, Drapeau wheeled out his model for the Olympic Stadium. The stadium, designed by French architect Roger Taillibert, came complete with a tall, stooping mast that resembled the ridiculed "poem in concrete" of 1964. According to Jean-Claude Marsan, former head of the Université de Montréal's school of architecture, that was the roof's fatal flaw. The roof, Marsan told Hubert Bauch, was essentially an afterthought, superimposed as a function of the tower instead of the other, logical way round, with the technical requirements of the roof the paramount consideration. No other covered stadium in the world, Marsan pointed out, required a tower to support its roof. "Down deep, what he wanted wasn't a roof but a tower," he said. "Instead of a functional roof we built a monument to illusion."[10]

An early warning about the dangers inherent in the projected retractable fabric roof for the stadium came from Otto Frei, designer of the German pavilion at Expo, who had pioneered the concept of suspended roofs. The proposed stadium roof, he said, was "audacious in the extreme." In the first place, the fabric structure would be ten times larger than any similar one extant, and then it would also have to withstand Montreal's punishing climate. A potential problem he wisely anticipated was "the displacement of membranes in the roof during windy periods."[11]

At the time, the projected cost of the Olympic installations was $120 million, but City Councillor Nick Auf der Maur ventured that they would cost a billion dollars, maybe more. He was right. "You didn't hear a lot of engineers denouncing the project," he told Bauch in 1991, "because they were too busy jockeying for the fat contracts that were being doled out for stadium construction. Instead of saying, 'Wait a minute, let's make sure this is going to work,' they were like sharks in a feeding frenzy."[12]

In any event, neither the tower nor the roof were in place in time for the Olympic Games in 1976. Back in 1973, Taillibert assured Montrealers that the roof would be made of "a strong synthetic fabric attached to cables suspended from the tower that [would] cover the central opening, folding and unfolding easily and quickly."[13] Then, in 1989, thirteen years behind schedule, the $52 million roof was actually installed. It never performed as promised. At the best of times, it took twice as long to open and close as did the retractable roof of Toronto's SkyDome. The roof lining tore in 1989 and again in the spring of 1991. Then, in a flash storm on June 28, 1991, it tore for the third time, leaving two massive triangular gaps, about thirty to forty-five meters wide. Since then, the roof has not been re-tracted even once, and then, on Friday, September 13, there was worse news. A fifty-ton, twenty-meter, nonstructural beam dropped more than nine meters into a space where visitors to the billion-dollar complex usually congregate. Fortunately, the beam collapsed at 7:45 a.m. before workers had reported to the site. But as a consequence, the safety of the stadium has been called into serious question and it is even possible that it will be demolished.

In an article that he published in *Le Devoir* in 1985, Jean-Claude Marsan suggested that the Olympic Stadium was the answer to a profound imperative in the French Canadian soul. The Québécois, he wrote, have historically shown a propensity for building spectacular monuments of limited functional value as a means of sublimating an ingrained sense of impotence in the face of the Anglo-North American juggernaut. "Here is the problem," he wrote. "Quebecers, who do not control what is real, have a visceral need to realize themselves in the imaginary. At the beginning of the 19th century, while the Anglophones were taking over the economy—dredging the harbor and dig-ging the Lachine Canal—French Canadians were building Notre-Dame, the biggest temple north of Mexico."

Montreal's St. Joseph's Oratory, one of the five largest shrines in the world, was, so far as Marsan was concerned, a display of the same tendency a century later.

"And now," he had written in 1985, "they are preparing to celebrate the apotheosis of their history by topping off the stadium, perhaps the most costly building in the history of humanity. Yet the Taillibert retractable roof doesn't have ten chances in one hundred of working."

Six years later, Marsan, who is now dean of the Université de Montréal's planning faculty, told Hubert Bauch, "In any other society, this foolish concept would not have gone beyond the drawing board, and the architect would have been sent home to play with his crayons.

"Here, to the detriment of screaming priorities, Quebecers have become hostages to their dream."[14]

Yes, but in a country where the realized Anglophone dream is too often a dredged harbor, the building of Notre-Dame is essential. Put plainly, we need each other if we are to create a Canada that is more than merely functional.

Twenty-five

A QUEBECER BORN AND BRED, I suffer from a recurring nightmare that all of us, French- and English-speaking, will one day be confronted by our grandchildren, wanting to know what our generation was about when the Berlin Wall crumbled, a playwright became president of Czechoslovakia, and, after seventy-four years, the Communist Party was overthrown in the Soviet Union and then the Soviet Union itself was dissolved. We will be honor bound to reply, why, in Quebec, we were hammering each other over whether or not bilingual commercial signs could be posted outside as well as inside. We were in heat, not only in this province, but throughout Canada, over whether or not Quebec could be officially crowned "a distinct society."

Our continuing quarrel—still unresolved, as I write—could yet lead to the dismemberment of this incredibly rich but ineptly governed country. Following many increasingly acrimonious decades of constitutional haggling, an exasperated English Canada has asked, "What does Quebec want?" And Quebecers, like latter-day Talmudists, have countered with a question of their own. "What does English Canada want?" I can answer both questions. Quebec, as usual, wants more. English Canada, fearful of being snookered, wants a little peace and quiet.

The constitutional pot is coming to the boil. Legislation already in place suggests that in 1992, Quebecers might be obliged to respond to a multiple-choice question. Simply put, we could be asked to choose among:

    a. something called "renewed federalism"
    b. sovereignty-association
    c. independence

On the evidence available so far, we would be expected to choose without the federal government ever having had the guts, or the Québécois *indépendantistes* the honesty, to lay out the real costs, emotional and financial, or to address the hard question of whether the province's vast northland, Nouveau-Québec, would belong to Canada or the new republic.

Meanwhile, friendly foreigners, American and European, continue to shake their heads in astonishment at what is happening in this overprivileged country. I don't blame them. Consider, for example, events that transpired in the pretty little town of Ayer's Cliff, in the Eastern Townships, on September 20, 1991. On that day, wrote the *Gazette's* Ingrid Peritz, inspectors from the offices of the Commission de protection de la langue française, acting on evidence sent to them by the young vigilantes of Action-Québec, were out searching the otherwise tranquil countryside for commercial signs, or even menus, with illegal words such as "sundae" or "milkshake." The inspectors, she noted, "encountered some unexpected resistance in the quiet border villages of the Eastern Townships, however: the solidarity of Francophones and Anglophones who had lived peacefully with one another for two hundred years."[1]

Roland Dupuis, a Rock Island snack bar proprietor, told Ms. Peritz, "They've taken down the Berlin Wall in Germany and now they want to put it up in Quebec between the English and French. I've lived here all my life and never had any problem with anyone. We're all equal."

The owners of Derusha Supplies in Beebe Plain proved not only equal, but also innovative, wrote Ms. Peritz:

> They were told the world "supply" must be removed from their sign, which reads: "Equipements Derusha Supply." So they asked the farmer across the road if they could plant a bilingual sign on his property pointing to their business.
> That's because the Canada-U.S. border runs right down the middle of the road—and the farmer's field is in the United States.[2]

A little less than two weeks later, the Canadian government presented Quebec with a new unity offer, which proposed, among other things, a free movement of labor and goods *within*

Canada. No, no, no, Quebec businessmen hollered. Although they had been fervent in their support of a free-trade deal with the U.S. only three years earlier, they seemed horrified by the prospect of a Canada that would allow a free movement of men and goods between its very own provinces. Go figure.

RENEWED FEDERALISM

Come the crunch, I still believe that Roland Dupuis, and other Quebecers of good will and common sense, will prevail and that renewed federalism, a loot bag that would yield still more sweets to the Quebec Cookie Monster, will be the choice of the majority. Most observers of the Canadian scene, however, feel that this time we have walked too far out on the plank for that. I am bound to agree that this time out, unlike 1980, federalism lacks a lustrous French Canadian champion. Alas, our cause now rests in the calculating hands of Premier Bourassa, a politician with no sentimental attachment to Canada, one who regards it, rather, as a convenience store which he is disposed to favor so long as it produces a quarterly dividend. On the other hand, he also seems to have grasped that in the short run—say, over the next decade at least—independence would be an economic nightmare for Quebec. But Bourassa is sadly without a moral anchor that could steady him against unfavorable winds. Based on past performance, he is most likely to tilt in whichever direction the opinion polls or renewed street theater blows him.

Renewed federalism—English Canada twisting itself into a political pretzel to oblige Quebec—would temporarily arrest but not end the tribal bleeding in the province. Young, bilingual Anglophones will continue to leave, unless, *pace* Auden, we are blessed with "a change of heart, new styles in architecture."

SOVEREIGNTY-ASSOCIATION

This solution to our troubled Canadian marriage, an idea once proffered by Bourassa and then burnished by Lévesque, is too clever by half. It was set in place to mollify a majority of Quebecers who are discomfited, to say the least, by the prospect of having to deal in their own currency. Sovereignty-association is the all-too-familiar plea, albeit writ large, of any pampered middle-class spouse who is willing to quit the farm so long as alimony payments (shared currency) are guaranteed, as well as dual custody of the marital properties (Air Canada, the St. Lawrence Seaway, Nouveau-Québec, and so forth). If this country of ours is to be dismembered it should not be allowed to happen by stealth, Quebec's move underwritten by a no-risk insurance policy issued by the rest of Canada. Ottawa should treat this proposal, at once chicken-livered and sly, with the contempt it so richly deserves.

INDEPENDENCE

If I thought for a moment that Francophone Quebecers were oppressed in Canada, I would be out there in the streets demonstrating with them. The truth is, I happen to believe the contrary. I believe that when Quebecers, as they are often inclined to do, compare their plight to that of blacks in the United States or, less frequently, to Zionists, it is revealing of their unquenchable thirst for self-pity and not, happily for them, a measure of their historical experience. English-speaking Canada, far from stifling Quebec, has acted—and could continue to act—as a committed partner, a buffer, shielding its culture from the rest of an English-speaking continent that Quebecers perceive as a threatening force. Educated Canadians in the rest of the country cherish French Canadian culture and recognize it as an essential ingredient of our own emerging national identity. But to be fair, I must also admit that many of us are also exasperated. We have been told again and again that the most vibrant and only original culture in Canada is French Canadian, while at the same time it is apparently so fragile that the mere sight of a bilingual street sign is sufficient to propel it into the nearest intensive care unit.

AFTER ALL IS SAID AND DONE, I sometimes fear that I may have missed the point about Quebec's independence. Possibly it's a mistake to try to sink with logic an ideological boat that is floated not on rational argument but on turbulent seas of emotion. Certainly, having read the books of Québécois nationalists on the subject (from Lévesque, through Vallières and Bourgault, to Latouche, Fournier, Mathews, and others), I was struck by their rage against Anglophones and their passion to be free of us at last. Then, in the late watches of the night, I tend to brood over some of their more chilling pronouncements, say Yves Beauchemin telling the Bélanger-Campeau Commission, "The obligation to share one's cultural space with a foreign language always expresses a defeat or a state of weakness for someone. If Adolf Hitler had won the war in 1945, France would be bilingual: French-German."[3] Mulling over that one, I readily grasp that it is far too late to tell Beauchemin that English is no more a foreign language in Quebec than French, and that only on an Animal Farm would he be more equal than I; and next I am inclined to think, if nothing but independence will make them happy, why not? What, as A. M. Rosenthal might say, does it matter?

Then I am overcome with doubts about my doubts, as it were. For the truth is I am convinced that separation or sovereignty or independence, whichever, is a Québécois bourgeois conceit and could only be brought about by politicians who are indifferent to the welfare of the province's working class and farmers and who, furthermore, would welcome the destruction of Quebec's once thriving English-speaking community. If Quebec's independence were a projected book, rather than a political cause, it could only be published by a vanity press. So Jean Chrétien got it right when he told the Bélanger-Campeau Commission, "I hope your main preoccupation will be to tell workers what price they will pay for independence. . . . In fact, only two thousand bourgeois will profit from it."[4] Put plainly, it would be very costly indeed for Quebec and would not come free of charge for the rest of Canada either. On the other hand, our continuing national drift also undeniably exacts a toll, emotional as well as financial.

So let me come out of the closet and say I am for a referendum in 1992, providing Ottawa has the guts and Quebec the honesty to explain to voters the potential cost of independence and the contentious issues involved. Unfortunately, nothing we have been presented with by either side so far is reassuring. Most recently, Jacques Parizeau, wearing his Tinker Bell suit, actually told a group of Université de Montréal students that independence would not cost a cent and, instead of heaving him out the window, the students clapped hands to show that they believed in fairies. Then there's Ottawa's minister of constitutional affairs, Joe Clark, the tiger in our tank. Even before presenting Quebec with his government's latest unity package, he assured the province that it was only an imperfect working document and if it wasn't to their taste, not to worry, we'll be right back with a better offer.

Several months later, our incomparable Joe announced that he would introduce enabling legislation for a *federal* referendum on the terms of a new constitutional deal, but—hold the phone, nobody was to worry—the results wouldn't count. Then, when even this toothless proposal inflamed the Tories' Quebec caucus, Joe, as was his habit, retreated in disorder: There would be no national referendum. Quebec could opt for renewed federalism in a referendum of its own, but the ROC wasn't entitled to say whether they found the terms acceptable. Put plainly, Quebec could stay or go, but it wasn't going to be evicted.

Before any Quebec, rather than national, referendum, Ottawa will have to stop playing the tart, showing too much leg by the roadside, hoping to hitchhike to a New (Canadian) Jerusalem. Instead, it will have to behave out of character and set out the real cost of separation to Quebecers, which I interpret as follows:

1. A republic of Quebec will be liable for one-quarter of Canada's national debt, a sum based on its share of the population.

2. Quebec will have to trade with its own currency, and its citizens travel on the republic's very own passports. However, filling the office of good neighbor, Canada should help Quebec

develop both currency and passports so that both can be in place on the first day of independence.

3. The Cree, and other First Nations, will not be abandoned by Ottawa. Even as the descendants of French-speaking immigrants, comparative latecomers to this land, are being offered an opportunity to choose, so the First Nations should also enjoy the right of self-determination on their traditional lands. Obviously, the PQ, committed democrats, would have it no other way.

4. Ottawa will reclaim all of Nouveau-Québec, which was a gift to the province so long as it was an integral part of Canada. This dispute should be settled without resort to arms by either side but through an appeal to an international court or by the intervention of mutually acceptable arbitrators. As such a dispute could drag on for years and years, it would be folly for Hydro-Québec to now proceed to invest billions in power developments on land where it may turn out to be no more than a tenant.

5. Quebec should be warned in advance that in any new trade deal it might seek with either the rest of Canada or the United States, it will be in a very vulnerable position, offering a piffling market of six million in exchange for free access to markets of eighteen million and two hundred and forty million. The interventionist policies of the Caisse and Hydro-Québec could also be brought into question.

6. Sadly, the thousands of Québécois now employed by the federal civil service, or serving with Canada's armed forces, will have to choose between Canadian or Quebec citizenship; and those who opt for the latter will obviously have to be discharged as born-again foreigners.

The Parti québécois, making its case, should not be allowed to get away with insulting the intelligence of Quebecers by pretending that independence would come free of charge. There will be a bill to settle, and Quebecers must be given the facts before they are asked to choose.

If a clear majority of Quebecers choose independence, then,

of course, it will be a sad day for Canada, but their decision must be honored. All I ask is that the new republic allow the remaining Anglophones time enough to pack and join their children in other provinces or the United States and that they be allowed to take their goods with them. Possibly anticipating such a large-scale exodus, Jacques Parizeau flirted with Anglophone concerns at a September meeting of the PQ on Montreal's West Island. Twenty years down the road in an independent Quebec, he suggested, it might just be possible to relax some of the language laws. He needn't worry. Twenty years from now in an independent Quebec the only Anglophones left in Montreal would not be able to cope with bilingual outside signs, the French predominant. They would require LARGE PRINT.

Finally, following an initial decade of economic sorrows, I have no doubt that a combination of Francophone ingenuity and imagination could make Quebec a viable little country. Its citizens would find it a decent place to live, *provided they were French-speaking*. But, without the rest of Canada acting as an increasingly bilingual buffer, it would become even more isolated from the North American mainstream, its standard of living diminished. Eventually, I suspect, it would revert to being a folkloric society. A place that people come from. Ireland without that country's genius.

Postscript

AN EXCERPT FROM THIS BOOK was published in *The New Yorker* last autumn, under the magazine's "Reporter at Large" rubric. For the most part, it recounted the political events that had led to the imposition of Bills 22 and 101, and, ultimately, the screwy Bill 178, but it also dealt briefly with the unfortunate history of anti-Semitism in Quebec. I had not expected the *New Yorker* piece to endear me to Québécois nationalists, but I was astonished by some of the reactions all the same, in English as well as French Canada. The most overheated, a Lise Bissonnette editorial in *Le Devoir*, struck me as the sort of letter many write in anger but usually have the wit not to mail. Ms. Bissonnette did not mention anywhere in her first bilious editorial on the subject that she was in fact reacting to my charge that *Le Devoir* was tainted by "a long and disgraceful history of anti-Semitism." But after I wrote an article in the Montreal *Gazette*, in which I pointed out this curious omission, she responded with a second editorial acknowledging my accusation, dismissing it as vicious, destroying *Le Devoir*'s reputation in a phrase.[1] She also noted—justifiably—that the charge in the *New Yorker* excerpt was proffered without qualifying evidence. This, I should explain, was due to limitations of space, not lack of material.

So let me now cite chapter and verse, beginning with the sensibility of Henri Bourassa, the founder of *Le Devoir*. On June 20, 1906, Bourassa told the House of Commons that he was not influenced by anti-racial motives. I assume that it was in order to prove his point that he then offered our parliamentarians the benefit of the following *pensée*: ". . . simply giving the experience of every civilized country . . . the Jews are the most undesirable class of people any country can have . . . they are vampires on a community instead of being contributors to the general welfare of the people. . . ."[2]

In 1915 Bourassa informed a French Canadian constituent that he had been cured of anti-Semitism. Well, not quite. "Perhaps I am mistaken," he wrote, "but the tendency of certain Catholics to explain *everything* [italics mine] as the action of Freemasonry and International Jewry has always seemed false to me."[3] In 1917 Bourassa wrote a letter to a Jewish MP, in which he protested that he was "not at all an anti-Semite. The best proof is that I was one of the MP's to protest against the excessive terms which the Sunday Law—prepared by the Liberal government and supported by a great majority of both parties—sustained against your co-religionists." It is true that Bourassa finally did vote against the bill that obliged Jewish shopkeepers to observe Sunday, not Saturday, as their sabbath. But, in doing so, he said, ". . . *while I think it wrong to encourage Jewish immigration* [italics mine again], the moment a Jew lands in this country and we collect his money, we owe him the same justice and equality that should govern every man in this country."[4]

To be fair to Bourassa, in 1929 he did condemn excessive nationalism in a pamphlet, *L'affaire de Providence et la crise religieuse en Nouvelle-Angleterre*, that sparked such anger in Quebec as to compel him to resign as editor of *Le Devoir*. So he was no longer in charge in the thirties, a decade which Ms. Bissonnette—uncharacteristically given to understatement this once—allows was not "the most glorious" in the newspaper's history.[5] In fact, it was a decade in which the racist effusions of *Le Devoir* more closely resembled *Der Stüermer* than any other newspaper I can think of. In those halcyon days—according to Esther Delisle's thesis *"Antisémitisme et nationalisme d'extrême droite dans la province de Québec, 1929-39"*—*Le Devoir* assumed the following editorial positions: Canadian nationality should not be granted to Jewish immigrants, Jews should be denied the right to vote, they should be issued a special passport, they should be obliged to live in ghettos, they should be deported. Mind you, none of this seems to have discomfited Pierre Anctil, head of French

Canadian studies at McGill. In a lengthy interview with *L'actualité*, he pronounced my comments on *Le Devoir* unjustified. "I have done research for my book about *Le Devoir*," he said, "and could find only twelve editorials hostile to Jews over ten years, in a very precise historical context."[6] Twelve editorials, maybe, but also hundreds of rabidly anti-Semitic articles blessed by that newspaper's editors. On the other hand, Anctil was absolutely right when he went on to describe *Le Devoir* as "a journal of ideas."[7] Following, a random sampling of these ideas, plucked from the pages of *Le Devoir*, circa 1929-39, by Esther Delisle:

"Charlie Chaplin is not English, he is a Jew."[8]

"Between 1910 and 1930 Montreal was flooded by the arrival of Austrians, Russians, or Poles, who were no more Austrian, Russian or Polish than you or I."[9]

Le Devoir's flock should avoid Jewish shopkeepers, who have "cheating and corruption in their bloodstream."[10]

"The mayor of New York, Fiorella La Guardia, has some Jewish blood in him."[11]

"Israel is king in Quebec."[12]

"Abraham, Isaac and Jacob wish to have a tenth province in Canada: the New Palestine."[13]

"In various federal government services, secretaries, office clerks and inspectors get their jobs because they can speak Yiddish."[14]

"The Jew Einstein made us accept on his word his theory of relativity."[15]

"If the 'anti-nazi refugees, be they Jewish or not,' came to settle in Canada, they would turn the country into 'Europe's dumping ground.'"[16]

"Why change one's name if one can't change one's nose?"[17]

In the world according to *Le Devoir*, Jews not only suffered from crooked noses but also from a distinctive body odor. "Even though it is not the nose that makes the Jew . . . it is often the nose that detects him."[18]

"Jack Benny smells strongly of garlic."[19]

I could quote many more examples of this sort of redneck

racism from the pages of *Le Devoir*, but I suspect that Lysiane Gagnon would still protest against "unfounded accusations of anti-Semitism flying all over,"[20] and Pierre Anctil would still insist, as he did in *L'actualité*, that even so this was "not enough to declare a newspaper anti-Semitic."[21] Actually, *Le Devoir* is not only tainted by a long and disgraceful history of anti-Semitism, but also has to answer for the pro-Vichy stance of its editor during World War II. In 1941, arguably one of the war's darkest years, a group of Québécois nationalists—so picayune as to interpret the struggle against Hitler as another British imperialist adventure—decided to form an organization that would oppose Ottawa's right to conscript young Canadians for military service overseas. "The usual elements flocked forth," wrote Conrad Black in *Duplessis*, "the St. Jean-Baptiste Society of Montreal, the Association catholique de la Jeunesse canadienne-française, the Junior Chamber of Commerce of Montreal. These and like-minded elements gathered around *Le Devoir* and organized a negative campaign for the upcoming plebiscite . . . the organization was given a name: La Ligue pour la défense du Canada."[22] Maxime Raymond, who became leader of this most incongruously named *ligue*, was seconded by Georges Pelletier, then editor of *Le Devoir*, and André Laurendeau, a future editor. On October 28, 1941, Pelletier, himself the author of numerous anti-Semitic diatribes in *Le Devoir*, introduced the now seventy-four-year-old Henri Bourassa to an audience at the Auditorium du Plateau. Bourassa proclaimed his longing for an "intelligent" peace whose participants would include "Pétain's France, Franco's Spain, Salazar's Portugal, and even Mussolini's Italy."[23] An unabashed admirer of the Marshal, he declared, "What France needs is not revenge against Prussia, but revenge against its own sins." He went on to say, "I believe that France is now passing through a period of attrition from which she will emerge morally and politically stengthened, provided that there are not too many traitors at her bosom nor too many of her sons seduced by foreigners into decrying abroad and at home their noble and aged leader."[24]

THE BLINKERED ANCTIL, once again limiting his research to editorials, could find no anti-Semitic material in *Le Devoir* after 1939. Possibly, he ought to look again. Meanwhile, I recommend he read *None Is Too Many, Canada and the Jews of Europe, 1933–1948*, by Irving Abella and Harold Troper. The authors write:

> On April 19, 1943, on the eve of the Jewish Passover and on the day when the final struggle of the doomed Jews of the Warsaw ghetto began, the Bermuda Conference opened. Canada had not been invited, but had been put on warning by the British government that it would be expected to admit two thousand refugees. It had also been put on warning by French Canada. *Le Devoir* castigated [Prime Minister Mackenzie] King for not demanding "avec insistance et fermeté" that Canada attend the conference in which Canada would likely be asked to accept refugees. Other Quebec newspapers cautioned the prime minister that he had best keep his guard up lest the Allies attempt to "dump" a large number of Jews in Canada's lap.[25]

After 1945, Anctil told *L'actualité*, ". . . *on ne trouve plus un mot sur les Juifs.*" (". . . you won't find another word about the Jews.")[26]

Think of it. Six million Jewish men, women, and children were shot or hanged or buried alive or boiled in their own fat or gassed or burned in ovens before the editors of *Le Devoir*, Quebec's brightest and best, scratched their heads, stroked their jaws, and came to the conclusion that it was no longer in good taste to print anti-Semitic bilge. We are not grateful.

ALTHOUGH ANDRÉ LAURENDEAU did not become editor of *Le Devoir* until 1958, he possibly qualified for the post by writing in *Les Cahiers du Jeune-Canada*, in 1933: "Everybody in the world knows that the Jews aspire to that happy day when they will dominate the world."

Among Laurendeau's many anti-Semitic articles there was at least one that dealt with the plight of the German Jews in the thirties:

Les Juifs ont convoqué, au commencement d'avril, une assemblée pour protester contre les prétendues persécutions d'Hitler contre leurs congénères. Je dis "prétendues," parce que des atrocités qu'on rapporte, rien n'est absolument prouvé. Il suffit de rappeler que toutes, ou presque, les agences de nouvelles sont entre les mains des Juifs, pour qu'un peu de scepticisme s'introduise en notre esprit quant à l'authenticité de ces persécutions.[27]

At the beginning of April, the Jews called an assembly to protest against Hitler's alleged persecution of their people. I say "alleged" because there has been no absolute proof of the reports of atrocities. If we remind ourselves that all, or almost all, the news agencies are in the hands of Jews, we become a little skeptical about the authenticity of these persecutions.

As late as 1964, as I have noted on page 94, Laurendeau upbraided the Montreal *Star* in his diary for pronouncing the Abbé Groulx, author of *L'Appel de la Race*, a racist. "It is unjust to attack him for things he is not guilty of," he wrote.[28]

As good at injustice collecting as anybody else in Canada, I could go on, on and on, but I have already been charged here, there, and everywhere with brooding on events long past; that is to say, outrages that occurred in the thirties and forties. This, astonishingly, from members of a people who have had *Je me souviens* stamped into every vehicle license plate in the province to remind us of events that happened more than two centuries ago. Or, put another way, *Moi aussi, je me souviens.*

Writing in *La Presse*, Lysiane Gagnon accused me of not taking into account the fact that Francophone attitudes toward Jews have changed since World War II. Responding in the Montreal *Gazette*, I wrote that Claude Ryan, for one, would not agree:

Addressing a Jewish audience in Montreal in the late sixties, he said, "I should like to mention for your consideration some of the opinions, or rather, the prejudices which seem to me to be still very much alive in the minds of most French Canadians as concerns Jews. In the eye of the average French Canadian, the Jew is still first and above all a money-maker. He is considered a person who will do practically anything in order to make a fast dollar."[29]

Lise Bissonnette, writing in *Le Devoir*, objected to the imprecision of my dating of Ryan's address as sometime "in the late sixties,"[30] and Professor Steven Davis, about whom more later, cast even more doubt on the origin of the quote, describing it as coming from "a speech *reportedly* made by Claude Ryan [italics mine]."[31] So let me now set the troubled minds of both Bissonnette and Davis at rest. Ryan's speech, "How French-Canadians See Jews," was included in *A Stable Society*, a collection of articles and speeches by the former publisher and editor of *Le Devoir*, edited and translated by Robert Guy Scully and Marc Plourde. It is introduced as follows on page 311:

> The following article, written in English almost ten years ago, for a Jewish audience, updates an important issue. The author refused to believe that French-Canadians are anti-Semitic [*sic*]. And he urges Jews to meet them halfway . . . on the neutral terrain of mutual understanding.

As *A Stable Society* was published in 1978, I assumed that Ryan had delivered his speech in either 1969 or 1970, describing honestly, if bluntly, what he understood to be the prejudices about Jews that still prevailed "in the minds of most French Canadians:" *and this, if Lysiane Gagnon is to be credited, some twenty years after these attitudes had supposedly changed.*

In Ryan's place, I might have taken advantage of my appearance before a Jewish audience to apologize for the racist trash earlier editors of *Le Devoir* had been guilty of peddling, and for the role the newspaper had played in protesting against Canada's becoming a "dumping ground" for Jewish refugees from Hitler. Instead, he told them that French Canadian prejudice "is nourished to a large extent—or was nourished in the past to a large extent—by lawyers, for instance, who used to specialize in certain aspects of the practice of their profession which were the least pleasant, such as collection of past accounts."[32]

Arguably, French Canadian prejudice against Jews had found far more nourishment in the past in the pages of *Le Devoir* than from contact with the occasional shyster of Jewish origin. Never mind. Ryan went on to say:

In addition, some Jews have tended to specialize in practices which leave much to be desired. I remember having read in the papers about notaries dealing in the land business, for instance, having developed all sorts of techniques: offices communicating by secret doors to facilitate rapid transactions on the operations that may be needed in order to make it possible for some names not to appear on official documents while the unnamed individuals actually still control all phases of the operation.[33]

Certainly not an anti-Semite himself, Ryan went on to talk about the "mentality and psychological attitudes" of many French Canadians:

Employers, Jewish employers, have the reputation of paying low salaries and being not too scrupulous about working conditions. This, again, can be explained by the fact that Jewish industrial leaders have not generally been involved in the most prosperous types of industry where the margin of profit is extremely limited as compared to heavy industry. But the prejudice still lingers in the French Canadian's mind that Jews have a tendency to exploit their workers and to exploit French Canadian manpower.[34]

2.

FOLLOWING THE PUBLICATION of my *New Yorker* article, Jean Dorion, president of the Montreal St. Jean-Baptiste Society, told reporters that I was "somebody who fundamentally doesn't like French Quebec. . . ."[35]

He was wrong on that count, but he could have argued quite accurately that I have nothing but contempt for his wretched society, which, in 1938, delivered to Parliament a petition signed by nearly 128,000 of its members, opposing "all immigration and especially Jewish immigration" to Canada.[36]

Responding to this sort of criticism, Steven Davis has reproached me for trafficking in "ancient history."[37] Well now, so far as I'm concerned ancient history is the nineteenth century, when the Jews of Rome were still locked into their ghetto every night and the Pope turned up in their synagogue once a year for a ceremonial spit on the chief rabbi's robes. On the other hand,

I consider it all-too-recent history that there are Jews, absent contemporaries of Steven Davis and myself, who could be alive today had not bigots conspired to deny them a haven in the thirties. In this shameful affair, let me hastily add, French Canadians were not alone. Let's just say they were in the vanguard and leave it at that.

Readers of Steven Davis's op-ed piece in the Montreal *Gazette* were informed that he was a professor of philosophy at Simon Fraser University in British Columbia, but there was no mention of the fact that he had a personal stake in the quarrel over my *New Yorker* piece: he also happens to be Lysiane Gagnon's husband. Some have suggested that it was devious of him not to acknowledge as much, but I prefer to think he was merely shy. It could be said, however, that his grasp of English is shaky. Professor Davis objected strongly to my alluding to *Le Devoir*'s "long and disgraceful history of anti-Semitism," because, he wrote, it implied to Americans that the newspaper was currently anti-Semitic. I implied no such thing. If the professor will consult his *Oxford English Dictionary*, he will find the first definition offered for "history" to be "narrative of past events."

ONE OF THE FIRST TO POUNCE on my *New Yorker* piece was Michel Bélanger, who rushed to judgment before he had even read it. "Foreigner is not the right expression for Richler," the banker told reporters. "I think the right expression is he doesn't belong."[38]

This, Lysiane Gagnon allowed in *La Presse*, did something to confirm my notion that, in an increasingly tribal climate, only *Québécois pure laine* were members of the family.[39] Ms. Gagnon also wrote that my article was vivid proof that I was a "poor political analyst."[40] Not being given to false modesty, I take this as a welcome opportunity to toot my own horn. Over the years my political pieces have been published, in England, in *Encounter*, the *Spectator*, the *New Statesman and Nation*, as it then was called, the *Sunday Times*, the *Guardian*, and the *Observer*;

and, in the United States (*The New Yorker* aside) in *Harper's*, *Atlantic Monthly*, the *New York Review of Books*, *Life*, and *Time*, among other publications. I would like to think all this is a tribute to my beautiful bod, but possibly, there were other considerations.

Ms. Gagnon also wrote that my article had been nasty, its accusations of anti-Semitism unfounded. Actually my accusations stemmed from a survey conducted by Professor Joseph Fletcher of the University of Toronto in 1987 in association with the Institute for Social Research of York University, also of Toronto. According to this survey, based on interviews with nearly 3,500 Canadians, anti-Semitism in Canada is most prevalent in Quebec. Speaking at the 22nd Plenary Assembly of the Canadian Jewish Congress held in Montreal in 1989, Professor Fletcher said that what made a difference in his survey of attitudes toward Jews, and a whopping difference, was region. "And where the problem is gravest is here in Quebec. On our index over seventy percent of Quebecers fell into our highly anti-Semitic category—not one-third, as one would expect on the basis of chance and as occurred in every other region. It is over 70 percent here. These findings indicate that while anti-Semitic sentiments are present in every region of the country, they are disproportionately concentrated in the province of Quebec. In this rather ominous sense, Quebec is truly a distinctive society."[41]

Since then, Lysiane Gagnon, returning to the subject in a December *Globe and Mail*, has pronounced the York University survey questionable, to say the least. On the other hand, there are now two more surveys that confirm the findings of York's Institute of Social Research. The first was analyzed in the lead article in a recent issue of *Viewpoints*, the literary supplement of *The Canadian Jewish News*. The data in this survey, culled from a random sample of 3,377 Canadians, originated in a 1984 National Election Study, which was funded by the Social Sciences and Humanities Research Council of Canada, and led to a paper that was published in *The Canadian Journal of Sociology*. That paper and the report in *Viewpoints* were both the work of Robert Brym, a professor of sociology at the University of Toronto, and Rhonda Lenton, an assistant professor of sociology at McMaster University, in Hamilton. They concluded that the overall level of anti-Semitism was quite modest in Canada as a whole. "The only populous province with a relatively high level of anti-Semitism (and a large Jewish population) is Quebec." They blamed this situation on the teachings of the Church, noting that it was Catholics of French origin who accounted for the tendency of Catholics to be more anti-Semitic than Protestants:

> "Ten percent of Catholics who spoke only English at home disliked Jews. That is 4 percent below the national figure for all Canadians. In contrast, 24 percent of Catholics who spoke only French at home displayed such attitudes: nearly twice the national figure. The latter figure was identical for Quebec considered alone."[42]

The second survey, its findings rooted in a seven-year study by Environics, was sponsored by the B'nai B'rith Canada League for Human Rights. Organized by Taylor Buckner, a professor of sociology at Concordia University, in Montreal, it polled more than 14,000 Canadians, just about four times as many as the separate surveys undertaken earlier, and surfaced— Lysiane Gagnon notwithstanding—with the same embarrassing news: anti-Semitic attitudes are more prevalent in Quebec, and particularly among Francophones, than elsewhere in Canada. The report concluded that a quarter of Quebec's respondents were tainted by anti-Semitic attitudes, by far the largest proportion for a province with a large Jewish population. It pointed out that 20 to 25 percent of all Quebec residents through the years studies stated that they would not vote for a Jewish candidate even if they were running for the party they normally support. In 1989, 19 percent of all Canadians agreed Jews had too much power; in Quebec, the figure was 26 percent. Discussing the report at a recent B'nai B'rith meeting, Stephen Scheinberg, chairman of that organization's League for Human Rights, noted, "[Quebec] nationalism, having been historically interwoven with anti-Semitism and when combined with a poor economy, is a cause for concern."

Ms. Gagnon also charged me with presenting "sloppy research," in "the October issue of *The New Yorker*,"[43] which suggested the magazine is a monthly. It is not. Furthermore, my article was published in the September 23 issue. In *La Presse*, Ms. Gagnon allowed that I had written that neither Lévesque nor Parizeau was an anti-Semite; but did that, she asked, imply that most other nationalists were subject to that malady? No. However, I would still insist that Quebec nationalism—from Groulx, through Georges Pelletier's *Le Devoir*, the Bloc populaire, the Ligue, and, most recently, Péladeau—has undeniably anti-Semitic roots. And so it follows that when thousands take to the streets, chanting *"le Québec aux Québécois,"* we can readily understand why our children continue to leave.

Writing in the *Gazette*, columnist Gretta Chambers, like Lysiane Gagnon, Steven Davis, and others, felt that the impression I had left "that Abbé Groulx is still an intellectual or social force in Quebec is deeply distressing to francophone Quebecers who have completely repudiated both his narrow Catholicism and the xenophobic society it called for."[44] In that case, Chambers, Gagnon, Davis, and God knows how many deeply distressed Francophone Quebecers disagree with René Lévesque, who, citing a pantheon of great *québécois* names, in *An Option for Quebec*, began with Etienne Parent and Lafontaine and ended with Abbé Groulx.[45] In that case, they disagree with André Laurendeau, who wrote, "We loved him dearly,"[46] when the eighty-nine-year-old bigot died in 1967. And they disagree with Claude Ryan, who wrote: "He was . . . the spiritual father of modern Quebec. Everything noteworthy, everything novel on the Quebec scene, carried the imprint of Groulx's thought."[47] Finally, they disagree with those nationalists who, far from repudiating Groulx, have named a major Montreal métro station after him, as well as a junior college, numerous schools, and a chain of mountains.

TO RETURN BRIEFLY TO MS. BISSONNETTE: *Le Devoir*'s editorial writer seems to be of the opinion that I was writing satire in *The New Yorker*. This is flattering, but honesty compels me to protest that no living satirist could improve on what has actually been happening here. However, I do appreciate Ms. Bissonnette's confusion. Whenever I have described Quebec's sign laws at dinner parties, whether in New York or London, the other guests have accused me of inventing the details. They have also warned me never to put it in a novel—nobody would believe anything so patently absurd.

Ms. Bissonnette's first editorial on the subject, titled "Vu du Woody's Pub," suggests that my article was "delivered with the flavour of a smoky bar at dawn, when paranoia embalms and reason nods."[48] Had she bothered to make inquiries, she would have discovered that my wife and I have been living in the Townships for the past five years and only get to Montreal once a week. On my day off in Montreal, she would have learned that I usually frequented Woody's, until it closed last winter, either for lunch or for a few drinks after five in the afternoon, at which time I strongly suspect Ms. Bissonnette sends out for a yogurt (flavored, if she is feeling really wicked).

THE DAY AFTER MY ARTICLE APPEARED, Gérard LeBlanc wrote in *La Presse* that I had been paid $40,000 (US) for it,[49] and this story was confirmed in the next morning's *Globe and Mail*, English Canada's paper of record. Of course, neither LeBlanc nor the *Globe* bothered to check this figure out with me. Unfortunately, it was wrong. Never mind: the subtext was that I had done the dirty deed for money. Seemingly, LeBlanc, Bissonnette, et al. can write out of inner conviction, but nobody would take issue with them unless there were big bucks involved. I understand this thinking. For, as Claude Ryan went on to say in his illuminating address to that Jewish audience in Montreal in the late sixties: "Whenever a French Canadian wants to pass a severe judgment on one of his compatriots, he will often be heard to say, 'He's a bad Jew'—meaning that he made a fast dollar at the expense of his compatriots, either in the practice of his profession, or the conduct of his business."[50]

I am sorry, then, to have to report that there is actually damn little money to be made writing about Quebec politics, favorably or unfavorably, for magazines or book publishers outside of Canada, all of whom justifiably consider the subject parochial. The fact that some columnists here, English and French, think this is how I support myself between novels is a measure of their provincial innocence. I wrote *The New Yorker* article and this book because—Michel Bélanger notwithstanding—this is my home and I care deeply about what is happening here. So I am more than somewhat baffled by those who have explained my article by saying I don't like living in Quebec or that I suffer from a nostalgia for the past. "My lost paradise," wrote Agnès Gruda in *La Presse*.[51]

What past? Which paradise?

The thirties, when *Le Devoir* was raging against the Jews?

The forties, when Marshal Pétain was being celebrated as a hero, and Francophones marched down The Main shouting, "Kill the Jews"?

Or maybe the fifties, when me and my chums on St. Urbain Street controlled the levers of financial power in the province and clapped hands every time the thuggish Duplessis sent his uniformed hoodlums out to crack strikers' heads?

SIFTING THOUGH RESPONSES to my article in the French press, I can identify several common threads.

If there are undeniably some Francophones who are anti-Semitic, several columnists wrote, then they are no more numerous than those to be found in English Canada. Well, no. Not according to that York University survey. And if that's the case, why have something like 30,000 Jews, born and bred in Quebec, many of them bilingual, quit the province for English Canada or the United States during the past twenty years?

While attacking *Le Devoir* for its anti-Semitic history, why didn't I also note that at the time McGill had a Jewish student quota? So, for that matter, did Sir George Williams College, as it then was, but I had already written about that more than once. In fact, in the past, I have been no less critical of WASP bigotry and English Canadian nationalism than I have been of Francophone follies.

I have also been singled out for not being bilingual myself after all these years, and it's true and it is deeply embarrassing. However, Lise Bissonnette is wrong when she writes that my French is so feeble I can't read her editorials. Unfortunately, I can read them.

I wish I could say as much for the ability of a number of French-speaking journalists to read my work. Agnès Gruda, for instance, charged me with writing in *The New Yorker* that Francophone Quebecers were becoming more and more unilingual,[52] but I had written no such thing. What I had done was to quote an English-speaking businessman, saying: "Years ago, if we placed an ad in the papers looking for a bilingual employee, a good many of the applicants were Francophones. Now they are for the most part Anglophones, Italians, or Greeks. The young Francophones are being forced to revert to unilingualism, which will deny them most jobs, whether this province separates, drifts out to sea, or whatever."[53]

Alain Dubuc, chief editorial writer for *La Presse*, was among the many who claimed that I had called Francophone grandmothers sows.[54] This was also untrue. What I had actually written was: ". . . in the past, [Francophone] families of a dozen children were not uncommon. This punishing level of reproduction, which seemed to me based on the assumption that women were sows, was encouraged with impunity from the sidelines by the Abbé Groulx, whose newspaper, *L'Action Française*, founded in 1917, preached *la revanche des berceaux* [the revenge of the cradles]. . . ."[55] Gretta Chambers, a columnist much given to soft-pedaling, put it differently. After protesting my choice of language, she demonstrated how the same thought could be sugar-coated and served up as fudge. "The reproductive hardships that their foremothers were called upon to assume," she wrote, "horrify many Quebecers today."[56] In my case, I was simply echoing the distinguished Québécois philosopher Jean Le Moyne, who wrote in *Convergences* that the

Catholic church in Quebec despised women. And I was amazed that, in the uproar that followed my comment, Francophone feminists did not rise to my defense. After all, it was their bodies I was defending against employment as factory farms for political purposes. It was the church, not I, that had no regard for their health.

It is sometimes difficult to fathom what Mrs. Chambers is about. She concludes her column by saying. "An article like Richler's encourages [young bilingual Anglophones] to feel there is no hope for them here,"[57] which was naughty of me. But then she goes on to say, "and the reaction to the Richler piece confirms their fears," which seems to suggest that I was right after all.

I also cannot allow a blast that was published in the *Globe and Mail* to pass without comment. Ray Conlogue's column began: "Every two or three years Mordecai Richler mounts the lucrative podium of a well-known American magazine to deliver himself of a thunderbolt directed against the province of Quebec."[58] Actually, I have written three other pieces about Quebec in the last fourteen years, the last one in 1984. Two of them appeared in *Atlantic Monthly* and one in *Geo*. Closer to the mark, Conlogue wrote, "Conspicuously absent from Richler's piece was a word about the flourishing Québécois culture."[59] Right. There was also not a word about Québécois hockey players, surgeons, restaurateurs, or gardeners, since the article was about the province's language laws. In his column, Conlogue also claimed that he had phoned *The New Yorker* and been told "that the magazine had been overwhelmed by a flood of hostile, and apparently unexpected, phone calls about the article."[60] I have also been in touch with *The New Yorker*. The only person in the editorial department whom Conlogue spoke to declined an interview, but on the understanding that what he would say was not for publication, he added that there had been *some* phone calls in praise of my article, and others from people displeased by it. He also had the foresight to write down immediately what Conlogue had said to him. Complaining about the fact that I had been commissioned to write the article,

Conlogue said: "You do understand that [Richler] is a disaffected, English-speaking, Jewish writer, outside the mainstream, and having him represent us is like having a Hispanic speak for all of America."

AND, A FINAL RESPONSE to those who maintain I have never had anything good to say about Quebec.

What follows, complete with its error about the state-of-health of the PQ, is the last paragraph of *Home Sweet Home*, a book of essays about Canada which I published in 1985:

"For all my complaints about the PQ, a nationalist aberration now in sharp decline, I could not live anywhere else in Canada but Montreal. So far as one can generalize, the most gracious, cultivated, and innovative people in this country are French Canadians. Certainly they have given us the most exciting politicians of our time: Trudeau, Lévesque. Without them, Canada would be an exceedingly boring and greatly diminished place. If I consider the PQ an abomination it's only because, should their policies prevail, everybody in Canada would be diminished. This is still a good neighborhood, worth preserving. So long as it remains intact."[61]

Appendix

The Sign Laws

58. Public signs and posters and commercial advertising, outside or intended for the public outside, shall be solely in French.

Similarly, public signs and posters and commercial advertising shall be solely in French:

(1) inside commercial centres and their access ways, except inside the establishments located there;

(2) inside any public means of transport and its access ways;

(3) inside the establishments of business firms contemplated in section 136;

(4) inside the establishments of business firms employing fewer than fifty but more than five persons, where such firms share, with two or more business firms, the use of a trademark, a firm name or an appellation by which they are known to the public.

The Government may, however, by regulation, prescribe the terms and conditions according to which public signs and posters and public advertising may be both in French and in another language, under the conditions set forth in the second paragraph of section 58.1 inside the establishments of business firms contemplated in subparagraphs 3 and 4 of the second paragraph.

The Government may, in such regulation, establish categories of business firms, prescribe terms and conditions which vary according to the category and reinforce the conditions set forth in the second paragraph of section 58.1.

1977, c.5, s. 58; 1983, c. 56, s. 12; 1988, c.54, s.1.

58.1 Inside establishments, public signs and posters and commercial advertising shall be in French.

They may also be both in French and in another language, providing they are intended only for the public inside the establishments and that French is markedly predominant.

1988, c. 54, s. 1.

— from Charter of the French language, updated to 1 August 1989
Last amendment: 1 July 1989

A week later, on August 8, 1989, the *Gazette officielle du Québec* published a clarification of 58.1:

Regulation facilitating the implementation of the second paragraph of section 58.1 of the Charter of the French language:

This regulation has been made without amendment by Order in Council 1130-89, 12 July 1989.
(1989) G.O. 2, p. 2779.

8 August 1989
Regulation facilitating the implementation of the second paragraph of section 58.1 of the Charter of the French language.

1. In public signs and posters and posted commercial advertising that are both in French and in another language, the French is markedly predominant where the text in French has a much greater visual impact than the text in another language.

2. The text in French is deemed to have a much greater visual impact in public signs and posted commercial advertising that are both in French and in another language on the same sign where the following conditions are met:

(1) the space allotted to the text in French is at least twice as large as the space allotted to the text in the other language;

(2) the characters used in the text in French are at least twice as large as the characters used in the text in the other language;

(3) the other characteristics of that sign or poster and that advertising do not have the effect of reducing the visual impact of the text in French.

3. The text in French is deemed to have a much greater visual impact in public signs and posters and posted commercial advertising that are both in French and in another language on separate signs of the same size where the following conditions are met:

(1) the signs bearing the text in French are at least twice as numerous as the signs bearing the text in another language;

(2) the characters used in the text in French are at least as large as the characters used in the text in the other language;

(3) the other characteristics of that sign or poster and that advertising do not have the effect of reducing the visual impact of the text in French.

4. The text in French is deemed to have a much greater visual impact in public signs and posters and posted commercial advertising that are both in French and in another language on separate signs of different sizes when the following conditions are met:

(1) the signs bearing the text in French are at least as numerous as the signs bearing the text in another language;

(2) the signs bearing the text in French are at least twice as large as the signs bearing the text in the other language;

(3) the characters used in the text in French are at least twice as large as the characters used in the other language;

(4) the characteristics of that sign or poster and that advertising do not have the effect of reducing the visual impact of the text in French.

5. This Regulation comes into force on the fifteenth day following the date of its publication in the *Gazette officielle du Québec* together with a notice indicating the date of its adoption by the Government.

Notes

ONE

1. A presentation to the Standing Committee of the Senate and the House of Commons on Official Languages, Mar. 28, 1990, by Ronald Leach, President, Alliance for the Preservation of English in Canada, p. 2.
2. Official Languages Act of Canada, Sec. 2.
3. A Brief Opposing Bill c-72, Proposed Official Languages Act for Canada, presented to the Legislative Committee on Bill c-72, Apr. 1988, by Ronald Leach, President, Alliance for the Preservation of English in Canada, pp. 1–2.
4. New Democratic Party MP Ian Waddell, as quoted by Hubert Bauch, in Montreal *Gazette*, Apr. 14, 1990.
5. Ibid.
6. J. V. Andrew, *Bilingual Today, French Tomorrow* (Kitchener, Ont.: Andrew Books, 1977), p. ii.
7. Ibid., p. 1.
8. Ibid., p. 89.
9. J. V. Andrew, *Enough! Enough French. Enough Quebec.* (Kitchener, Ont.: Andrew Books, 1988), p. 9.
10. Ibid., p. 5.
11. Toronto *Globe and Mail*, Oct. 22, 1990.

TWO

1. Lord Durham Report, as quoted in *Canada*, by Brian Moore, p. 87.
2. Roy MacLaren, *Canadians on the Nile, 1882–1898* (British Columbia: University of British Columbia Press, 1978), p. 167.

3. Toronto *Globe and Mail*, Aug. 4, 1990.
4. Sheila McLeod Arnopoulos and Dominique Clift, *The English Fact in Quebec* (Montreal: McGill-Queen's University Press, 1980), pp. 56–57.
5. Léandre Bergeron, *The History of Quebec, A Patriote's Handbook* (Toronto: New Canada Publications, 1971), p. 118.
6. Canada Act, 1982, Fundamental Freedoms. 2 (b)
7. Donald Johnston ed., *Pierre Trudeau Speaks Out on Meech Lake* (Toronto: General Paperbacks, 1990), p. 29.
8. René Lévesque, *An Option for Quebec* (Toronto: McClelland & Stewart, 1968), p. 14.
9. René Lévesque, *Memoirs* (Toronto: McClelland & Stewart, 1986), p. 186.
10. *Time* (Cdn Edition), Jan. 13, 1975.
11. Montreal *Gazette*, Sept. 9, 1982.
12. Ibid., Aug. 19, 1989.
13. *Le Devoir*, Oct. 4, 1986.
14. John Sawatsky, *Men in the Shadows* (Toronto: Doubleday, 1980), p. 133.

THREE

1. Rod McQueen, *Blind Trust, Inside the Sinclair Stevens Affair* (Toronto: Macmillan of Canada, 1987), p. 27.
2. Ibid., p. 144.
3. Ibid., p. 146.
4. Herbert Marx, MNA, "Quebec in the 70s: Looking Backwards," based on Marx's 1978 Corry Lecture at Queen's University, Kingston, Ont. *Viewpoints*, Vol. 10, No. 4, Spring 1980 (Montreal: Canadian Jewish Congress), p. 18.

5. Montreal *Gazette*, Sept. 22, 1987.
6. Mordecai Richler, *Home Sweet Home* (Toronto: Penguin Books, 1985), p. 255.
7. Ibid.
8. Montreal *Gazette*, Aug. 18, 1987.
9. Ibid., Mar. 11, 1988.
10. Ibid., Mar. 25, 1988.
11. Ibid., Nov. 29, 1988.
12. Montreal *Star*, May 14, 1964.

FOUR

1. Toronto *Globe and Mail*, Dec. 2, 1988.
2. Montreal *Gazette*, Dec. 3, 1988.
3. Ibid., Dec. 16, 1988.
4. Ibid.
5. Ibid., Dec. 19, 1988.
6. Toronto *Globe and Mail*, Dec. 20, 1988.
7. Mordecai Richler, "A House Divided," *Geo*, August 1980.
8. Montreal *Gazette*, Dec. 21, 1988.
9. Ibid.
10. Ibid., Dec. 22, 1988.
11. Ibid., Dec. 23, 1988.
12. Ibid.
13. Ibid., Dec. 31, 1988.
14. Ibid., Feb. 1, 1989.
15. Ibid.

FIVE

1. Montreal *Gazette*, Jan. 21, 1989.
2. Ibid.
3. Ibid., Feb. 6, 1989.
4. Charles Dickens, *American Notes and Pictures from Italy* (London: Oxford University Press, 1957), p. 210.
5. Rosemary Pitcher, *Château Frontenac* (Toronto: McGraw-Hill Ryerson, 1971), p. 13.
6. Ibid.
7. Joseph Sansom, Esq., *Travels in Lower Canada* (London: Sir Richard Phillips & Co., 1820), p. iii.
8. Ibid., p. iv.
9. Ibid., pp. 41–42.
10. Ibid., pp. 47–48.
11. Montreal *Gazette*, Feb. 8, 1988.
12. Ibid.

SIX

1. Montreal *Gazette*, Feb. 15, 1990.
2. Ibid., Mar. 26, 1991.
3. *Saturday Night* magazine, Apr. 1991.
4. Louis Falardeau in *La Presse*, Feb. 11, 1989.
5. William Johnson in Montreal *Gazette*, Feb. 15, 1989.
6. Ibid., Feb. 17, 1989.
7. Ibid., Feb. 21, 1989.
8. Ibid., Feb. 22 and 23, 1989.
9. Ibid., Mar. 13, 1989.
10. Ibid., Mar. 15, 1989.
11. Ibid., Mar. 1, 1989.
12. L. Ian MacDonald, *From Bourassa to Bourassa: A Pivotal Decade in Canadian History* (Montreal: Harvest Press, 1984), p. 34.
13. Ibid., p. 18.
14. Ibid., p. 79.
15. Claude Ryan, *A Stable Society*, trans. Robert Guy Scully, with Marc Plounde (Montreal: Editions Héritage, 1978), p. 148.
16. Ibid., p. 134.
17. Montreal *Gazette*, Mar. 21, 1989.
18. Ibid., Sept. 9, 1989.
19. Ibid., Mar. 17, 1989.
20. Ibid., May 2, 1989.
21. Robert McCrum, William Cran, and Robert MacNeil, *The Story of English* (New York: Penguin Books, 1989), pp. 19–20.
22. Montreal *Gazette*, May 4, 1989.
23. Ibid.
24. Ibid.

SEVEN

1. Mrs. C. M. Day, *Pioneers of the Eastern Townships* (Montreal: John Lovell, 1863), p. 161.
2. William Bryant Bullock, *Beautiful Waters* (Newport, Vt.: Pigwidgeon Press, 1985), p. 18.
3. Day, *Pioneers of the Eastern Townships*, p. 164.
4. Ibid., p. 166.
5. Ibid., p. 168.

6. Sherbrooke *Record*, May 22, 1989.
7. Mrs. C. M. Day, *History of the Eastern Townships* (Montreal: John Lovell, 1869), p. 150.
8. Ibid., pp. 152–53.
9. Ronald Rudin, *The Forgotten Quebecers, A History of English-Speaking Quebec, 1759–1980* (Montreal: Institut québécois de recherche sur la culture, 1985), p. 52.
10. Sherbrooke *Record*, May 23, 1989.
11. Walter Stewart, *True Blue, The Loyalist Legend* (Toronto: Collins, 1985), p. 175.
12. Bernard Epps, *Tales of the Eastern Townships* (Lennoxville, Que.: Sun Books, 1980), pp. 99–100.
13. Pearl Mailloux Grenier, *The Lost Nation* (Knowlton, Que.: The Brome County Historical Society, 1976), p. 105.
14. Dorothy Williams, *Blacks in Montreal 1628–1986: An Urban Demography* (Cowansville, Que.: Les Editions Yvon Blais Inc., 1991), p. 12.
15. Sherbrooke *Record*, May 23, 1989.
16. Montreal *Gazette*, July 6, 1989.
17. Sherbrooke *Record*, Aug. 18, 1989.

EIGHT

1. Montreal *Gazette*, Mar. 20, 1989.
2. *La Presse*, May 14, 1962.
3. Montreal *Gazette*, Sept. 7, 1989.
4. Ibid.

NINE

1. Bergeron, *The History of Quebec*, p. 184.
2. Montreal *Gazette*, Sept. 24, 1988.
3. Ibid.
4. Toronto *Globe and Mail*, Jan. 29, 1989.
5. Ibid.
6. Montreal *Gazette*, Sept. 24, 1988.
7. Ibid.
8. FDR letter as quoted in Jean-François Lisée's *In the Eye of the Eagle* (Toronto: HarperCollins, 1990), p. 5.
9. Montreal *Gazette*, Sept. 24, 1988.
10. *La Presse*, Jan. 28, 1989.

TEN

1. Erna Paris, *Jews, An Account of Their Experience in Canada* (Toronto: Macmillan of Canada 1988), p. 52.
2. Bergeron, *The History of Quebec*, p. 75.
3. Miriam Chapin, *Quebec Now* (Toronto: Ryerson Press, 1955), p. 85.
4. Ibid., p. 162.
5. Ramsey Cook, ed., *French Canadian Nationalism, An Anthology* (Toronto: Macmillan of Canada), p. 201.
6. Abbé Groulx, *Variations on a Nationalist's Theme*, ed. Susan Mann Trofimenkoff (Toronto: Gage, 1983), pp. 40–41.
7. Stuart Rosenberg, *The Jewish Community in Canada*, Vol. I (Toronto: McClelland & Stewart, 1983), p. 145.
8. Ibid.
9. Mason Wade, *The French Canadians*, Vol. II, 1911–1967 (Toronto: Macmillan of Canada, 1968), p. 497.
10. Ibid., p. 498.
11. Montreal *Gazette*, Apr. 29, 1990.
12. André Laurendeau, *Witness for Quebec*, tr. Philip Stratford (Toronto: Macmillan of Canada, 1973), pp. 178–79.
13. Bergeron, *The History of Quebec*, p. 187.
14. Victor Teboul, *Mythe et images du Juif au Québec* (Montreal: Editions de Lagrave, 1977), p. 181.
15. Ibid., pp. 181–82.
16. Bergeron, *The History of Quebec*, p. 183.
17. Laurendeau, *Witness for Quebec*, pp. 71–72.
18. Bergeron, *The History of Quebec*, p. 184.
19. Brian McKenna and Susan Purcell, *Drapeau* (Toronto: Clarke, Irwin, 1980), p. 375.
20. Ibid., p. 189.
21. André Laurendeau, *The Diary of André Laurendeau, 1964–1967* (Toronto:

Lorimer & Co., 1991), p. 48.
22. Ibid., p. 51.
23. Ibid.
24. Ibid., pp. 76–77.
25. Teboul, *Mythe et images du Juif au Québec*, pp. 173–74.
26. McKenna, Purcell, *Drapeau* p. 63.

ELEVEN

1. As quoted in Teboul, *Mythe et images du Juif au Québec*, p. 38.
2. Laurendeau, *The Diary of André Laurendeau*, p. 98.
3. Stewart, *True Blue*, p. 4.
4. Conrad Black, "Can't Build New Canada on Appeasement," *Financial Post*, Feb. 6, 1991.
5. McKenna and Purcell, *Drapeau*, p. 106.
6. *Seminar on French Canada* (Montreal *Star* transcript, May 1963), p. 8.
7. Ibid., pp. 2–3.

TWELVE

1. Laurendeau, *The Diary of André Laurendeau*, p. 94.
2. Luc d'Iberville-Moreau, *Lost Montreal* (Toronto: Oxford University Press, 1955), p. 7.
3. Montreal *Gazette*, Sept. 30, 1989.
4. Ibid.
5. Ibid.
6. Ibid., Apr. 6, 1990
7. Ibid.
8. Ibid.
9. *Globe and Mail Report on Business Magazine*, Sept. 1987.
10. Ibid.
11. Ibid.
12. *La Presse*, Apr. 14, 1990.
13. Montreal *Gazette*, Apr. 19, 1990.
14. Ibid., June 14, 1990.

THIRTEEN

1. Parti Québécois, *La Souveraineté: Pourquoi? Comment?*, May 1990.
2. Ibid.
3. Montreal *Gazette*, February 23, 1991.

4. Jacques Langlais and David Rome. *Jews and French Quebecers*. Original source, J.P. Gaboury, "Le nationalism de Lionel Groulx, Aspects idéologiques," *Cahiers des sciences sociales, No. 6* (Ottawa: Editions de l'Université d'Ottawa, 1970), pp. 35–36.
5. As quoted in William F. Shaw and Lionel Albert, *Partition, The Price of Quebec's Independence* (Montreal: Thornhill Publishing, 1980), p. 16.
6. Ibid, p. 23.
7. Ibid., p. 25.
8. Ibid.
9. Ibid., pp. 28–29.
10. Ibid., pp. 105–06.
11. Montreal *Gazette*, July 10, 1990.
12. Montreal *Gazette*, September 15, 1990.
13. Ibid., April 9, 1991.
14. *New York Times*, June 24, 1990.

FOURTEEN

1. Sherbrooke *Record*, May 18, 1990.
2. Montreal *Gazette*, May 19, 1990.
3. Toronto *Globe and Mail*, May 19, 1990.
4. MacDonald, *From Bourassa to Bourassa*, p. 239.
5. Montreal *Gazette*, May 19, 1990.
6. Ibid., Sept. 29, 1990.
7. Laurendeau, *The Diary of André Laurendeau*, p. 21.
8. Mordecai Richler, "Oh! Canada," *Atlantic Monthly*, Dec. 1977.
9. Elliot J. Feldman and Neil Nevitte, eds., *The Future of North America: Canada, the United States, and Quebec Nationalism* (Cambridge, Mass.: Harvard University Press, 1979), p. 61.
10. Ibid., p. 63.
11. Georges Mathews, *Quiet Resolution: Quebec's Challenge to Canada* (Toronto: Summerhill Press, 1990), p. 58.
12. Feldman and Nevitte, eds., *The Future of North America*, p. 64.
13. Ibid., p. 65.
14. Ibid., p. 66.

15. Ibid., p. 64.
16. Montreal *Gazette*, June 21, 1990.
17. Ibid., Sept. 25, 1990.
18. Ibid., Sept. 29, 1990.
19. Ibid.
20. Ibid., Dec. 16, 1988.
21. Ibid., Sept. 29, 1990.
22. Ibid., Oct. 5, 1990.
23. Ibid.
24. Ibid.
25. Ibid.

FIFTEEN

1. Montreal *Gazette*, Jan. 20, 1988.
2. *Condé Nast Traveler*, Jan. 1988.
3. Ibid., Oct. 1987.
4. Montreal *Gazette*, July 12, 1989.
5. Ibid.
6. Ibid.
7. Ibid.
8. As quoted in Peter Brimelow, *The Patriot Gome: National Dreams and Political Realities* (Toronto: Key Porter, 1986) p. 12.
9. *New York Times*, July 16, 1982.
10. Notes for an address by Jacques-Yvan Morin, Sept. 1, 1982.
11. Mordecai Richler, *New York Times* Sports section, Sept. 29, 1985.
12. J. L. Granatstein and David Stafford, *Spy Wars* (Toronto: Key Porter Books, 1990), p. 200.
13. Ibid., p. 203.
14. Ibid.
15. Ibid.
16. Lisée, *In the Eye of the Eagle*, p. 2.
17. Ibid., p. 2.
18. Ibid., p. 285.
19. Ibid.
20. Ibid., p. 292.
21. Ibid.
22. Ibid., p. 293.
23. Ibid., p. 294.
24. Ibid.
25. Ibid., p. 300.
26. Ibid., p. 302.
27. Ibid., p. 210.
28. Ibid., p. 66.

SIXTEEN

1. Montreal *Gazette*, June 23, 1990.
2. Ibid.
3. Ibid.
4. Toronto *Globe and Mail*, June 23, 1990.
5. Ibid.
6. Montreal *Gazette*, June 24, 1990.
7. Ibid.
8. Andrew Cohen, *A Deal Undone: The Making and Breaking of the Meech Lake Accord* (Toronto and Vancouver: Douglas and McIntyre, 1990), p. 64.
9. Ibid, p. 74.
10. Ibid.
11. Toronto *Star*, May 28, 1987.
12. Ibid.
13. Pierre Bourgualt, *Now or Never! Manifesto for ann Independent Quebec*, trans. David Homel (Toronto: Key Porter Books, 1991), p. 14.
14. Philip Resnick, *Letters to a Québécois Friend* (Montreal and Kingston: McGill-Queen's University Press, 1990), p. 3.
15. *Globe and Mail*, January 7, 1988.
16. Ibid.
17. Pierre Fournier, *A Meech Lake Post-Mortem*, trans. Sheila Fischman (Montreal and Kingston: McGill-Queen's University Press, 1990), p. 63.
18. Bourgault, *Now or Never!* p. 14.
19. Ibid., p. 111.
20. Fournier, *A Meech Lake Post-Mortem*, p. ix-x.
21. Mathews, *Quiet Resolution*, p. 32.
22. Fournier, *A Meech Lake Post-Mortem*, p. x.
23. Ibid., pp. 3–4.
24. Mathews, *Quiet Resolution*, p. xii.
25. Sherbrooke *Record*, June 12, 1990.

SEVENTEEN

1. Toronto *Globe and Mail*, May 23, 1990.
2. Ibid.
3. Ibid.
4. Montreal *Gazette*, April 1, 1988.
5. Ibid.
6. Ibid.

7. Ibid., June 18, 1988.
8. Ibid., Aug. 6, 1988.
9. Ibid., Sept. 1, 1989.
10. Toronto *Globe and Mail*, May 18, 1991.
11. Montreal *Gazette*, May 23, 1990.
12. Ibid.
13. Ibid.
14. Ibid.
15. Toronto *Globe and Mail*, June 27, 1990.
16. Ibid., June 30, 1990.
17. Montreal *Gazette*, July 4, 1990.
18. Ibid.
19. Toronto *Globe and Mail*, July 26, 1990.
20. Montreal *Gazette*, Aug. 14, 1990.
21. Ibid., Aug. 23, 1990.

EIGHTEEN

1. Montreal *Gazette*, Aug. 9, 1990.
2. Ibid., Aug. 10, 1990.
3. Toronto *Star*, July 25, 1990.
4. Ibid.
5. Montreal *Gazette*, Aug. 27, 1990.
6. *La Presse*, Sept. 1, 1990.
7. Montreal *Gazette*, Sept. 26, 1990.
8. Ibid., Sept. 7, 1990.
9. Toronto *Globe and Mail*, Aug. 30, 1991.
10. Montreal *Gazette*, Sept. 8, 1990.

NINETEEN

1. Montreal *Gazette*, Oct. 27, 1990.
2. Ibid., Nov. 13, 1990.
3. Ibid.
4. Montreal *Gazette*, Aug. 14, 1990.
5. Ibid., Nov. 24, 1990.
6. Ibid., Jan. 30, 1988.
7. Ibid., Nov. 14, 1990.
8. Ibid., Nov. 15, 1990.
9. Ibid., Dec. 2, 1990.
10. Ibid., Dec. 5, 1990.
11. Toronto *Globe and Mail*, Dec. 24, 1990.

TWENTY

1. Montreal *Gazette*, Oct. 22, 1990.

2. Ibid.
3. Ibid.
4. Ibid., Sept. 18, 1990
5. Ibid.
6. Ibid., Sept. 8, 1990.
7. Ibid., Dec. 18, 1990.
8. Toronto *Globe and Mail*, Dec. 18, 1990.
9. Ibid.
10. Montreal *Gazette*, Dec. 1, 1990.
11. Ibid., Dec. 29, 1990.
12. Ibid., Jan 12, 1991.
13. Ibid., Feb. 16. 1991.
14. Ibid., Dec. 12, 1990.
15. Sherbrooke *Record*, Dec. 12, 1990.
16. Montreal *Gazette*, Dec. 20, 1990.
17. Ibid., Dec. 21, 1990.
18. Ibid.
19. Ibid., Dec. 31, 1990.
20. Ibid.

TWENTY-ONE

1. *L'actualité*, Jan. 1991.
2. Montreal *Gazette*, Jan. 8, 1991.
3. Ibid.
4. Ibid.
5. Ibid., Jan. 5, 1991.
6. Toronto *Globe and Mail*, Jan. 25, 1991.
7. Montreal *Gazette*, Jan. 17, 1991.
8. Ottawa *Citizen*, June 28, 1991.
9. Ibid.
10. Toronto *Globe and Mail*, Jan. 31, 1991.
11. Ibid.
12. Ibid., Feb. 7, 1991.
13. Ibid., Feb. 1, 1991.
14. *Financial Post*, Feb. 6, 1991.
15. Ibid.
16. Ibid.
17. Montreal *Gazette*, Feb. 12, 1991.
18. Ibid.
19. *Maclean's*, Jan. 7, 1991.
20. Montreal *Gazette*, Feb. 9, 1991.
21. Toronto *Globe and Mail*, Feb. 11, 1991.
22. Ibid.
23. Montreal *Gazette*, Feb. 8, 1991.
24. Ibid., Feb. 19, 1991.

25. Ibid.
26. Quebec Charter of Rights, Article 10.
27. Montreal *Gazette*, Mar. 6, 1991.
28. Ibid.
29. Ibid.
30. Ibid., Mar. 7, 1991.
31. Ibid.
32. Montreal *Gazette*, Mar. 26, 1991.
33. Toronto *Globe and Mail*, Mar. 26, 1991.
34. Ibid.
35. Ibid., Apr. 26, 1991.
36. Ibid., May 1, 1991.

TWENTY-TWO

1. Ibid., Mar. 11, 1991.
2. Ibid., Mar. 1, 1991.
3. Ibid., Mar. 19, 1990.
4. Ibid.
5. Ibid., Apr. 4, 1991.
6. Ibid.
7. Ibid., Mar. 8, 1991.
8. Ibid., Dec. 20, 1990.
9. Montreal *Gazette*, Mar. 17, 1990.
10. *La Presse*, Mar. 14, 1990.
11. Montreal *Gazette*, Mar. 25, 1991.
12. Ibid., Apr. 27, 1991.
13. *La Presse*, June 10, 1991.
14. Ibid., Apr. 28, 1991.
15. Montreal *Gazette*, May 18, 1991.
16. *Le Devoir*, May 18, 1991.
17. Montreal *Gazette*, June 2, 1991.
18. Montreal *Gazette*, June 15, 1991.

TWENTY-THREE

1. Montreal *Gazette*, Mar. 14, 1991.
2. Toronto *Globe and Mail*, June 17, 1991.
3. *L'actualité*, June 15, 1991.
4. Ibid.
5. Montreal *Gazette*, June 8, 1991.
6. Ibid.
7. Ibid., June 14, 1991.
8. *Report of the Group of 22*, June 1991.
9. Montreal *Gazette*, June 21, 1991.
10. Ibid.
11. *Time*, July 9, 1990.

12. Montreal *Gazette*, June 25, 1991.
13. Ibid., June 18, 1991.
14. Ibid., June 25, 1991.
15. Ibid.
16. Toronto *Globe and Mail*, June 25, 1991.
17. Montreal *Gazette*, June 25, 1991.
18. Ibid., June 26, 1991.
19. Ibid., June 18, 1991.
20. Toronto *Globe and Mail*, Aug. 5, 1991.
21. Ibid.
22. Montreal *Gazette*, Aug. 7, 1991.
23. Ibid.
24. Ibid., Aug. 6, 1991.
25. Toronto *Globe and Mail*, Aug. 7, 1991.
26. Ibid., Aug. 8, 1991.
27. *Le Journal de Montréal*, Aug. 16, 1991.
28. Montreal *Gazette*, Aug. 22, 1991.
29. Ibid., Aug. 27, 1991.
30. Ibid., Aug. 28, 1991.
31. Ibid., Aug. 29, 1991.
32. Ibid., Aug. 2, 1991.
33. Ibid.
34. Ibid., Aug. 13, 1991.
35. Ottawa *Citizen*, June 29, 1991.
36. Ibid.
37. Citizens' Forum on Canada's Future, Report to the People and Government of Canada (Ottawa: Ministry of Supply and Services Canada, 1991). p. 1.
38. Ibid., pp. 6–7.
39. Ibid., p. 144.
40. Montreal *Gazette*, July 20, 1991.
41. Ibid.
42. Ibid, July 17, 1991.
43. Ibid, Aug. 26, 1991.
44. Ibid.
45. Ibid., Sept. 5, 1991.
46. *Maclean's*, Sept. 9, 1991.
47. Montreal *Gazette*, Sept. 8, 1991.
48. Toronto *Globe and Mail*, Sept. 12, 1991.

TWENTY-FOUR

1. Montreal *Gazette*, Aug. 14, 1991.
2. Ibid.

3. Ibid., Aug. 15, 1991.
4. Ibid., Sept. 11, 1991.
5. Ibid.
6. Sherbrooke *La Tribune,* Aug. 3, 1991.
7. Montreal *Gazette,* Sept. 7, 1991.
8. Ibid., Aug. 10, 1991.
9. Ibid.
10. Ibid.
11. Ibid.
12. Ibid.
13. Ibid.
14. Ibid.

TWENTY-FIVE

1. Montreal *Gazette,* Sept. 21, 1991.
2. Ibid.
3. Ibid., Dec. 29, 1990.
4. Ibid., Dec. 18, 1990.

POSTCRIPT

1. *Le Devoir,* Oct. 2, 1991.
2. Stuart Rosenberg, *The Jewish Community in Canada,* Vol. I, p. 145.
3. Ibid., p. 225.
4. Ibid.
5. *Le Devoir,* Oct. 2, 1991.
6. *L'actualité,* Dec. 1, 1991.
7. Ibid.
8. *Le Devoir,* Apr. 6, 1931.
9. Ibid., Sept. 29, 1933.
10. As quoted in Montreal *Gazette,* Apr. 29, 1990.
11. *Le Devoir,* Nov. 17, 1938.
12. Ibid., June 21, 1933.
13. Ibid., Mar. 10, 1936.
14. Ibid., Mar. 24, 1936.
15. Ibid., Feb. 15, 1932.
16. Ibid., Oct. 18, 1938.
17. Ibid., Feb. 28, 1934.
18. Ibid., July 6, 1933.
19. Ibid., Jan. 10, 1938.
20. Toronto *Globe and Mail,* Sept. 21, 1991.
21. *L'actualité,* Dec. 1, 1991.
22. Conrad Black, *Duplessis* (Toronto: McClelland & Stewart, 1977). p. 251.
23. Ibid., p. 258.

24. Ibid.
25. Irving Abella and Harold Troper, *None Is Too Many, Canada and the Jews of Europe, 1933–1948* (Toronto: Lester & Orpen Dennys, 1982), p. 142.
26. *L'actualité,* Dec. 1, 1991.
27. Laurendeau, in *Les jeune-Canada: politicians et juifs.*
28. Laurendeau, *The Diary of André Laurendeau,* p. 77.
29. Montreal *Gazette,* Sept. 28, 1991.
30. *Le Devoir,* Oct. 2, 1991.
31. Montreal *Gazette,* Oct. 2, 1991.
32. Ryan, *A Stable Society,* p. 314.
33. Ibid., p. 315.
34. Ibid.
35. *La Presse,* Sept. 18, 1991.
36. Abella and Troper, *None Is Too Many, Canada and the Jews of Europe, 1933–1948,* p. 18.
37. Montreal *Gazette,* Oct. 2, 1991.
38. Ibid., Sept. 20, 1991.
39. *La Presse,* Sept. 29, 1991.
40. Toronto *Globe and Mail,* Sept. 21, 1991.
41. Joseph F. Fletcher, "Canadian Attitudes Toward Jews: Results of a Recent Survey," a lecture delivered at the Queen Elizabeth Hotel, Montreal, May 7, 1989.
42. Toronto *Globe and Mail,* Sept. 21, 1991
43. Ibid.
44. Montreal *Gazette,* Sept. 26, 1991.
45. Levesque, *An Option for Quebec,* p. 14.
46. Abbe Groulx, *Variations on a Nationalist Theme,* p. 212.
47. Ibid.
48. *Le Devior,* Oct. 2, 1991.
49. Ibid.
50. Montreal *La Presse,* Sept. 17, 1991.
51. Ryan, *A Stable Society,* p. 213.
52. *La Presse,* Sept. 19, 1991.
53. Ibid.
54. *The New Yorker,* Sept. 23, 1991, p. 66.
55. *La Presse,* Sept. 28, 1992.

56. *The New Yorker,* Sept. 23, 1991, p. 46.
57. Montreal *Gazette,* Sept. 26, 1991.
58. Ibid.
59. Toronto *Globe and Mail,* Sept. 23, 1991.
60. Ibid.
61. Mordecai Richler, *Home Sweet Home,* p. 291.

Selected Bibliography

1. BOOKS

Abella, Irving, and Harold Troper. *None Is Too Many: Canada and the Jews of Europe, 1933–1948*. Toronto: Lester & Orpen Denys, 1982.

Andrew, J. V. *Bilingual Today, French Tomorrow*. Kitchener, Ont.: Andrew Books, 1977.

————— *Enough! Enough French, Enough Quebec*. Kitchener, Ont.: Andrew Books, 1988.

Arnopoulos, Sheila McLeod, and Dominique Clift. *The English Fact In Quebec*. Montreal & Kingston: McGill-Queen's University Press, 1980.

Axworthy, Thomas S., and Pierre Elliott Trudeau, eds. *Towards A Just Society, The Trudeau Years*. Toronto: Viking, 1990.

Behiels, Michael D., ed. *The Meech Lake Primer*. Ottawa: University of Ottawa Press, 1990.

Belkin, Simon. *Through Narrow Gates*. Montreal: The Eagle Publishing Company, 1966.

Bercuson, David, J., and Barry Cooper. *Deconfederation*. Toronto: Key Porter Books, 1991.

Bergeron, Léandre. *The History of Quebec, A Patriote's Handbook*. Toronto: New Canada Publications, 1971.

Berton, Pierre. *Why We Act Like Canadians*. Toronto: McClelland & Stewart, 1982.

Black, Conrad. *Duplessis*. Toronto: McClelland & Stewart, 1977.

Bourassa, Robert. *Power from the North*. Toronto: Prentice-Hall, 1985.

Bourgault, Pierre. *Now or Never! Manifesto for an Independent Quebec*, Translated by David Homel. Toronto: Key Porter Books, 1991.

Brimelow, Peter. *The Patriot Game*. Toronto: Key Porter Books, 1986.

Bullock, William Bryant, ed. *Beautiful Waters*, Vol. I. Newport, Vermont: Memphremagog Press, 1926. Facsimile edition, Ayers Cliff, Que. and Derby Line, Vermont: Pigwidgeon Press, 1985.

—————, *Beautiful Waters*, Vol. II. Newport, Vermont: Bullock Publishing Group, 1938. Facsimile edition, Ayers Cliff, Que. and Newport, Vermont: Pigwidgeon Press, 1985.

Chapin, Miriam. *Quebec Now*. Toronto: Ryerson Press, 1955.

Clark, Gerald. *Canada: The Uneasy Neighbor*. New York: David McKay Co., 1965.

————— , *Montreal the New Cité*. Toronto: McClelland & Stewart, 1982.

Cohen, Andrew. *A Deal Undone: The Making and Breaking of the Meech Lake Accord*. Toronto and Vancouver: Douglas & McIntyre, 1990.

Collard, Edgar Andrew. *Montreal's Yesterdays*. Toronto: Longman's, 1963.

Cook, Ramsay, ed. *French Canadian Nationalism, An Anthology*. Toronto: Macmillan of Canada, 1969.

Côté, Jean, and Marcel Chaput, eds. *The Little Red Book, Quotations from René*

Lévesque. Translated by Robert Guy Scully and Jacqueline Perrault. Montreal: Editions Héritage, 1977.

Day, Mrs. C. M. *History of the Eastern Townships*. Montreal: John Lovell, 1869.

_____, *Pioneers of the Eastern Townships*. Montreal: John Lovell, 1863.

Desbarats, Peter. *The State of Quebec, A Journalist's Guide to the Quiet Revolution*. Toronto: McClelland & Stewart, 1965.

_____. *René, A Canadian in Search of a Country*. Toronto: McClelland & Stewart, 1976.

d'Iberville-Moreau, Luc. *Lost Montreal*. Toronto: Oxford University Press, 1975.

Eggleston, Wilfrid. *The Queen's Choice, A Story of Canada's Capital*. Ottawa: The National Capital Commission, 1961.

Epps, Bernard. *Tales of the Townships*. Lennoxville, Que.: Sun Books, 1980.

_____ *More Tales of the Townships*. Lennoxville, Que.: Sun Books, 1985.

Fournier, Pierre. *A Meech Lake Post-Mortem*. Translated by Sheila Fischman. Montreal and Kingston: McGill-Queen's University Press, 1990.

Fraser, Blair. *The Search for Identity*. New York: Doubleday, 1967.

Freed, Josh, and Jon Kalina, eds. *The Anglo Guide to Survival in Quebec*. Montreal: Eden Press, 1983.

Gibbon, Ann, and Peter Hadekel. *Steinberg, The Breakup of a Family Empire*. Toronto: Macmillan of Canada, 1990.

Gibbon, John Murray. *Our Old Montreal*. Toronto: McClelland & Stewart, 1947.

Granatstein, J. L., and David Stafford. *Spy Wars*. Toronto: Key Porter Books, 1990.

Gratton, Michel. *"So What Are the Boys Saying?": An Inside Look at Mulroney in Power*. Toronto: McGraw-Hill Ryerson, 1987.

Greber, David. *Rising to Power, Paul Desmarais & Power Corporation*. Toronto: Methuen, 1987.

Grenier, Pearl Mailloux, *The Lost Nation*. Lennoxville, Que.: Brome Historical Society, 1976.

Gwyn, Richard. *The Northern Magus: Pierre Trudeau and the Canadians*. Markham, Ont.: Paperjacks, 1981.

_____, *The 49th Paradox, Canada in North America*. Toronto: McClelland & Stewart, 1985.

Holden, Richard B. *Québec au travail: 1970 Election Quebec Crucible*. Montreal: Editions Ariès Inc., 1970.

Hoy, Claire. *Friends in High Places: Politics and Patronage in the Mulroney Government*. Toronto: Key Porter Books, 1987.

Hutchison, Bruce. *Canada: Tomorrow's Giant*. New York: Alfred A. Knopf, 1961.

Jacobs, Jane. *Quebec and the Struggle over Sovereignty, The Question of Separatism*. New York: Random House, 1980.

Jenkins, Kathleen. *Montreal, Island City of the St. Lawrence*. New York: Doubleday, 1966.

Johnston, Donald, ed. *Pierre Trudeau Speaks Out on Meech Lake*. Toronto: General Paperbacks, 1990.

Kattan, Naim, ed. *Les Juifs et la communanté française*. Montreal: Editions du Jour, 1965.

Kilbourn, William. *The Making of a Nation*. Toronto: McClelland & Stewart, 1965.

Langlais, Jacques and David Rome. *Jews and French Quebecers, Two Hundred Years of Shared History*. Waterloo, Ontario: Wilfrid Laurier University Press, 1991.

Laporte, Pierre. *The True Face of Duplessis*. Montreal: Harvest House, 1960.

Laurendeau, André. *Witness for Quebec*. Translated by Philip Stratford. Toronto: Macmillan of Canada, 1973.

———. *The Diary of André Laurendeau, 1964–1967*. Translated by Patricia Smart and Dorothy Howard. Toronto: Lorimer & Co., 1991.

Leacock, Stephen. *Leacock's Montreal*. Toronto: McClelland & Stewart, 1963.

Le Moyne, Jean. *Convergence, Essays from Quebec*. Translated by Philip Stratford. Toronto: Ryerson Press, 1961.

Lévesque, Réne. *An Option for Quebec*. Toronto: McClelland & Stewart, 1965.

———. *Memoirs*. Toronto: McClelland & Stewart, 1986.

Lipset, Seymour Martin. *Continental Divide*. New York: Routlege, 1990.

Lisée, Jean-François. *In the Eye of the Eagle*. Translated by Arthur Holden and Käthe Roth and Claire Rothman. Toronto: HarperCollins, 1990.

MacDonald, Ian. *From Bourassa to Bourassa*. Montreal: Harvest Press, 1984.

Macdonald, Capt. John A. *Troublous Times in Canada, A History of the Fenian Raids of 1866 and 1870*. Toronto: W. S. Johnston & Co., 1910.

MacLaren, Roy. *Canadians on the Nile, 1882–1898*. Vancouver: University of British Columbia Press, 1978.

McGoogan, Kenneth. *Canada's Undeclared War*. Calgary: Detselig, 1991.

McKenna, Brian, and Sheila Purcell. *Drapeau*. Toronto: Clark Irwin, 1980.

McNaught, Kenneth. *The Pelican History of Canada*. Harmondsworth, Middlesex, Eng.: Penguin Books, 1969.

McQueen, Rod. *Blind Trust, Inside the Sinclair Stevens Affair*. Toronto: Macmillan of Canada, 1987.

Milne, David. *The Canadian Constitution, From Patriation to Meech Lake*. Toronto: Lorimer, 1989.

Moore, Brian. *Canada*. New York: Life World Library, 1963.

Morf, Gustave. *Terror in Quebec, Case Studies of the FLQ*. Toronto: Clark Irwin, 1970.

Mulroney, Brian. *Where I Stand*. Toronto: McClelland & Stewart, 1983.

Newman, Peter. *The Canadian Establishment, Vol. 1*. Toronto: McClelland & Stewart, 1975.

———. *The Acquisitors, The Canadian Establishment, Vol. II*. Toronto: McClelland & Stewart, 1981.

Paris, Erna. *Jews, An Account of Their Experience in Canada*. Toronto: Macmillan of Canada, 1980.

Pitcher, Rosemary. *Château Frontenac*. Toronto: McGraw-Hill Ryerson, 1971.

Radwanski, George. *Trudeau*. Toronto: Macmillan of Canada, 1978.

Resnick, Philip. *Letters to a Québécois Friend*. With a Reply by Daniel Latouche. Montreal & Kingston: McGill–Queen's University Press, 1990.

———. *Towards a Canada-Quebec Union*. Montreal & Kingston: McGill–Queen's University Press, 1991.

Rosenberg, Stuart. *The Jewish Community in Canada, Vols. 1 & 2*. Toronto: McClelland & Stewart, 1970–71.

Rudin, Ronald. *The Forgotten Quebecers, A History of English-Speaking Quebec, 1759–1980*. Quebec City: Institut québécois de recherche sur la culture, 1985.

Ryan, Claude. *A Stable Society*. Translated by Robert Guy Scully with Marc Plourde. Montreal: Editions Héritage, 1978.

Sansom, Joseph. *Travels in Lower Canada*. London: Sir Richard Philips and Co., 1820.

Sawatsky, John. *Men in the Shadows*. Toronto: Doubleday, 1980.

Scowen, Reed. *A Different Vision, The English in Quebec in the 1990s*. Toronto: Maxwell Macmillan Canada, 1991.

Shaw, William F., and Lionel Albert. *Partition, The Price of Quebec's Independence*. Montreal: Thornhill Publishing, 1980.

Simpson, Jeffrey. *Discipline of Power, The Conservative Interlude and the Liberal Restoration*. Toronto: Personal Library Publishers, 1980.

Smith, Denis. *Bleeding Hearts . . . Bleeding Country*. Edmonton: Hurtig Ltd., 1971.

Stacey, C. P. *A Very Double Life, The Private World of Mackenzie King*. Toronto: Macmillan of Canada, 1976.

Stewart, Walter. *Shrug, Trudeau in Power*. Toronto: New Press, 1971.

————. *True Blue, The Loyalist Legend*. Toronto: Collins, 1985.

Story, Norah. *The Oxford Companion to Canadian History and Literature*. Toronto: Oxford University Press, 1967.

Sullivan, Martin. *Mandate '68, The Year of Pierre Elliott Trudeau*. Toronto: Doubleday, 1968.

Teboul, Victor. *Mythe et images du Juif au Québec*. Montreal: Editions de Lagrave, 1977.

Tiffany, Orwin Edward. *The Canadian Rebellion, 1837–38*. Buffalo: The Buffalo Historical Society, 1905.

Trofimenkoff, Susan Mann. *The Dream of Nation: A Social and Intellectual History of Quebec*. Toronto: Gage Publishing, 1983.

————, ed. *Variations on a Nationalist Theme*, by Abbé Groulx. Translation by Joanne L'Heureux and Susan Mann Trofimenkoff. Toronto: Copp Clark, 1973.

Trudeau, Pierre Elliott. *Federalism and the French Canadians*. Toronto: Macmillan of Canada, 1968.

————. *Approaches to Politics*. Toronto: Oxford, 1970.

Vallières, Pierre. *White Niggers of America*. Translated by Joan Pinkham. Toronto: McClelland & Stewart, 1971.

Vastel, Michel. *The Outsider, The Life of Pierre Elliott Trudeau*. Translated by Hubert Bauch. Toronto: Macmillan of Canada, 1990.

Wade, Mason. *The French Canadians, Volume One, 1760–1911*. Toronto: Macmillan of Canada, 1968.

————. *The French Canadians, Volume Two, 1911–1967*. Toronto: Macmillan of Canada, 1968.

Wilson R. D., and Eric McLean. *The Living Past of Montreal*. Montreal and Kingston: McGill-Queen's University Press, 1976.

2. MANIFESTOS, DOCUMENTS, REPORTS, SPEECHES, BRIEFS, SEMINARS

Seminar on French Canada. The Montreal *Star*, 1963. Limited distribution. Among those taking part, André Laurendeau, Gérard Pelletier, Abbé Gérard Dion, Marcel Faribault and the Hon. René Lévesque.

Quebec-Canada: A New Deal. The Québec government proposal for a new partnership between equals: sovereignty-association. Published by Conseil exécutif, Gouvernement du Québec, Quebec City, 1979.

The Task Force on Canadian Unity, A Future Together. Co-chairmen Jean-Luc Pepin and John P. Robarts. Ottawa, 1979.

L'union monétaire et l'union politique sont indissociables, by Robert Bourassa. Parti libéral du Québec, 1980.

Report of the Federal Cultural Policy Review Committee, Government of Canada,

1982.

Summary of briefs and hearings, Federal Cultural Policy Review Committee, Government of Canada, 1982.

Trading With Canada, The Canada-U.S. Free Trade Agreement, by Gilbert R. Winham. A Twentieth Century Fund Paper. Priority Press Publications, New York, 1988.

Montreal Jewish Community 1986 Census Summary, published by Allied Jewish Community Services, Montreal, 1989.

A Brief Opposing Bill c-72, Proposed Official Languages Act for Canada, April 1988, to the Legislative Committee on Bill c-72, presented by Alliance for the Preservation of English in Canada at the House of Commons, Ottawa.

La Souveraineté: Pourquoi? Comment? Published by Service des Communications du Parti québécois, Montréal, 1990.

Charter of the French Language, updated to 1 August 1989. Editeur officiel, Québec.

Regulation respecting the language of commerce and business, updated to 26 April 1983. Editeur officiel, Québec.

Regulation facilitating the implementation of the second paragraph of section 58.1 of the Charter of the French Language 8 August 1989. Excerpt from the *Gazette* officielle du Québec, Editeur officiel, Québec.

The Political and Constitutional Future of Québec. Report of the Bélanger-Campeau Commission, March 27, 1991.

The Meech Lake Accord, An Address to the Canadian Club of Montreal by the Honourable Clyde K. Wells, Premier, Newfoundland and Labrador. January 19, 1990.

A Presentation to the Joint Committee of the Senate and the House of Commons on Official Languages, March 28, 1990, House of Commons, Ottawa. Presented by Ronald P. Leitch, National President, Alliance for the Preservation of English in Canada.

A Québec Free to Choose. Report of the Constitutional Committee of the Québec Liberal Party, January 28, 1991. Also known as the Allaire Report.

The Legacy of Oka, by Maurice Tugwell and John Thomson, published by the Mackenzie Institute, Toronto, 1991.

A Presentation to the Standing Joint Committe of the Senate and the House of Commons on Official Languages, February 26, 1991, House of Commons, Ottawa. Presented by Ronald Leitch, President, Alliance for the Preservation of English in Canada.

Some Practical Suggestions for Canada. Report of the Group of 22. June 1991.

For a Future Together, Alliance Québec, *Mémoire présenté à la Commission sur l'avenir politique et constitutionnel du Québec,* December 1990.

Citizens' Forum on Canada's Future, Report to the People and Government of Canada, with a Chairman's Foreword by Keith Spicer, June 27, 1991.

Report of the Auditor General of Canada to the Senate of Canada, Audit of the Administration of the Senate of Canada, March 1991.

The Senator's Handbook, 1991.

Commissioner of Official Languages. *Annual Reports.* Ottawa: Minister of Supply and Services.

A Cultural Development Policy for Quebec, 1978.

Une Politique de la Culture et de Arts, par le Groupe-conseil sous la présidence de M. Roland Arpin, June 1991.

3. ARTICLES

"Bad Boy Made Good," by Harvey Enchin, *Report on Business Magazine*, September 1987.

"Quebec in the '70s: Looking Backwards" by Herbert Marx, MNA. *Viewpoints*, Canadian Jewish Quarterly, Vol. 10, No. 4, Spring 1980.

Permissions

Grateful acknowledgment is made to the following for permission to reprint previously published material:

The Diary of André Laurendeau: 1964–1967 by André Laurendeau ©1991. Used by permission of Lorimer & Co.

From *IN THE EYE OF THE EAGLE* by Jean-Francois Lisée. Copyright ©1990 by Les Editions du Boréal and Lisée Leconte Inc. English translation ©1990 by HarperCollins Publishers Ltd. Published by HarperCollins Publishers Ltd.

A Meech Lake Post-Mortem by Pierre Fournier ©1990. Used by permission of McGill-Queen's University Press, Montreal, Quebec.

Article by William Johnson. Used by permission of the *Gazette*.

Articles printed in *The Globe and Mail*. Used by permission.

A Stable Society by Claude Ryan ©1978. Used by permission of Les editions Heritage Inc., St-Lambert, Quebec.

Drapeau by Brian McKenna and Susan Purcell ©1980. Used by permission of Stoddart Publishing Co. Limited, 34 Lesmill Road, Don Mills, Ontario, Canada.

Excerpts from *The Story of English* by Robert McCrum, William Cran, and Robert MacNeil. Copyright ©1986 by Robert McCrum, William Cran, and Robert MacNeil. Reprinted by permission of Viking Penguin, a division of Penguin Books USA Inc.

Excerpt from Daniel Latouche used by permission of the author.

The New Republic: Excerpt from an article by Michael Kinsley. © The New Republic Inc. Reprinted by permission of *The New Republic*.

The History of Quebec, A Patriote's Handbook by Léandre Bergeron ©1971. Used by permission of NC Press, 345 Adelaide Street West, Toronto, Ontario M5V 1R5.

A NOTE ABOUT THE AUTHOR

Mordecai Richler was born in Montreal, Canada, in 1931. He moved to England in 1954 and lived there until 1972, when he returned to his native city. While best known as a novelist, Mr. Richler is also esteemed as an essayist and a writer of filmscripts. His novels include *The Apprenticeship of Duddy Kravitz* (1959), *Cocksure* (1968), *St. Urbain's Horseman* (1971), *Joshua Then and Now* (1980), and *Solomon Gursky Was Here* (1990). Among Mr. Richler's essay and short-story collections are *The Street: Stories* (1969) and *Home Sweet Home: My Canadian Album* (1984). He has edited the international anthology *Writers on World War II* and is also the author of two successful children's books, *Jacob Two-Two Meets the Hooded Fang* (1975) and *Jacob Two-Two and the Dinosaur* (1987). Mr. Richler has been the recipient of several awards, including a Canada Council Senior Arts Fellowship and a Guggenheim Fellowship, and he has twice received the Governor-General's Award for Fiction, Canada's highest literary award. He divides his time between Montreal and Quebec's Eastern Townships.

A NOTE ON THE TYPE

The text of this book is set in Garamond No. 3. It is not a true copy of any of the designs of Claude Garamond (1480–1561), but an adaptation of his types, which set the European standard for two centuries. It probably owes as much to the designs of Jean Jannon, a Protestant printer working in Sedan in the early seventeenth century, who had worked with Garamond's romans earlier, in paris, and who was denied their use because of the Catholic censorship. Jannon's matrices came into the possession of the Imprimerie Nationale, where they were thought to be by Garamond himself, and so described when the Imprimerie revived the type in 1900. This particular version is based on an adaptation by Morris Fuller Benton.

Composed by Graphic Perfections Inc.

Printed and bound by The Haddon Craftsmen, Inc. Scranton, Pennsylvania